Infidelity
on the
Internet

Virtual Relationships and Real Betrayal

Marlene M. Maheu, Ph.D.,
and Rona B. Subotnik, M.A., MFT

Forewords by Alvin Cooper, Ph.D.,
and Shirley Glass, Ph.D., ABPP

SOURCEBOOKS, INC.
NAPERVILLE, ILLINOIS

This publication is designed to provide accurate and authoritative information in regard
to the subject matter covered. It is sold with the understanding that the publisher is not
engaged in rendering legal, accounting, or other professional service. If legal advice or
other expert assistance is required, the services of a competent professional person
should be sought.—*From a Declaration of Principles Jointly Adopted by a Committee
of the American Bar Association and a Committee of Publishers and Associations*

Trademarks: All brand names used in this book are trademarks, registered trademarks,
or trade names of their respective holders. Sourcebooks, Inc., is not associated with any
product or vendor in this book.

Published by Sourcebooks, Inc.
P.O. Box 4410, Naperville, Illinois 60567-4410
(630) 961-3900
FAX: (630) 961-2168
www.sourcebooks.com

Library of Congress Cataloging-in-Publication Data

Maheu, Marlene M.
Infidelity on the Internet: virtual relationships and real betrayal / by Marlene M. Maheu
and Rona B. Subotnik.
    p. cm.
    Includes bibliographical references and index.
    ISBN 1-57071-722-2 (alk. paper)
    1. Adultery. 2. Computer sex. 3. Man-woman relationships. I. Subotnik, Rona
    II. Title.

HQ806 .M34 2001
306.73'6'02854678—dc21

             2001032240

Printed and bound in the United States of America
VP 10 9 8 7 6 5 4 3 2 1

To Laura, for her loving presence.
—MMM

To Norman, for all the joy he has brought to my life.
—RBS

Also by Marlene M. Maheu, Ph.D.
E-Health, Telehealth, and Telemedicine:
A Guide to Start-Up and Success
(with Pamela Whitten, Ph.D., and Ace Allen, M.D.)

The Mental Heath Professional Online:
New Questions and Answers for Practice Today

Also by Rona B. Subotnik, M.A., MFT
Surviving Infidelity: Making Decisions,
Recovering from the Pain
(with Gloria Harris, Ph.D.)
First Edition, 1994
Second Edition, 1999

Acknowledgments

We wish to thank all of our colleagues and friends who have helped us in the creation of this book. Their thoughts, suggestions, and generous support have been invaluable: Rosalie Ackerman, Martha Banks, Azy Barak, Judy Berman, Jean Chin, Gail Bernstein, Nina Breygin, Laura Brown, Peter Campos, Ellen Cole, Linda Cole, Yvette Colon, Alvin Cooper, Michael Erickson, John Economos, Shirley Glass, Barry Gordon, David Greenfield, Mary Gregerson, Eric Griffin-Shelley, Robin Hamman, Ellen Halpern, John Ingram, Kent Johnson, Cleo Kiernan, Marty Klein, Sally LeBoy, Kristin Levine, Claire Maheu, Shirley McNeal, Mardeene Mitchell, Tim Nelson, Hillary Norfleet, Camille Pierce, Les Posen, Dana Putnam, L. Dale Reed, Tracy Reed, Jennifer Schneider, Laura Struhl, Norman Subotnik, Denice Szafran, Manny Tau, Ryan Thurman, Denise Twohey, Thomas Williams, Miryam Williamson, Erica Wise, Cristina Versari, Kimberly Young, and Star Vega.

Our very special thanks go to our talented and experienced editors, Hillel Black and Peter Lynch of Sourcebooks, Inc., and to our reliable and steadfast agent, Julie Castiglia of Del Mar, California.

We thank Tim Mount for his astute observations, thoughtful suggestions, and careful preparation of this manuscript for publication.

A final note of acknowledgment and appreciation goes to the men and women who have shared their stories with us, and who taught us many lessons in courage and character throughout the years. In particular, we wish to thank the readers of *SelfhelpMagazine* for their contributions.

Table of Contents

Foreword

by Alvin Cooper, Ph.D.

The Internet's influence is permeating our daily lives. As people spend time on the Internet to play, learn, and work, it is not surprising that they are forming relationships with those with whom they are interacting. The Triple A Engine (accessibility, affordability, and anonymity) helps "turbocharge" the power of online interactions, making cyberspace a place where communication and sexuality blend as never before.

Sitting alone at a computer, people are revealing secrets more quickly to others who offer a sympathetic ear, day or night. Forums for countless types of discussions already exist. The means to find any aspect of fantasy, romance, and sex are available at the click of a mouse.

In this fast-moving world, feelings of intimacy can develop in a flash and easily transition to sexual innuendo. People often find themselves "cybering" before they fully get a chance to consider potential real-world implications. The secrecy that surrounds online sexual activity adds to the mystery and eroticism, as well as to the feelings of curiosity and excitement of these interactions. All too often, the virtual sex winds up having a dramatic impact on real-life romantic relationships.

What remains to be seen is whether these virtual relationships ultimately have a positive or negative impact on the lives of the participants. Journalists and reporters are always asking, "Is this new world of cyber-sex a good thing or a bad thing?" Of course, the answer is neither. The Internet is a vehicle and a means to an end. It is powerful, but not inherently either good or bad. Values that drive the people using the Internet are the factors that lead to its positive or negative impact. The responsibility for good or bad action resides in the individual, not the Internet.

Clarifying those personal values is the purpose of this important book. It has been written to provide millions of cyberspace travelers with a road map, to help them understand the terrain, navigate the dangers, and safely get to their destination. The authors carefully and methodically take us on a journey detailing the various ways that romantic and sexual interactions can occur in cyberspace, as well as how innocent exchanges and casual banter can easily cross the line to frank sexual exchanges.

Dr. Maheu is known internationally as a leader in the development of health care on the Internet. She has done pioneering work in delivering services both to consumers and professionals by building vibrant networking communities for both groups online. Her expertise has been sought by professionals since 1994, and in her first book, she gave a comprehensive overview of the impact of the Internet upon health care. Now she has turned her attention to one of the primary concerns she has heard from consumers, and is addressing infidelity on the Internet.

Rona Subotnik has been a successful author in the area of infidelity. Her book, currently in its second edition, is a bestseller on this topic. Now these successful authors have come together as authors and clinicians to provide a practical blend of theory and practice to anyone interested in the fascinating topic of cyber-infidelity.

In this book, infidelity is defined and an overview is provided as to how particular behaviors constitute infidelity. The various types of cyber-sexual activities are explained, as well as when such activities are considered compulsive. Next, the reader is helped to identify and prepare for discussions about cyber-infidelity, and meaningful suggestions are offered for how to recover from its pain. Finally, the reader is instructed how best to make use of self-help materials, and when it is necessary to seek the assistance of a professional.

The book is lively and fast paced. It starts with a review of the pertinent scientific literature, moves to practical considerations, and throughout, provides useful case examples taken from an essay contest conducted in the first private mental health website to have been constructed for consumers, *SelfhelpMagazine*. As a blend of professional theory, scientific data, and hundreds of real-life examples taken from a worldwide, interactive community website, this book is truly the first of its kind. It is a riveting "must read" for anyone wanting or needing information about infidelity on the Internet.

> — Alvin Cooper, Ph.D., is Director of the San Jose Marital and Sexuality Centre, and Coordinator of the Training Program of Counseling and Psychological Services at Stanford University. Dr. Cooper's publications can be accessed via <www.sex-centre.com>.

Foreword

by Shirley Glass, Ph.D., ABPP

The seduction of Internet relationships has created a new breeding ground for extramarital emotional affairs. Individuals with no intention of betraying their marriages find themselves sliding down the slippery slope of infidelity on the Internet. Internet relationships can be so captivating that they threaten committed relationships despite the absence of physical contact. Sharing sexual experiences and sexual fantasies in virtual space can be more arousing and feel more intimate than actually having sexual intercourse at home with one's partner.

The placement of appropriate boundaries to keep platonic friendships from becoming romantic is particularly relevant on the Internet. Protecting the commitment to our chosen partners requires not only dedication, but awareness of where to draw the line. Infidelity occurs without sexual contact when expectations about the primacy of the emotional bond are violated. In fact, Internet infidelity is a classic example of extramarital emotional involvement because it meets all three criteria for an emotional affair: emotional intimacy, secrecy, and sexual chemistry (Glass and Wright, 1997). Emotional intimacy can quickly become stronger on the Internet than in the home because of the freedom from distractions and lack of social constraints. The wall of secrecy that soon surrounds the Internet communications leads to lying and covert activities. Sexual chemistry is intensified by the titillating exchanges and barriers to physical contact.

Friendships that begin in chat rooms develop quickly when individuals connect with someone who appears to be not only interested in the same things but unbelievably empathic. The first line is crossed when they begin sharing information about problems in their primary relationship, because this signals vulnerability and potential availability. Furthermore, the marriage is endangered when marital problems are discussed with someone who is not a friend to the marriage. The computer itself can function as a virtual diary in which no restraint is necessary. Individuals often feel closer to members of the same message board than to friends and family members because of the perception of openness and understanding. When these Internet pals move outside the public arena to share their innermost feelings in private chat rooms and Instant Messages, they enter a concealed world of kindred spirits and soulmates.

The romantic idealization that characterizes new relationships is greatly enhanced by computer communication. Falling in love is easily accomplished when there are no annoying personal habits or distractions from daily routines. The appeal is not only what we can project onto the other person, but that we can be anyone we wish to be. One of the attractions of extramarital relationships is the opportunity to experience oneself in a new role. Internet relationships offer an infinite range of possible roles because of the insufficient tools for reality testing.

The betrayed partner's initial concern is about the involved partner's newfound obsession with the computer and growing detachment from family life. This concern shifts to suspicions, which are vehemently denied. The detective work that follows usually unearths evidence of a sexually charged and emotionally intimate relationship. The revelation is often followed by intense conflict regarding their disparate perceptions about the extent that this online friendship stepped over the line. The involved partner minimizes their actions while the betrayed partner feels that their commitment to exclusivity has been broken.

Betrayed partners commonly feel that their world has collapsed. The basic assumptions of honesty and trust have been shattered, and these shattered assumptions lead to traumatic reactions in the betrayed partner. The traumatic reactions that follow the disclosure of infidelity include hypervigilence regarding activities associated with the infidelity, intense emotions that vacillate between extremes of passion and despair, flashbacks, and intrusive thoughts. A healing process of recovery must begin with establishing safety. In cases of Internet infidelity, recovery cannot begin until ground rules are established to provide safety in the use of the computer.

Readers of this book will be alerted to the detours on the information highway and the pathways to recovery. This book brings together the combined expertise of two women who are experienced clinicians and prominent experts on the Internet and infidelity: Marlene Maheu is widely known and respected for her knowledge of the virtual world, and Rona Subotnik has coauthored a book on surviving infidelity which I consider a classic. Their book, *Infidelity on the Internet*, is a valuable resource at this time of accelerating infidelities which launch on the computer screen and make a crash landing in our marriages and families.

—Shirley P. Glass, Ph.D., ABPP, is a Diplomate in Family Psychology and is in private practice in Owings Mills, Maryland.

A Word from the Authors

Marlene M. Maheu, Ph.D.

Cyber-infidelity is one of the most frequently mentioned and explored topics among the readers of *SelfhelpMagazine* (www.selfhelpmagazine.com), a community meeting place for thousands of people who want information about personal matters, emotional issues, and information about how to help themselves. As the founder and editor in chief of this psychology magazine, I manage one of the world's first and largest consumer mental health websites.

Since 1994, our readers have asked questions that might raise your eyebrows or make your ears burn with embarrassment. Nonetheless, they are seeking solid answers to honest questions about everyday problems—often things they would not dare ask a physician or confidant. The anonymity of the website allows them to not only ask their questions, but also get a variety of answers about topics such as:

- ❍ having their spouse learn of an online affair;
- ❍ having their children find their love notes to a stranger;
- ❍ their gay or lesbian fantasies; and
- ❍ their devastation over reading a private love letter made public by a disgruntled ex-virtual lover.

They also want to know:

- ❍ if they should take the free plane ticket to meet their phantom lover in a faraway city;
- ❍ how to turn off their yearning to read email from someone who brought them passion yesterday, but guilt today; and
- ❍ how to break off a cyber-affair and pay attention to finding satisfaction in their family life.

Cyberspace pioneers are asking their innermost questions—especially when they have gone too far and are recoiling from their experiments. You will gain an appreciation of their successes, failures, insights, and confessions by reading the "Cyber-Infidelity Essay Contest" stories provided in this book.

Given my clinical work as a licensed psychologist with couples facing infidelity, along with my work at the magazine, I have devoted myself to bringing comfort and understanding to the many people who are struggling with relationship issues, including cyber-infidelity.

We have changed names, aliases, addresses, and modified stories to protect the identities of all contributors. You will hear stories from these cyber-pioneers, peek into their lives, experience their thrills, feel their pain—and learn.

I invite you, the reader, to contribute your thoughts about cyber-infidelity through an open discussion on an active listserv called Cyber-affairs <http://www.selfhelpmagazine.com/subscrib.html>.

Our great-grandparents would never have believed what has become possible today. In fact, when I showed my ninety-six-year-old grandfather our *SelfhelpMagazine* website, he took a step back and said, "It's a miracle." And it is....

Let us begin our miraculous travels into this brave new world.

Rona B. Subotnik, M.A.

When Dr. Maheu asked me to join her in this enterprise, I realized it was a daunting endeavor, because the need for information on this topic is so very great. More and more people are being drawn to the Internet as a means of finding romance in their lives. The motives of others are not so genuine. Some are searching for an affair, even though they are in a committed relationship offline, and yet others are criminals searching for victims.

As a therapist for the past eighteen years, I have never lost my fascination with human relationships. The part the Internet plays is complex, and information is needed to help people stay out of trouble. Infidelity online is no less harmful than offline, and in some cases it can be worse. Because of my work in the field of infidelity, my interest in helping people survive infidelity continues to grow, even as the means to cheat expands. One day, a couple came into my office and the wife told me, "I didn't want to come, but he made me. I am leaving him tomorrow. I found love online." I knew we were seeing the tip of a new and formidable iceberg. What you shall read soon will bear that out.

That is why I hope that this book will bring information and comfort to you, as we make our way through cyberspace together.

Authors' View

Our view of cyber-infidelity is based on over forty-five years of combined research and practice of psychotherapy. As clinicians, we see most cyber-infidelities as ineffectual attempts to remedy family or individual problems.

Rather than resolving problems, cyber-infidelity typically causes emotional pain to everyone involved, including extended family members. We have tried to achieve and present an appreciation of the diversity of beliefs held by people using the Internet worldwide. This new technology is global in its reach, and therefore requires critical thinking when discussing issues related to a previously inaccessible and unexamined audience. With this in mind, we have created a new definition of infidelity that allows for diversity and a global outlook. It also provides a means for couples to understand each other and guard against infidelity in the future.

The paradox of the Internet is that it can have effects both globally and within the family unit. It is for this reason that we have used family systems theory as the theoretical basis for understanding the phenomenon of cyber-infidelity. The effects of one person's actions are not limited to that individual, but to all members of the family, both in the present and for future generations.

Understanding one another, recognizing the effects of family history, and becoming aware of current stressors will help couples discover the conditions that led to cyber-infidelity. Individuals touched by cyber-infidelity will need skills to cope with its painful aftermath, and find the tools to reconstruct their relationship. These tools include honesty and the willingness to experience emotional pain as they work together to resolve underlying problems.

The discovery of infidelity creates a crisis. As with all crises, it can be the motivation for change. It is possible for an individual to survive infidelity, even if the relationship does not. One can grow and benefit, even if the experience seems devastating. The couple also can survive infidelity, and become closer and stronger than ever before, because they will achieve a better understanding of each other, themselves, and develop true intimacy. We believe the journey through cyber-infidelity, despite its often searing pain, can help forge a deeper, more intimate, and satisfying relationship for those who have the courage to face themselves and their partners.

Introduction

There's a new kid in town—the Internet—and not many people know what to make of her. She is intriguing, but also complex. One thing is for sure: she can't be ignored!

The purpose of *Infidelity on the Internet: Virtual Relationships and Real Betrayal* is to help you understand relationships as they are influenced by the telecommunication technologies. This book will give you the tools to understand that power and how to make them work for you.

The outcome of a unique project, *Infidelity on the Internet* combines the authors' expertise in treating cyber-infidelity with the real-life experiences of people struggling with online affairs. Common themes are illustrated by essays collected through a *SelfhelpMagazine* interactive exchange, known as the *SelfhelpMagazine* Cyber-affairs Essay Contest. The authors also reach into uncharted territory by supplying a definition of cyber-infidelity that is both reflective of the global diversity of Internet users yet practical for individuals who have behaved in ways that threaten their committed relationships. To assist the reader in coping with the challenges and emotions related to cyber-infidelity, this book provides suggestions for self-help and therapeutic interventions.

Infidelity on the Internet will show you that love blooms wherever people gather, and so the Internet has become the dating center for a global population of romantics. Freed of limitations posed by physical bodies, identities, reputations, or accountability, people are experimenting with new types of relationships and expressions of love and romance on the Internet.

Connecting in this new world, people are engaging in love and romance at astonishing rates, and often with disregard for their monogamous offline relationships. They and their loved ones are often not sure if they are cheating or just experimenting. *Infidelity on the Internet* will come alive for you with many personal stories and individual conversations that help you understand how people have fallen in love—or what they believe to be love. It will outline their paths to virtual romance and cyber-infidelity. You will hear their experiences, share their joys, cry at their heartbreaks, and somewhere in these stories find answers to your questions.

This book is a survival guide. We will examine motivations and benefits, as well as repercussions and long-term effects of experimenting with cyber-infidelity. We will discuss how to understand and deal with the eleven types of virtual lovers, and we will reveal their motivations. Some people are sincere, some are harmless, and some are dangerous.

You will learn to understand the components of love and the behaviors that enhance relationships. You will discover how self-validation and intimacy can flourish in a relationship, and how anxiety and obsession can be reduced. This book will also help you understand sexual impulses that go "haywire." You will be able to identify sexual compulsivity online, and discover strategies that will make your life manageable again if you or a loved one suffers from this problem.

Infidelity on the Internet will help you define cyber-infidelity. We will look at the various types of cyber-affairs. We will also show you how the virtual world differs from the real world. Quizzes will help you decide if your behavior has slipped or could slip into cyber-sexual compulsivity or cyber-infidelity. We will also provide you with a checklist of signs of a cyber-affair. If your suspicions are correct, we will explain the normal course of emotional reactions to cyber-affairs, and teach you techniques to manage your reactions.

We will discuss how to deal with the discovery of a cyber-affair, how to cope with the emotions that typically follow, and how to recover from its often-devastating blows. After the discovery of cyber-infidelity, decisions must be made about the future of your relationship. *Infidelity on the Internet* will help you think through the important considerations involved with those decisions. We will help you through the path of recovery by teaching you how to deal with the strong and often troubling reactions experienced by both the faithful and unfaithful partners. We will suggest ways in which the unfaithful partner can help restore trust and intimacy in the relationship. *Infidelity on the Internet* will show you what constitutes an apology for cyber-infidelity, and how to bring closure to these painful episodes. We will also provide you with a number of resources to help you find added support and direction both online and offline. Throughout, this book will serve as a guide to understanding and developing the values needed to function in a world being shaped by technology.

At the end of our book, you will find two appendices. They have been added to help you understand the Internet and how people communicate using it for romance, as well as infidelity. In the first appendix, you will find a brief navigational map for understanding where people go and what they do online. Then, you will find a list of emoticons and acronyms in Appendix B that facilitate communication on the Internet.

So, come with us on this journey through virtual romance, real betrayal, and recovery from infidelity on the Internet.

Prelude to Infidelity

1

Cyber-Affairs: Lighthearted Flirting, Hot Chatting, or Infidelity?

Sara in Toronto is ending her email conversation with Edward in Australia.

Sara: It's been wonderful ;-) [wink]
Edward: Can't believe we found each other. Dream of seeing you some day.
Sara: Sex maniac from Down Under drives up-and-coming jazz singer nuts.
Edward: You love it.
Sara: I do. LOL [laughing out loud]
Edward: You are my world.
Sara: I feel so close to you. I feel as though we have reached an intimacy that can only increase as time goes by. This relationship has made me feel more alive than I ever thought possible. When we're together, we are alone, safe, and excited! I love it!
Edward: Let's do it again, right now. I picture you lying down. I am running my hand down your smooth back, and when I...
Sara: [interrupts] no, no—have to go—don't have time. I just remembered I need to pick up a friend at the airport.
Edward: Honey, it won't take long. Just one more?
Sara: tomorrow—same time—ok?
Edward: ok, :-* [kiss]

Sara shuts off her computer. She reaches for her purse, takes out her car keys, and goes to the garage to hop into her van. She drives six blocks to a nearby school, parks, and walks to the side door. When the children are dismissed, two little girls with ponytails run toward her.

"Mommy, Mommy!" they greet her with hugs and kisses. "We're so excited! Let's go get Daddy at the airport."

Sara is maintaining a secret love affair on the Internet. Neither her husband nor her lover knows about the other. But since Sara and Edward have never met, is she, in fact, cheating on her husband?

From apartments on the lower east side of Manhattan to laptops on Caribbean beaches, the Internet culture is unprecedented, unlimited, unregulated, and global. Sparked by anonymous and relatively safe communication technologies, online romantic relationships are exploding. Strangers are meeting and developing sexual relationships online. The Internet provides group and individual chat rooms, dating websites, and audio-video connections—technologies that challenge traditional concepts of an intimate encounter. This ability to interact romantically, seductively, and sexually online is creating an upheaval in social mores. A completely new culture is evolving. When sexuality is combined with the newfound freedoms of technology-based communication and social networking, you have a mixture that is even more enticing than the back seat of a Chevy on a late summer evening.

Unbounded by geographic distance, language, culture, religion, social conventions, or what is generally considered common decency, online flirtation can evolve very quickly into cyber-infidelity. Some people invest so much emotional energy online that they find that they are living in two worlds—online and offline. They may have lovers in both worlds. Some of these questions show the confusion that occurs when technology and tradition collide:

⊃ Am I guilty of infidelity if I merely proposition someone?

⊃ Am I being unfaithful to my partner if I have an orgasm when talking to someone online?

⊃ Why can't my partner understand that I consider his online dating to be cheating, even if they never meet?

⊃ How can I tell if someone online is sincere, and not just looking to cheat?

⊃ My spouse never makes love to me. Is it wrong to find someone who excites me in cyberspace?

⊃ If I have a cyber-romance with someone of the same sex, does that mean I am a homosexual, and is it considered cheating on my spouse?

For some, the Internet has delivered convenient and inexpensive new ways of meeting potential partners, exciting ways to explore oneself in relation to a variety of new people, and safe avenues for courtship. For others, it has spawned questions regarding traditional and committed relationships.

Stories and *SelfhelpMagazine* Contributors

As part of the research effort to gather information for this book, many stories were gathered in an Internet project hosted by *SelfhelpMagazine*, an Internet magazine founded and edited by Dr. Marlene Maheu, one of this book's authors. As the first private mental health publication to be established for consumers on the Internet, its objective is to deliver reader-friendly psychology to the daily life of the Internet user. Since November 1, 1994, many of *SelfhelpMagazine*'s readers have shared their stories through letters and through a "Cyber-Affairs and Dialogue Essay Contest" that invited participants to describe their experiences with cyber-infidelity. Many of these experiences have been included in this book, with the permission of the contributors.

In other cases, fictional stories have been created based on the authors' years of experience working with infidelity and cyber-infidelity. In all comments and stories, names and information have been changed, compiled, and occasionally supported by clinical observations by the authors to protect the confidentiality of all contributors.

Who Is Looking for Love Online?

The Internet is quickly becoming the next best thing to being there, and when it comes to romance, it can be safer, too. You can mingle, see who has something interesting to say, and who may be interested in you. You can meet people in specialized places, regardless of how specific or out of the mainstream your interests might be. Strangers can conveniently screen potential new partners, flirt, play, and test interpersonal limits and sexual boundaries. The Internet opens the door for everyone to meet.

There are reports of successful connections between people who find soulmates with shared values, goals, and dreams from all corners of the globe. People in abusive relationships can have positive interactions with those who treat them respectfully, care about their opinions, and look forward to their contact. Shy people can meet possible romantic partners and experiment with flirtation. Isolated people can find partners who share common experiences, humor, and pain.

The typical Internet user is between thirty-two to thirty-six years old, and has an above-average income. While recent surveys estimate that equal numbers of men and women go online, men seem to spend more time online. When we shift our attention from the general Internet population to those who are involved with virtual dating, the picture becomes even more fascinating.

Dating Websites

A study conducted by Jupiter Media Metrix at the end of 2000 and reported by *ABC News* found that visits to websites with romantic content increased by just under 50 percent in one year. The latest polls indicate that up to 30 million people are logged on to dating websites. Why is there such an interest in these sites? Here are a few reports from respondents to our *SelfhelpMagazine* essay contest:

➔ Marianne, a forty-six-year-old researcher, explained, "Because I don't drink and don't enjoy the 'bar scene,' I was having trouble meeting

people, and placed an ad in the personals on America Online, after lots
of infighting with my conscience about it feeling 'desperate.' My ad
didn't have my picture, wasn't particularly provocative, and I was
amazed at the response I received. It was overwhelming."

❍ Chantal, a twenty-five-year-old horse trainer, wrote, "I placed an ad
because it was easy and inexpensive to get access to lots of different
types of people."

❍ Renée, a thirty-six-year-old reporter, said, "When I applied to the
online dating service it was because I knew if I didn't find a person
who satisfied my needs in real life, I would always be lonely."

In the article, "Online Love," *ABC News* reported that Netizens (people
who frequently use the Internet) are notorious for falsifying their personal
information. The cyberwaves are abuzz with people falling in love with
those who pretend to have desirable characteristics.

Seeking romance has become one of the most popular activities in cyberspace. We can only conclude that the Internet is not only a communication
technology, but also a massive social experiment. As such, it is creating new
opportunities for interpersonal exploration, as well as new relationship
problems, including infidelity.

Indeed, married people comprise a surprisingly high percentage of visitors to the most popular dating websites. Virtual lovers are all too often in
a committed relationship in real life and looking for a little something on
the side. Unfortunately, we do not have information about how many married or otherwise committed people are roaming the dating websites with
false descriptions of themselves, using anonymous names, or more likely,
both.

How can married people feel so free to date online? How can their intentions be so easily masked? Do others care if they are married? It is evident
that our values are changing. Without rules of propriety to slow them down,
and without the restraints of physical bodies to keep them sane, strangers can
now have emotional or sexual affairs—immediately and without touching
another human being. But the looming question is: "Do cyber-sex and virtual
relationships constitute infidelity?"

Real vs. Virtual Dating

Dating on the Internet can give the illusion of real dating because it seems
to create a meeting place. In fact, this novel aspect of a technology-
mediated virtual world contributes to the fact that the Internet is becoming
known as a social network as well as a communication network. Cyberspace
is a place where people can meet, hang out, or hide out. In his book, *The
Media Lab*, Steward Brand quotes Howard Rheingold describing the Internet
experience, "It's like having the corner bar, complete with old buddies and

delightful newcomers and new tools waiting to take home and fresh graffiti and letters, except instead of putting on my coat, shutting down the computer, and walking down to the corner, I just invoke my telecom program and there they are. It's a place."

Within this newly formed cyberspace, developers of technology are reproducing closer and closer approximations of offline romantic experience. In dating websites, people can post pictures of themselves for others to view, along with other information about themselves. They can send a picture as an email attachment and leave voice messages. People can also augment their email and chat room conversations by sending their private website address, where their pictures, voice clips, and video clips are posted. These visual and auditory representations allow individuals to have greater control over how they represent themselves to others in cyberspace. They also maintain a safe distance from one another.

Nonetheless, there are differences between the experiences of a virtual meeting and a real meeting. One difference is that members do not always see their companions and probably do not know where they live—which could be anywhere on the planet. They also do not dress up for the occasion—no perfume, no aftershave. They just plop down at the computer and start typing.

Another difference of note is that given this new meeting place, people are unsure how to think about the events that might happen there. They are unsure about whether experiencing romance or sexuality in cyberspace is the same as it is in the real world, or if the differences are important.

The other confusing aspect to the development of this new cyberspace is that people do not just stay there. Netizens are moving in and out of cyberspace, as if it were similar to any other type of place. Virtual lovers pick up the phone, send a fax, send real flowers, or hop a plane and have a face-to-face visit. People do not typically communicate or live exclusively in the virtual or real worlds. They combine both and move from one to the other. As technology has now provided a social gathering place, virtual lovers are enjoying the fluidity and convenience of moving from one mode of contact to another, one parallel world to another, and all too often, without the knowledge of their real-life or virtual lovers.

Infidelity and the Internet

The issues raised by virtual relationships and mutual sexual gratification are complex. A few other basic concepts will help us gain clarity. The inner drive to meet like-minded or like-spirited people for a romantic relationship is as primal as breathing and walking. The Internet provides an escape to millions of people who otherwise cannot see a reasonable way to transform their difficult relationships. They may be too overwhelmed to work on a difficult relationship, end a bad marriage, or pursue a mate. Their religious beliefs may prohibit divorce. They may find themselves financially, geographically, or emotionally stuck. Whatever their reasons, they seem to be hungering for easy access to companionship and sex.

Determining a reliable estimate for the number of marriages that have been touched by infidelity, and for the percentage of men or women having affairs, is very difficult to accomplish. There have been many studies over the last fifty-five years to find the answer, but the findings are inconsistent. The difficulty is due to many factors, such as the population polled, the honesty of the participants, their ages, the length of the marriage, the circumstances under which the questions were asked—such as who was in the room and whether the answers were written or oral—and the definition of infidelity as defined by the researchers.

For example, Sherry Hite's results from a non-randomized survey of magazine questionnaires and shopping mall interviews showed that 70 percent of women and 76 percent of men reported having extramarital sex.

The University of Chicago sponsored a study in which 80 percent of those polled responded. It was a randomized national sample for several major studies during the 1990s, and was conducted by the National Opinion Research Center. Participants were asked, "Have you ever had sex with someone other than your husband or wife while you were married?" The incidence of extramarital intercourse was 22.7 percent of men, and 11.6 percent of women.

Psychologist Shirley Glass, M.D., who has been doing research on infidelity for over twenty-five years, has reported in the *Clinical Handbook of Marriage and Couples Intervention*, edited by W.K. Halford and H.J. Markham, that 25 percent of wives and 44 percent of husbands had cheated on their spouses. These figures are consistent with previous reports by the Kinsey Institute, which report infidelity by 26 percent of wives and 50 percent of husbands; Athanasiou, et al, who report infidelity among 36 percent of wives and 40 percent of husbands; and Janus and Janus, who found that 26 percent of women and 35 percent of men committed adultery.

Although these studies are of sociological interest, and future studies will no doubt include cyber-sex as a form of infidelity, the pain of infidelity nevertheless is very piercing. Suffice it to say that infidelity is a problem for many relationships, and indications are that the use of the Internet will likely add to the complexity of this problem.

We believe that it is important for individuals to understand the type of affair, the reasons for the affair, the dynamics of relationships, and the power of the Internet to help them recover from the pain and reconstruct their relationship.

Today, those who use secrecy and denial to have their way are now empowered with technologies that are better, faster, and more clandestine. The Internet is making it easier for the deceitful to hide their infidelities. But where exactly are the lines between lighthearted flirting, hot chatting, and infidelity? Unfortunately, ambiguity is further clouded when romantic and sexual interactions do not involve the sense of touch, and technology allows people to simultaneously live in two worlds.

Living in Parallel Worlds

Psychologist David Greenfield, Ph.D., author of *Virtual Addiction*, was quoted in *Newsweek* magazine on the topic of cyber-infidelity. He said, "Is the Internet to blame? It may be a great communications medium, but it is also an intoxicating parallel universe with real world implications."

The Internet is in fact a parallel world, providing real world activity with few repercussions, and at the speed of electricity. It provides an alternative place to go, with people to meet twenty-four hours a day, seven days a week. Moving in and out of this virtual world is as easy as sitting at one's desk or going to the library. Individuals bring their desires, unconscious needs, personalities, and goals to this world, and interact with people they will never need to face.

Parallel is a particularly appropriate term for the discussion of cyber-infidelity because many unfaithful partners lead two lives simultaneously, two parallel existences—one in a real-life, committed relationship and the other online, in a cyber-affair. While the unfaithful partner goes about the daily business of living, the virtual lover can be only a few fantasy-filled clicks away.

Deb Levine, M.A., health education consultant from San Francisco, in the article, "Virtual Attraction: What Rocks Your Boat," says that online flirting differs from face-to-face flirting. "In real life, there is much more flirting between people....Online, flirtation more often leads to erotic satisfaction, as there is a mental ability to disassociate the online sex with anything having to do with a person's real life." Many people are finding it increasingly easy to live in these parallel worlds and to act as if their behavior in one world is completely separate from their behavior in the other world. Technology allows a shifting from one world to another, one that is both private and immediate.

Interestingly, a report of more than seven thousand people who answered a survey on MSNBC.com found that over 60 percent of those surveyed considered cyber-sex *not* to be infidelity. Indeed, some people believe cyber-sex with another human being does not constitute infidelity, but consider it to be similar to pornography. If people find sexual relief by looking at pornography and do not consider such behavior to be infidelity, why should interacting with a stranger online be different?

Cyber-infidelity and cyber-sex are such new, yet vague terms that they have different meanings for different people, and therefore are often difficult to define. However, for purposes of this book, we will offer our definitions, and hope you will make your own thoughtful decisions.

Given the complexities involved, we have developed the most basic of definitions for cyber-infidelity. *Cyber-infidelity occurs when a partner in a committed relationship uses the computer or the Internet to violate promises, vows, or agreements concerning sexual exclusivity.* Such a basic definition takes into account the diversity of people using the Internet. The premise of this definition is the need for couples to extend their relationship contracts to include the use of technology for sexual expression.

To get a better understanding of what is happening when people are sexual online, let us take another look at Sara and Edward, the couple we mentioned at the beginning of this chapter. The answer to whether their secret, sexual liaison is cheating depends on the agreement Sara has with her husband. If we assume that Sara has promised sexual exclusivity to her husband, as most people do when they marry, then her virtual romance has all the elements of traditional infidelity: shared intimacy, secrecy, deception, sexual fantasy, and sexual response.

The fact that all her contacts with Edward take place in cyberspace is not the point. Bringing herself to orgasm without physically touching someone who stimulates her does not make it less sexual. Just because she did not share physical touch with Edward does not mean she has kept her promise of fidelity to her husband. She has been having a sexual relationship with Edward. Her promise of sexual exclusivity has been buried in the confusion that clouds the parallel world created by the Internet; it may seem to Sara that having a phantom lover whom she meets somewhere in cyberspace has no bearing on her promise of fidelity to her husband.

The Internet Enigma
As we will discuss throughout this book, many paradoxes exist because of the powers of the Internet. The following conditions illustrate some of the paradoxes that are manifested by the capability of the Internet:

- ⊃ **Contact.** The most profound and far-reaching paradox of the Internet is that we can reach out to literally millions of people while being completely alone. This is the first time in history that contact is able to be simultaneously global and solitary.
- ⊃ **Intimacy.** The Internet can create a powerful feeling of closeness to someone whom we have never met or seen.
- ⊃ **Time.** The Internet changes our concept of time. While it allows us to do things more quickly, it also allows us to lose track of time, create illusions with time, and waste time.
- ⊃ **Honesty.** On the Internet, it is easier to be honest, and, at the same time, to be more deceitful. It is often less embarrassing to be honest when we may never see that person face-to-face, and for the same reason, it is just as easy to be deceitful.

- ⮕ **A Meeting Place.** The Internet allows us to create a place to meet without ever leaving home.
- ⮕ **Disengagement.** The Internet gives us an experience of one another, while disengaging that experience from our bodies. We connect with only our thoughts and emotions.
- ⮕ **Safety.** Because of the distance between us there is a sense of safety, yet it may be false because we do not know the other person or his or her intentions.
- ⮕ **Interpretation.** Because we put such credence on the written word, believing its meaning is clearer than the spoken word, we believe there is less chance for misinterpretation. The paradox is that this is untrue. Email and chat room messages are more easily misinterpreted than the spoken word.
- ⮕ **Attention.** On the Internet, we feel that we have the complete attention of the other person, and yet he or she can be involved in many other activities of which we are not aware.

We consider these and many other interlocking effects to be the "Internet enigma." The Internet can become a tool which allows us to expand the freedom of choice, and thus be pulled in many opposing directions. These paradoxes are more than interesting—they are enigmas of the Internet. They represent extraordinary conditions that can affect our lives in personal and dramatic ways.

The paradox of intimacy is very important in understanding the development of infidelity on the Internet. Many people have described the feeling of intimacy on the Internet, even though they are worlds apart. Sara, who we met in the beginning of the chapter, explained this feeling of intimacy in her relationship with Edward. "I feel so close to him," Sara says. "I feel as though we have reached an intimacy that can only increase as time goes on. This relationship, even though it is only online, has made me feel more alive than I ever thought possible. When we're together, we are alone, safe, and excited. I love it!"

However, the nature of this paradox is that although Sara sits secluded in her home with her computer, typing her very private thoughts to Edward, who is also alone, they feel connected, as if they are the only two people in the world. At that moment, they experience only each other, and this accounts for the illusion of intimacy they feel.

In this parallel world, lovers can produce a sense of intimacy. This sense of intimacy is different from the true intimacy experienced in real love.

The Rapid Shift to Cyber-Sex
The paradox of the Internet can foster a remarkably quick shift from a sense of intimacy to sexuality. This shift is so rapid, and the parallel world can

become so intertwined with reality that traditional customs and timelines may blur. The course of attraction, connection, and passion can change dramatically. While some people have months of email contact, eventually share photographs of themselves, progress to telephone contact, and perhaps meet in the real world, other people meet and have cyber-sex within five minutes.

To give you a better idea of how this happens, we offer our definition of cyber-sex for your consideration. *Cyber-sex occurs when people use computerized content (text, sounds, or images obtained from software or the Internet) for sexual stimulation.* They usually start by typing provocative and sometimes erotic words to each other. They might also send voice files to one another, describe their fantasies, or show each other pictures or videos of themselves or other people. Whichever technology they use, the individuals create a shared sexual excitement and usually end with masturbation.

Cyber-Sex and Infidelity

As technology gives us the ability to simulate real contact in a parallel world, the lines between fidelity and infidelity blur, raising many unanswered questions. For example, how is cyber-sex different from having phone sex with paid "receptionists"? These are not easy questions, so let us look at cyber-sex in more detail as we try to help you come to your own conclusions.

A large-scale study conducted on MSNBC.com by psychologist and researcher Alvin Cooper, Ph.D., and colleagues examined many different areas of cyber-sex. Among their amazing findings was the fact that approximately nine million users (15 percent of the online population) had accessed one of the top five adult entertainment websites.

Test your beliefs about cyber-romance against the findings of these researchers in their 1998 MSNBC Online Sexuality Survey.

Test Your Sex-Surfing IQ

	True	False
1. Twenty-five percent of the people using the popular sexual websites are sexually compulsive.	❏	❏
2. Ten percent of the general population is sexually compulsive.	❏	❏
3. Women are as interested as men in visual erotica on the Internet.	❏	❏
4. Equal numbers of men and women participate in sexual or romantically related chat rooms.	❏	❏
5. Some people visit cyber-sex sites while at work.	❏	❏
6. The majority of people are truthful about their race when seeking cyber-sex.	❏	❏
7. Many people lie about their gender when seeking cyber-sex.	❏	❏

	True	False
8. People often lie about their age when visiting sexual sites online.	❏	❏
9. Most people spend about ten hours or less online in sexual pursuits.	❏	❏
10. People tend to be secretive about how much of their time was spent online for sexual activities.	❏	❏

Answers

1. **False.** According to the respondents, only 8 percent were sexually compulsive.
2. **False.** Approximately 5–10 percent of the general population is sexually compulsive. These statistics do not support the common perception that people suffering from sexual compulsivity are the primary users of the Internet.
3. **False.** Women skip the erotica in favor of chat rooms. According to the survey, an estimated 23 percent of women surf for visual erotica as compared to 50 percent of males.
4. **False.** Almost the reverse is true. Forty-nine percent of women reported seeking sexual or romantic contact in chat rooms, as compared to 23 percent of men.
5. **True.** An estimated 20 percent of people go to cyber-sex sites on the job, and 70 percent of visits to adult sites take place between 9:00 A.M. and 5:00 P.M.— normal business hours.
6. **True.** But 38 percent of the respondents to the study did say they were untruthful about their race when seeking cyber-sex.
7. **False.** There is some deception about gender online, but only 5 percent of respondents said they had lied about this. Lying about gender is referred to as "gender-bending."
8. **False.** The study showed that only about 20 percent of the survey respondents were "often" untruthful about their age. However, 60 percent said that they "occasionally" lied.
9. **True.** The survey showed that 91.7 percent of respondents spend less than ten hours a week on sexual pursuits. Less than 8 percent spent eleven or more hours per week engaging in online sexual activities. Those who reported spending eleven or more hours on sexual activities were more likely to say that cyber-sex "interfered with" or "jeopardized" the quality of their lives, and were classified as sexually compulsive by Dr. Cooper and his colleagues.
10. **True.** About three out of four respondents keep secrets about the time spent online, and 87 percent of those reported never feeling guilty.

Researchers in the MSNBC study found that an estimated 20 percent of all Internet users engage in some kind of online sexual activity; half the people said that online sexual activity has changed real-world sex with their partner; and approximately 13 percent of respondents identified negative effects on their relationships due to online sexual activity.

Nearly two-thirds of the people engaging in some type of online sexual activity are married or in a committed relationship. Of the remaining third, more than half are involved in a romantic or sexual relationship. This means that only about 16 percent of those reporting to be engaging in online sexual activity are not in committed relationships!

While cyber-sex as a topic has been sensationalized by the media, ongoing research is showing it to be much less of a problem than commonly depicted when handled appropriately. Most people report the use of the Internet for sexual expression does not interfere with their lives, but rather is a beneficial source of education and experimentation.

In spite of the number of people who believe that cyber-sex does not constitute infidelity, Dr. Cooper, in a personal communication, explained that many spouses of people who pay for phone sex with "receptionists" consider it a violation of their relationship contracts. Phone sex and cyber-sex, then, are the same, in that partners often consider it a violation of their relationship agreements.

It may be that as technology evolves, systems such as the Internet are making it easier to engage in such activities without awakening the sensitivities associated with other types of compulsive sexuality. In fact, understanding the power of sexual material on the Internet is fundamental to understanding the Internet's role in infidelity.

Triple A Engine

Something about the Internet is blowing open the ancient doors that have kept sexual impulses under check. In Dr. Cooper's book, *Cybersex and Sexual Compulsivity: The Dark Side of the Force*, he and his colleagues have identified three factors that seem to make cyber-sexuality so prevalent—accessibility, affordability, and anonymity. Together, these are known as the "Triple A Engine."

Accessibility

Easy access means much less effort is needed to find a sexual partner. Immediate gratification is available for anyone with access to the internet. A computer search for a possible partner can take two minutes and yield hundreds of potential matches. An affair in the real world requires more effort.

Real-world affairs also generate more guilt. The ride home from a face-to-face fling can be very tense, filled with worries about being caught. Walking away from a computer after cyber-sex is easy. There is very limited time to reflect and consider what has just been done. To make things even easier, there is no last call or closing time online—the festivities can continue as long as desired. If one partner is tired, another can be found within minutes. The lights are on any time, day or night.

Affordability

There is always an "Internet cocktail party," so to speak, with no cover charge, no minimum age—just the monthly charge to an Internet service provider. If a specialty service is desired, competitive pricing is driving those costs down, too. Many dating and erotic services are free. Whatever your fancy, there is no need to dress for the occasion, drive an expensive car, or pay for dinner. Where else can you get so much for so little?

Anonymity

Exploring the arts of flirtation and seduction in a scaled-down environment is now possible through anonymity on the Internet. Typical obstacles to intimacy vanish when identity can be masked and cloaked. Anonymity also provides the safety of camouflaging potentially undesirable aspects of one-self, from social class to physical appearance and age. It also eliminates the heartache that comes from being rejected at first sight.

Many Internet users assume a pseudonym as part of anonymity. Anyone can be behind the pseudonym, from a child to a senior citizen. The person can be single or married. He or she can lie about gender, race, religion, nationality, or any other personal characteristic. A fourteen-year-old boy can pose as a thirty-three-year-old woman.

By using a pseudonym, a person can feel safe in sharing his or her secret desires, roles, and thoughts. For example, individuals may assume a pseudonym to experience the sadistic side of their personalities. By exploring their feelings in websites or other discussion areas devoted to sadism, they can avoid the stigma and rejection typically associated with such people in the real world.

Types of Virtual Lovers

There are many kinds of people on the Internet. When you understand their different motivations, you will gain an appreciation of the complexity of issues brought about by the Internet, including cyber-infidelity. Given the novelty, anonymity, and global nature of the Internet, the following group-ings are not scientifically derived, but identified by the authors to help you understand who is navigating the Internet. We cannot estimate how many Netizens are in each category. Some people you meet can fit in more than one category, and some can be cyber-cheaters. The groups are listed in probable order of sincerity:

- ➊ The Seeker
- ➋ The Explorer
- ➌ The Romantic
- ➍ The Escapist
- ➎ The Fibber

- The Lurker
- The Seducer
- The Compulsive
- The Dumper
- The Criminal

The Seeker

Anna and Jodie are having lunch on the terrace of the Los Angeles County Museum of Art. Both art lovers, they lunch there once a month and browse the collection. After their orders are taken, Jodie asks, "So, what's this big news?"

"Well," Anna replies, "where should I start? I've met a guy that I think I really like. I think the days of going to bars and answering personal ads are finally over. My mother keeps telling me, 'You're not getting any younger.'"

Jodie nods. She understands. They are both thirty-three, and although Los Angeles is a tough city in which to meet nice guys, from what she hears, it's not easy anywhere. "So, tell me. Where did you meet him? What's he like?" she asks.

"I met him on the Internet in a chat room for singles." Anna smiles and waits for the reaction.

"What?!" Jodie is intrigued.

"I want to find someone. I want to find someone and settle down, and have kids. In fact, if you were single, I'd encourage you to do this too, especially since you're a lesbian. In fact, from what I hear, it's a great way for gay and lesbian folks to screen new people. You just talk and get to know each other. I talked to about six guys so far, and soon knew they weren't right for me. It's easier than getting dressed up and going through an agonizing first date. I just go online. There are no distractions. Sex is not a problem. You just talk until you feel like you want to meet."

Anna fits the category of Seeker. She wants to find a sincere relationship. If Anna finds another Seeker online, they have the potential to form a happy and healthy relationship offline. The Seeker, in her sincere attempts, may unwittingly be drawn into cyber-infidelity. As you read on, you will see that the success of a relationship depends upon meeting the right type of partner.

The Explorer

"As odd as it seems," Rhoda says, "I think I've led a rather sheltered life. I am in college now, and I have a boyfriend from high school days, back home. I can tell from listening to everyone up here at school that my boyfriend and I really act like kids that come from a small town, like we do. I can tell from everything people do here that I am different. I am definitely not cool.

"So I am trying things out online. Why not? I've got nothing to lose. It's fun. I talk to a lot of guys. They are not boyfriends. I tell them I've got a boyfriend back home. Meanwhile, I am learning a lot from them. I also joined a sex-only chat room. One man pounced on me. This would have driven me to tears in person, but I got a chance to respond. I didn't have to run out of the room or anything. We've been chatting like crazy...don't know if it will go anywhere else. It's fun for now. I feel like I am learning a lot, getting into the world. So I am getting to know a lot about myself as well. But mainly I know I've got my basic values."

Rhoda is using the Internet to experiment with different sides of herself. When Rhoda went to college in a big city, she realized that that she was inexperienced compared to her peers. Her personal development was limited. The Internet is giving her the opportunity to meet many types of people and to experiment with new behaviors. Rhoda seems to have her feet planted firmly on the ground, even though her thoughts and fantasies are roaming the Internet. She is using the Internet for personal growth. Employing the Internet to explore different parts of oneself is a legitimate use of the technology.

The Romantic

"I dreamed of meeting a sensitive, sweet man who would be very romantic," Beijing Flower said. "I had never been able to have relationships with men before, but I know what I want. I like attention, appreciation. I would like love notes—little touches that make me feel special.

"I did meet a man online who seemed to be what I dreamed of. He was very romantic. He said that he could not live without me. I felt I really knew him. Besides being romantic, we shared the same cultural background.

"One spring break from college, and after having spoken to him for four months online, I went to his city, San Francisco, to meet him. I was scared. It was risky, but I felt I had to do it. I fell in love with him He is in person what he is online. He is everything I know I need. We are going to keep seeing each other and 'talk' online."

"Beijing Flower" is, as her alias suggests, a romantic woman seeking a romantic partner. Luckily for Beijing Flower, she met such a guy who, like all Romantics, dreamed of sweeping someone away. So far, things worked out well for her in her quest.

Romantics must pay attention to "red flags," those nagging doubts about what is being said or inconsistencies in the story. They tend to feel transformed by love and often lack skills to stand up for themselves, and can find themselves in trouble or hurt if they come across the Seducer, the Dumper, or the Compulsive.

The Escapist

"I picked the name 'Orchid' because it's kind of how I saw myself—beautiful, exotic. It can be so dark and cold where I live I don't even want to go outside. I have no social life. Period. Sometimes I think there isn't really anybody out there for me in the real world. I had a horrible experience dating a man that I work with a few years ago. I'm fed up with the dating scene, but I get cabin fever sitting in the house alone. I don't want to meet anyone online for a real relationship offline. I just want to have some fun. My friend loves meeting guys online, and she got me to try it out. I guess it's nice to at least have someone to talk to. Talking on the Internet helps me forget my boredom. This way, I get to 'go out' and not worry about the bad side of relationships."

Like many people who are lonely, Orchid is reaching out through cyberspace to connect with someone. She finds satisfaction with a limited relationship, one in which she will never meet her partner face-to-face. For Orchid, this relationship fills an emotional need, while still letting her remain emotionally distant and safe. She may occupy her life with work and other obligations, and convince herself that she "doesn't have time" for a full relationship. She sees herself as "needing warmth," but not wanting the entrapments of a marriage or family. Knowing she can go online to find a connection fills a void and brings her what she seeks. Orchid is one of the people whose motivation for using the Internet is loneliness.

Escapists also use the Internet to help cope with emotional problems. Most people need to connect with others, and if they find that they cannot do so successfully in their everyday real world, they can now search the Internet for contact with others. Sometimes, unresolved anxieties or personal problems motivate people to reach out but maintain a distance. If interpersonal skills are at a minimum, the Internet becomes an avenue for the Escapist to have a relationship that works, limited as it is. Escapists, however, could easily be caught in a trap set by the the Seducer, the Dumper, the Compulsive, or the Criminal.

The Fibber

Marcus told us, "I choke when I try to talk to a girl face-to-face. My friends told me to get some practice on the Internet. They told me to call myself 'sledgehammer' or something like that, but I couldn't....

"A girl online is as interested in history as I am. When she asked what I look like, I told her I have brown hair and am of 'medium build.' That was a stretch since I am over 230 pounds...but what if she wouldn't want to talk with me anymore? Why wreck a good thing?"

Fibbers present themselves as thinner, better, smarter, or otherwise different from whom they are in the real world. They can be in a committed relationship or not. They can get away with their lies, exaggerations, and minimizations in text-based environments because no one can see them or verify their statements. Their lies, while deceiving, are not usually meant to be malicious. They may be dishonest and insincere, but have convinced themselves that their lies will not hurt anyone.

Of course, the situation changes if they attract someone who seriously falls for their story. They may experience further damage to an already low self-esteem if they are first accepted for their self-projected image, only to be rejected when the truth is revealed. They may be seeking emotional or sexual connection, or both.

The Lurker

Elusive people, Lurkers rarely engage others actively online, and when they do, their involvement is minimal. As Lucinda put it, "He just hangs out. It makes me really nervous, having a bunch of people just watching us and hardly saying anything."

It is difficult to assess whether or not Lurkers are sincere. While caution is in order, it is likely that most of these people are shy. But without information to confirm this suspicion, it is best to avoid these people and not try to engage them. If you do, notice how they might try to entice you to communicate and reveal information about yourself. Be smart. Reveal nothing personal to a Lurker who comes out for a brief moment in a sexualized Internet environment. Along with Escapists and Fibbers, Lurkers may be recreational, at risk, or compulsive cyber-sex users. These users are described in more depth in Chapter Four.

The Seducer

Joanna told us her story in tears.

"I met him online," she began. "He called himself 'chef4u.' I knew from that name that he was going to cook something special for me! I have never married and didn't get out much because of taking care of a sick relative for years. When a friend suggested I try the Internet, I had a social life for the first time in years! I had fun talking with several men, but this one really captured my interest. He opened himself up to me and sent me his picture. He wasn't spectacular looking, but nice. I loved the way he kept asking me about my favorite foods...he said he wanted to cook for me.

"I finally sent him a picture and it went from there. He asked if he could phone me. I was glad he did. His voice was so nice....He never brought up phone or cyber-sex, so he seemed like a gentleman. It got so I couldn't wait for his phone call. So I was ready when he asked if he could pay all the expenses and come and visit me....

"I talked to my friends online. That's when I heard he does this all the time. 'He loves the seduction,' they told me. He's visited a whole chain of women, and he never sees them a second time. This guy can't make a commitment."

The Seducer can be either male or female. Joanna is a Seeker looking for a serious life partner. She is very much like Nancy, the Seeker, not married and wanting a family. She is using the Internet to screen people, in search of Mr. Right. Joanna had the misfortune to meet the Seducer, who enjoys seduction as a sport.

Seducers can also be married. Despite reaching chronological adulthood, these people still need endless attention and acceptance from others to feel a sense of self-worth. Adult Seducers are immature. Their marriage may be troubled, or they may be troubled themselves. They may be unable to understand the impact on others and are likely to be narcissistic. Seducers are not seeking a relationship, but self-confirmation from others. These individuals have not learned to calm their own anxieties. They most likely cannot see exchanges from both points of view. They are likely to vacillate from feeling too self-centered to feeling very upset that others are not willing to validate them. Because they may think the world revolves around them, they tend to believe others are there to meet their needs. He or she may also be sexually compulsive, or an at-risk user.

The Compulsive

"It's all over, Sam. Clear out your desk and leave by 3:00 P.M., today! We are a baby products business, and we have no place for this kind of stuff around here."

Sam was caught red-handed. He had been looking at pornography on his computer when the office manager walked into his office. There he sat, in the beautifully furnished office of the firm he'd made his sanctuary for the last three years. He felt as though he couldn't breathe. His boss continued, "Look, Sam. You have been warned twice, and you're still doing it. Go to personnel now."

"Jim, give me another chance" Sam pleaded.

"We've given you other chances."

"I promise, Jim. I'll stop."

"That's just it, Sam. Apparently, you can't stop."

It was difficult for Sam to get out of his chair. The weight of what had happened fell heavily upon him. He saw his hard-earned career falling apart, and the possibility of losing his wife. He'd neglected her for so long, explaining that this job was their ticket to a happier life. How could Ellen ever understand, when he himself could not begin to explain what was happening. He wouldn't be able to hide it anymore. Everyone would find out.

Sam fell victim to his personal problems that surfaced when he was tempted by the accessibility and anonymity of the Internet. The information highway is not the only road being traveled in cyberspace. Other paths are being explored, new people are being met, and new behaviors are being tried. Sam was cyber-sexually compulsive.

He coped with temporary anxieties by practicing daily rituals. For example, he would find himself regularly logging on to check for new messages and sharing intimate, personal details with others online. These activities absorbed a great deal of his time. He allowed his compulsive activities to interfere with his occupational functioning. Although he tried to focus on work, what became apparent was that he was trying to avoid real-life intimacy and reduce his personal anxiety through cyber-sex.

We will have much more to say throughout the book to help you identify this pattern of behavior. If indeed someone is cyber-sexually compulsive and they want to stop, treatment can help them do so and the real-life relationship can be saved.

The Dumper

April recalls, "Christmas Eve felt very lonely to me last year. I remember I was going to the annual big dinner party at my parents' home, which is a family tradition, and I was feeling pretty let down. I had hoped that Jonathan would join us, but he couldn't because his parents were just getting in from the airport about the time my parents' dinner was to start. I met Jonathan in a chat room for singles and we hit it off beautifully. We had not met and I was hoping we could meet face-to-face at Christmas. He meant a great deal to me. We had cyber-sex regularly, and I thought I had found the right guy."

I was dressing when the phone rang and a voice said, "April?"

"Yes," I replied.

"This is Jonathan's wife. Merry Christmas!" she said in a tight, angry voice.

"What?!"

"You heard me! Jonathan's wife."

"Are we talking about Jonathan XXXX?"

"That's the one!"

"It can't be. He's not married!"

"Oh, April, dear. He is very married."

"I don't believe this."

"We're married. We have two adorable daughters. And we're mortgaged up the wazoo. Are you saying you aren't aware of this?"

"It can't be. We are going..."

"To Florida," she interrupted.

"Yes, but I can't believe this. How do you know about Florida? How do you know about me? Why would he do this? What is going on? I don't understand what is happening."

"I know you because he left your last email on the desk. Why? To make me miserable. Our life together hasn't been a bed of roses. He's done this before. I won't give him a divorce, but he just keeps trying."

"I can't believe this."

"You want to talk to him? He's right here," she said.

"Right there? I thought he was picking his parents up at the airport."

"Picking his parents up? They've been dead for years."

So that was my Christmas! I really thought I had been so lucky to meet the man of my dreams on the Internet. I feel so used.

Jonathan is a Dumper. He is trying to exit his marriage by using the Internet to have an affair. He hopes his wife will discover the affair, get angry, and divorce him. He does not have the skills to deal with his dissatisfaction openly and seek resolution with his wife. He sees divorce as the easiest way out of his difficult situation.

There are some variations on this type of person. For example, some Dumpers have an affair so that there is someone to lean on through the difficult process. Others have an affair to bring the couple into therapy so the therapist can help the partner adjust to the departure.

Although the Dumper is cheating, his or her motivation differs from the Seducer. The Dumper wants to leave the relationship and chooses to do so by cyber-infidelity. The Seducer does not necessarily want to leave his or her committed relationship, but is acting from other needs, such as boosting his or her self-esteem, coping with feelings of emptiness, or attempting to solve other emotional problems.

The Criminal

Criminals exist in far too many places in the real world. It is not surprising that they appear on the Internet. Cloaked in the anonymity of the Internet, they take advantage of the weak, the innocent, and the unsuspecting. Some of the criminals online are sexual predators. They seek to meet their needs without the consent of their victims. For example, some seek to satisfy themselves through interaction with minors. The following is a true story of how a sexual predator used the Internet to attract the attention of Katie Tarbox, a thirteen-year-old girl.

Katie Tarbox wrote her memoir, called *Katie.com: My Story*, about an online encounter with a man struggling with pedophilia. She met Frank Kufrovich, a forty-one-year-old businessman from Southern California, in an AOL teen chat room. The anonymity of the Internet allowed him to hide his identity from her. He told her was a twenty-three-year-old college student named Mark. "Valley Guy" was his alias. In their online discussions, he minimized her concern about their age difference.

Kufrovich suggested they meet when she was scheduled for a swim meet in Dallas. Katie agreed and met him in his hotel room. She was surprised to find a middle-aged man, not a college student. She did not know he was a pedophile. He kissed and fondled her, but his plans went awry when her mother and the police arrived at the door.

After her mother had discovered Katie was missing, she was able to discover her whereabouts by asking her friends. The Dallas police arrested him. An FBI investigation showed he had several sexual relationships with younger girls and boys. Kufrovich pleaded guilty to two federal crimes and was sentenced to prison for eighteen months. He was freed in June 1998.

Katie was an Explorer, a minor who was using the Internet to learn social skills. She thought she was in contact with a young, single man, and instead discovered a Criminal. Fortunately, Katie did not hide her whereabouts from her friends. Because these friends were honest with her mother, Katie was saved.

Deep Trouble or Simple Exploration?

In making your own decisions about cyber-infidelity and the Internet, it may be important for you to know that the Internet itself cannot hurt you. When used appropriately, the Internet can be a source of unparalleled learning and creativity, opening a door to unseen worlds and experiences. People have successfully connected with others, received support, and fallen in love online.

Nevertheless, people can hurt themselves and those they love by misusing the Internet. The same can be said of inappropriate use of telephones, televisions, or automobiles. Technology has no virtue or vice in and of itself. As human beings, we bring morality, or a lack of it, to these tools.

Therefore, the Internet can be used to give free expression to an undeveloped, misunderstood, and harmful part of our selves. Our online impulses must be kept in check, just like the desire to hang up the telephone when upset, to watch too much television, or to drive recklessly. With regard to fidelity, the Internet allows those who wish to be deceitful and betray their commitments of monogamy to do so more easily.

Special Themes

A number of other special themes are central to understanding infidelity on the Internet. These themes have been woven throughout the book, but are being highlighted here for your ease of identification as you explore this brave new parallel world with us, where freedom of choice creates illusion and reality at the same time.

Men and Women

You will notice that we frequently describe the differences between men's and women's uses of the Internet. As with all statements about the genders, our statements must be imbued with an understanding that gender is not absolute. That is, there are varying degrees along the continuum of masculinity and femininity. We intend to portray this continuum as it occurs in nature, rather than simply as male and female, heterosexual, bisexual, or homosexual.

Nonetheless, general observations about genders and orientations are being made by researchers, and they will be discussed as they are described by their reports. For now, let us introduce this theme by noting that researchers have also differentiated between the types of sexual websites of interest to men and women. In general, men seem to prefer sexually explicit materials, while women prefer more interaction and relationships. Men tend to predominate the areas that offer erotica, such as websites and newsgroups. Women tend to be primarily drawn to dating chat rooms and other discussion areas.

International Flair
Users of the Internet represent different cultures, religions, social groups, and sexual orientations. They use the Internet to communicate and to relate. The Internet is not only a communication network, but also a global social experiment. This international aspect makes the Internet truly revolutionary.

With respect to infidelity, such global diversity suggests that most Netizens will understand infidelity and sexuality from their own particular cultural and religious norms. When it comes to definitions of infidelity, conservative suburbanites may differ from their more outrageous children, Mormons may differ from Catholics, and African villagers may differ from couples in Iceland. We therefore have attempted to take a conservative approach in our definitions of these phenomena, but also recognize that different people have different beliefs.

Two such colleagues are psychologists Azy Barak, Ph.D., and Marilyn P. Safir, Ph.D., of the University of Haifa in Israel. They wrote an article entitled "Sex and the Internet: An Israeli Perspective," in which they discussed how "sex-related" Internet behavior represents a global phenomenon. They looked at Israel, which has a mix of old and new traditions, secular and religious groups, a variety of cultures, and a complex political system, with a small population in a compact geographic area.

They described Israeli websites for pornography, escort services, sex magazines, sex shops, chat rooms, and dating services. The authors concluded that the interests of Israeli users "are quite similar to what is available in the West. The contents of verbal messages in chat rooms or graffiti on walls all strongly resemble American, Indian, British, Dutch, French, or Japanese sex-related websites and their functions."

Such early reports give evidence that online romantic and sexual communities are proliferating worldwide, developing their own languages, functions, and creativity. While sociologists examine these newly-forming communities, psychologists look at interactions between people, and ethnographers examine written aspects of these developing cultures.

Throughout this book, we will offer you our views, as well as those of many researchers, sprinkled with the voices of many Internet explorers who have responded to our *SelfhelpMagazine* essay contest. This will give you an opportunity to draw your own conclusions regarding cyber-infidelity.

Love at the Speed of Electricity: The Power of Virtual Attraction

In England, at the end of the day when people want to unwind, they often go down to the village pub and laugh about life with their neighbors. In warmer climates such as Mexico and Italy, people visit the village square and exchange pleasantries. In Israel, people stroll Dizengoff Square to the circle, where they watch the Adam fountain sculpture spill water, shoot fire, and make rings. Music plays and they "schmooze."

The more things change, the more they remain the same. For centuries, lovers have met in public places, only to seek private places together. They breathlessly share secrets, dreams, and fantasies. Today, people on the Internet meet in public websites, email discussion lists, and a variety of other gathering places. They then move to private places, such as chat rooms or direct email messaging. Their love messages are amplified and transported electronically by cell phones, beepers, audio- and videostreaming websites, digital monitors, and transcontinental email—all at the bat of a bedroom eye.

Lovers have also invented many secret codes through the years—endearments, *noms de plume*, and pet names. All of these can now be used in email secured by digital signatures to prevent the delivery of love-struck messages to the wrong address. Millions of people using the Internet now have many convenient communities to "scroll," rather than "stroll," and quicker access to private meeting places once they have found someone with whom to share sweet nothings, deep secrets, and orgasms. To understand how cyber-affairs can develop and thrive online, we must understand why people seek relationships online, the various powers of the Internet, the components of love, and the dynamics of relationships.

Why Do People Seek Relationships Online?
People bring different motivations to the Internet. Socially isolated people may seek those who share their language or culture, single parents may want to find other single parents without the problems involved with childcare, and senior citizens reach out to other computer-savvy seniors to share their golden years. Some enjoy the buzz of talking to many

different people in a very short amount of time. Many people, dissatisfied with their committed relationships, look for companionship online. Some find the attraction so strong that they become involved in a cyber-affair. Yet, there are others who go online specifically for the purpose of having a cyber-affair.

"I like the chat rooms because I meet people who fall for my charade," Richard, an eighteen-year-old clerk explained. "I pretend to be a big rock star. I know a little about music, so I can pull it off. Some people go along with it, but I think they're on to me. Anyhow, its fun."

Abby, a seventy-three-year-old retired librarian, reported, "I have met the most wonderful people online—and even had a few romantic flings. It helps break up the monotony of my life. I may be older than a lot of these people, but I'm not out of commission. It makes me feel young again!"

Elsewhere, people are finding it increasingly permissible to put personal ads on dating websites, email lists, and other singles areas of the Internet. For example, Swoon, the popular dating and romance website, receives millions of visitors per week.

As always, there are those dissatisfied with existing relationships. Many of these people lack the skills to make the needed changes. The Internet provides an escape for millions who otherwise cannot find a reasonable way to transform their lives. They may feel trapped by a history of poor choices, bad luck, or conflicting values, or feel suffocated by what they perceive to be unchangeable living circumstances. Without upsetting their daily lives, they use the Internet to develop a parallel world in which they are freer, more alive, and yes, single.

For many, the Internet has also become a social laboratory for examining oneself in relation to others. The Internet allows people to separate their interactions from their bodies with the goal of exploring various parts of their personalities. They are finding virtual romance and learning about themselves in the process. People who have participated in the *SelfhelpMagazine* Essay Contest have expressed some of these feelings.

Trudy, a twenty-three-year-old administrative assistant, told us, "I know I have some fears. I don't trust too easily. This seems to be a way to start for me."

Jon, a twenty-something computer programmer, said, "I can talk dirty online and if she doesn't like it, she can leave the IM (Instant Message). It's a lot better than in the real world, where she would tell everybody."

As Phyllis, a forty-two-year-old farmer, told us, "What I like sexually, I have discovered, is a turn-off to almost anyone I meet. So online I don't have to play the dating game and get rejected. I just tell them what I want. Shutting me down online doesn't bother me the way it does face-to-face."

However, there are people who look for romance and sexuality online, despite the fact that they are in committed, monogamous relationships.

Barney, a thirty-four-year-old car salesman, said, "I use the Internet to fool around. I'm married and don't want any other commitments."

Tom, a fifty-three-year-old plumber, wrote, "I don't know what led up to it besides boredom in my relationship."

Patti, a twenty-nine-year-old social worker, reflects, "I wasn't really looking, not consciously. But I did find online what I lacked in real life."

The Internet is a powerful aphrodisiac. This power comes from its ability to add new dimensions to the written word and to alter the experiences of time, space, and social connections—conditions that are missing from the real world, but are unique to the virtual world. An exploration of these unique characteristics will help us understand the mystique of virtual attraction.

The Written Word

Correspondence has enticed eager lovers for years. Now it can whirl through cyberspace and delicately be delivered onto someone's desktop within seconds of being composed. Tenderly and passionately written, love letters have made the heart grow fonder for centuries. Technology adds unique advantages that make it a powerful aphrodisiac.

The Internet allows you to control your message, and, at the same time, prevents the intrusion of reality. Bad breath, dirty fingernails, or an irritating tendency to interrupt are irrelevant in email of chat rooms. Lovers are not distracted by physical attributes, allowing them to listen with their inner selves—their souls.

As Ellen said, "Sometimes I have to laugh at what I am writing and the way I look. Hey, my hair is wet, I'm wearing sweats, and my room is a mess, but I'm writing about romantic getaways in the Bahamas."

Email and chat rooms also tap into a different function in human communication—inner dialogue. People tend to find it easier to communicate deeply-felt emotions through writing rather than speaking. Couples often write notes after a fight, or send a card to express difficult emotions.

The written message is something tangible, something held onto, referred to years later, read and reread, even after the sender is gone. Love letters have been cherished for decades. With computers, email love letters or records of chat room discussions can be saved on a hard drive. However, they are not always accurately read.

Accuracy of reading the written word also plays a part in how successfully you can navigate romances developed primarily in email and chat rooms. If your emotions override your logical mind, you can misread messages and get hopelessly lost in your fantasy of what the other is saying. Perceptual inaccuracies are common when reading the written word. For example, count the number of times the letter *F* appears in the following sentence:

FINISHED FILES ARE THE RESULT OF YEARS
OF SCIENTIFIC STUDY COMBINED WITH THE
EXPERIENCE OF MANY YEARS OF EXPERTS.

Just to be sure, go slowly and count them again. The letter *F* appears seven times in the above paragraph. Most people count five or fewer, and are convinced they are right until they are asked to look at the *F* in the word "of." Simple reading errors, increased reading speed, and heightened emotion lead to inaccuracy when reading email and chat discussions. People often react not to what is written, but to what they imagined was written. When they get upset about what they imagined and refuse to take another look at the facts, they can create havoc in their relationships.

We will discuss this at length later in this book, but for now, just note that the written word in email and chat rooms can be inaccurately read. That is, a significant amount of distortion can take place, and people can feel hurt and be hurtful to others when they act on their perceptions rather than the facts.

The Experience of Time
Americans went from waiting for their love letters by Pony Express to waiting for their neighborhood postal carrier. The paradox is that today's messages can be transmitted more quickly than ever, yet can more easily camouflage the length of time actually taken for composition. Email can be sent in almost real time, or can sit for days and months, only to be answered when the other party is ready. Imperfections in the system allow for more tolerance for delayed responses, too. Either way, email allows for more breathing room than offline meetings. Its text-based nature allows extroverts to share all their personal details ahead of time and introverts to move at a slower pace.

After dates, people often wish they had not said this, or would have said that. However, time can feel suspended on the Internet because there is a newfound opportunity to think about, compare, and change messages.

Writing also typically slows the reaction of the recipient, and gives him or her more time to prepare a thoughtful response. On the other hand, the immediacy of email or chat room transmission can lead to impulsive responses. Once again, the Internet enigma is that this new technology can move us in opposite directions, more quickly or more slowly, depending on our preferences. People can use email and chat in ways they regret. They can impulsively send love messages to people they hardly know and sit anxiously until they receive a response. They can send sexual fantasies to people who will use them in unintended ways.

When upset, impulsive people can also send angry messages to individuals or groups, and when they have calmed themselves, feel overly exposed.

They sometimes get angry reactions in response, and a cycle begins until it is resolved or someone has the strength to walk away. The tendency to send angry email messages is so prevalent that some of the leading software now has a warning feature that allows the user to know when incoming or outgoing messages contain hostile or provocative words. Impulsivity, then, is being slowed by software. While the delivery system is speeding interactions, software is being developed to signal people to reflect. Without the time needed to write, address, stamp, and mail an envelope; or dial, ring, and speak to a person, people are finding that they are quickly damaging their relationships and hurting others needlessly.

Email and chat rooms seem to accelerate romance and seduction. Frequent contacts change our perception of intimacy. For instance, whether you have three exchanges with someone spread over three days, three weeks, or three months generally makes a difference in how close you will feel after the third date. Many contacts over a short time may contribute to a rapid sense of intimacy. Getting to know people through frequent contact on the Internet can create a strong sense of bonding, just as it does in the real world. Lovers can have "pillow talk" from thousands of miles apart, and do it for hours, day or night.

Interruptions in time also are easily covered in email, which leads to several other interesting features of this world. Email creates not only strong bonding because of frequent contact, but also increases it because of the greater sense of quality contact. Your lover can interrupt the conversation with a number of meaningless distractions, and you would never know it. When you get an email, the impression is usually that it was all written in one sitting.

Some people use this feature to their advantage. They may claim their computer was down, and meanwhile they were writing, editing, and reediting for hours or days. People can craft an email that took hours to write, but appears as if it were written quickly and casually. While such deceit is not the norm, with cyber-affairs you cannot always expect honesty. Alternatively, interruptions in chat rooms are much more obvious, yet still leave the recipient eagerly waiting for more, and wondering if the delay is a technical glitch or simply the result of the communicator's distraction with other chat room discussions, incoming email, or fixing dinner.

Regardless of the degree of honesty shown by different people, uninterrupted messages can feel more personal and more sensitive than when interrupted. Email and private chat rooms can easily provide a false sense of "you are here and I'm focusing only on you."

On the other hand, email and chat room communication can be sent impulsively, whipped up and whisked off within a matter of seconds. Only the writer knows for sure. The obsessed lover, then, can send a series of short but well-written messages to heighten the experience of the recipient, and never reveal the time and energy that go into the effort. Taken to a new high, or low, depending on your perspective, insincere people can craft a series of romantic email notes and send them to dozens of potential lovers with a few simple clicks of the mouse.

However, it is also possible that fewer distractions are taking your lover's attention away from you. Typing email and chat room messages are most often solitary experiences, which means writers can have fewer competing cues from moment to moment. That's the mystique of having a love affair with someone you can't see—you never know what they're doing. Lovers can be less distracted by someone who is interrupting them or otherwise limiting their flow.

People online who are not interrupted or distracted often discuss much more than they would offline. They report talking about their personal histories, future goals, past accomplishments, families, jobs, education, health, finances, and other such personal and intimate topics sooner than they might if dating in the real world. Time spent at a movie, sporting event, or shared task may not feel as intimate as time spent together on the Internet, sharing personal information. When they are honest about themselves, people can get to know more about one another online than they do when spending the same number of hours together offline.

Love and romance are similar in many ways, whether online or offline. But each technology (email, chat rooms, video) offers special features that can be used to enhance or diminish specific qualities of the sender.

As Chloe, a thirty-year-old real estate sales agent, wrote, "I can't believe it! I met the most wonderful guy online. He's not a nerd. He just never had time to develop a relationship. Online it was easier. We are offline sometimes and still online at other times. The last time we met offline, he gave me the most beautiful engagement ring."

Expressing Emotion

The Internet has its own conventions, and in some respects, its own language. When conversing through text-based parts of the Internet, such as chat rooms or email, symbols and abbreviations are used as shortcuts. Commonly used symbols, called "emoticons," are provided for you in Appendix B. They are combinations of keyboard symbols used to express feelings. Some of these symbols will be used in the stories throughout this book. Here are of some basic emoticons: "smileys" :-) :] :-} "frowns" :-(:[or a "kiss" :-* (turn your head to the left and use your imagination to see a facial expression).

Appendix B also lists many common acronyms, which are abbreviations used to quickly type frequently used expressions. For example, "LOL" means "laughing out loud." Others might include "BTW," which means "by the way" and "ROFL" means "rolling on the floor laughing." BRB means "be right back" and is often used in chat rooms when someone needs to leave the keyboard. These symbols help fill in the lack of visual cues.

Emotions are also expressed by drawing verbal pictures of emotions, such as:

::::::hands on hips, tapping foot:::::::

or

~~~sliding into the chair, right next to you~~~~.

People can make "I" statements about their feelings, and reveal deeply personal events and feelings. Creative types make their own symbols and expressions on the fly. <:^)

Pace

Offline, people meet quickly and slowly get to know each other over time. Online, they learn about each other quickly and slowly move toward meeting face-to-face, often months or years later. For many people, real-life meetings never happen. Offline, people usually get an immediate sense of each other's bodies; online, they cannot, regardless of their desire.

Another unique aspect of email is that a rapid succession of contacts can feel less intrusive than receiving the same number of phone calls or visits from a lover. For example, if a virtual lover dropped several short "I love you" emails over the course of the workday, the recipient would probably feel less intruded upon than by receiving several visits at work. Getting multiple calls throughout the day from someone saying, "I love you" is likely to raise more concern about someone's emotional stability than to win your affection.

The quick pace of many email and chat room contacts over short periods also allows a couple to rapidly develop a shared language, a private understanding of each other, the relationship, and their future. It may contain personal jokes or other nuances that enhance the belief that they share closeness, something deemed "our love" that is exclusively theirs.

Emma writes, "It's interesting. I once met this guy who sent me flowers three times a day for two days in a row. I was harassed and annoyed, and finally got him to stop. Now I get emails five times a day from Ralph and I really like it."

Silence alters pace, and it is also experienced differently in email and chat rooms. Long silences can be interpreted to mean that the person has left the discussion to do something else. Long, unannounced silences are not easily tolerated in online courtship. Comfort is found in consistent communication. Keeping the pace is important.

People also get accustomed to the rapid pacing of email or chat room romance. If messages suddenly stop, either for the evening or altogether, the experience can be upsetting. Moving from frequent contact to no contact at all can add to the anxiety people often feel when a cyber-affair ends. The discrepancy between several contacts and an empty inbox can elicit feelings of helplessness and depression.

The difference in pace between frequent love notes and their sudden cessation can serve as a reoccurring reminder that the affair has ended. A person may find themselves obsessively checking an empty inbox or dating website throughout the day, only to reexperience the pain of lost love, the lover's refusal to respond, and the sheer hopelessness of the situation. For people caught in a love triangle with someone who is married and simply having a cyber-affair, this loss is unavoidable and can be very painful.

People experiencing this pain also have difficulty finding the support they otherwise would find for a lost relationship. Family and friends often do not understand the intensity of such feelings for someone whom they consider a stranger, who never came to dinner, who does not have a recognizable physical presence, face, or voice.

Insincere people who regularly engage in affairs have always left a path of broken hearts. When empowered by the Internet, these people can quicken the pace, get what they want, and break more hearts than ever before.

Altered Social Conventions

Dating on the Internet eliminates social pressures found in the real world. Virtual lovers are not bothered with eating habits, grooming, social graces, or meeting each other's friends and family. People are not as focused on style. They need not worry about a bad hair day, wearing the right clothes, or whether they can dance. Lacking the physical aspect of a real-life encounter, other skills are needed in virtual romance and seduction.

Charm on the Internet

Virtual lovers must use their intellect to charm and win the attention of potential partners. Many people are being forced to develop the skills of written communication.

Wendy reports, "Yes...we sometimes meet face-to-face, BUT...we talk every day on the Internet—it's cheaper than phone calls! I think being online for a while has *helped* our relationship because it is based on communication, which is a big problem with most couples. We share everything and sometimes it's easier to be on a computer, typing."

Not only do people need to communicate effectively with the written word, but the "what-is-beautiful-is-good stereotype" is not as prevalent online as it is offline. While it is true that someone who is focused on appearance is likely to seek partners whose photos are readily available, some people choose to not offer their photos. They prefer to concentrate on written exchanges with suitors before sharing their photos. By not focusing on appearance, they allow themselves a much wider range of possibilities to explore.

As they do offline, people on the Internet try to hide their lack of charm. Email and chat rooms force the writer to communicate, and eventually, one's written skills, or lack thereof, are revealed. People with poor written communication skills may be passed over for those who can charm with a quick retort, a whimsical thought, or a soothing anecdote. Then again, if they lack the skill to turn a catchy phrase, they can put a sexy picture of themselves (or someone else) on a dating website and draw lots of attention without being good writers.

Deciding When to Tell

If a virtual romance shifts the emphasis in a relationship from outward appearances to inner thoughts and feelings, people experience freedom to make decisions regarding when and how to reveal information about themselves that causes them anxiety. Research has shown that there is no "golden rule" in timing self-disclosure of negative aspects of oneself online. Some people prefer to reveal such information early on. Others choose to wait.

"I have been very lonely since my wife's death five years ago from breast cancer, a disease which struck with a vengeance. We had two bad years before she died. I am raising my kids alone. My three little girls have been through a lot. They are being raised by me, a housekeeper, and a wonderful grandmother—my wife's mother. She wants me to start looking for 'companionship,' as she put it.

"I went online. No one was right until I started communicating with Casablanca. We hit it off, because we both love old movies and that flick was a favorite for both of us. She started calling me Rick, Humphrey Bogart's name in the movie.

"We talked for two months—no sex. When I said I wanted to meet her, she agreed. When we met I could tell she was very nervous. She eventually revealed that she had a physical disability, one that made it hard for her to walk. I assured her that it did not matter to me.

"We've been married a year now. I'm writing to you in celebration."

Casablanca did not reveal her disability until after months of discussion with Rick. Her intent was obviously to protect herself from the possibility of rejection. In this case, her fibbing was not destructive. In other cases, it can be. People experiment with where to draw the line between telling the truth and allowing their new romance to languish in the anonymity provided by the Internet. The inability to see and hear one another in email and chat rooms can mask many physical disabilities and emotional problems.

As video capabilities become more commonplace, they may bring their own complications. For now, it is safe to assume that both sincere and insincere people are using the Internet as a way to find romance and as a way to have cyber-affairs. In such a world, it is wise to know yourself, your own motivations, and your own vulnerabilities.

Intrigue

Sparking intrigue is another one of the Internet's fundamental draws. A soulmate might be a click away, and after several weeks of steamy correspondence, so is the possibility of falling in love. On the other hand, this same person could be a voyeur. Sharing personal secrets, even sexual ones, with someone who is nameless, faceless, and without a physical presence is tantalizing for many people.

Private chat rooms and email, perhaps heightened with an occasional picture, are breeding grounds for fantasy. As in real life, intrigue on the Internet is more a matter of imagination than fact. The turn of a phrase, the half invitation, and the mention of a passing thought can allow the reader to add his or her own spice to the mix.

A message can be fuzzy or precise, depending on the motivation of the sender. Fuzzy information can be used to hide something or create curiosity, while precision can be used to pinpoint facts and reveal one's true self. For people such as the Seducer, the Dumper, the Fibber, and other insincere people on the Internet, intrigue may serve the purpose of hiding the real self.

These people are likely to communicate in ways that are fuzzy, that leave questions in the mind of their readers. They may intentionally want to remain unknown, not want to reveal the details of their situations, or know the specifics of the person with whom they are interacting.

The Escapist and the Seducer tend to look for and offer less detail. They often are more suggestive, leaving something to the imagination. They search for an image to stimulate their romantic or sexual fantasies. Often, these people present themselves as wanting something more lasting, but in truth, they deceive those who are looking for serious relationships.

Romance has had risk of deception through the ages, but the Internet adds new twists and capabilities. Meeting electronically allows people to push normal social limits a bit farther, both within themselves and with others. People can be more deceptive than ever, and others may mistake their motivations. The solution to this problem is to ask very precise questions and evaluate the quality of the response. Avoiding deception online is tricky, but those who seek to be vague can be uncovered if they react inappropriately to a series of very pointed and direct questions about how they feel and what they are thinking.

Absence of a Physical Presence

The average American juggles many changing identities during the day: mom, wife, commuter, boss/employee, cook, housekeeper, student, and/or lover. The roles merge and separate, calling upon various parts of ourselves to step to the forefront and command a particular situation, then retreat while we prepare to deal with the tasks of the next situation. These changing roles occur in the real world where our physical bodies are relatively unchanging.

However, the Internet successfully allows us to create an illusion for ourselves as well as for other people. When online, identity can exist simply as an email address, and whatever other information or profile we choose to give of ourselves. Therefore, we can assume roles or identities that are quite different from the roles we take when identified with a body. For example, the shy, retiring, petite woman can become an aggressive tyrant online. The kind gentleman can become a sexual deviant. The shy boy can try to become an experienced Don Juan. The sense of self as either portrayed or experienced online can change from window to window, alias to alias, message to message. Chuck, a thirty-three-year-old nurse, wrote, "I am heavy and the women I meet are turned off by my appearance. All my friends think I am a great guy and include me in their activities, but none of the women want to date me. But I have the same sexual feelings that thin guys do. So, for me the virtual world is better than the real world."

Beyond the obvious experimentation that many people are enjoying online, some people are affected emotionally by the revelations they have as they experience themselves in various roles. This new ability to move from a full-bodied sense of self in real time and space to a fluid and bodiless identity, freed through technology, is leading some people to add new dimension to the ageless philosophical questions of who, why, and what they are.

Even more intriguing is how some people manage to find online experiences without being damaged emotionally, while others get hopelessly lost. Self exploration is healthy and necessary to understand one's needs and preferences. Knowing how to explore oneself without violating one's commitments is one of the secrets of success. Linda concluded about navigating these dangerous but exciting avenues, "People with unresolved emotional issues can become irreversibly tangled in a web of problems. Anonymous relationships are not only easier to get into, but they create the false impression of being easy to get out of. People don't realize that emotional ties can be even greater because of the rapid rate of communication."

More precisely, we are discussing issues of identity and the complications that can arise when identity is not yet fully formed. Psychology theorists such as well-known Margaret Mahler, Ph.D., have defined identity as, "the earliest awareness of a sense of being; of entity—a feeling that includes in part, we believe, a...body with...energy. It is not a sense of *who* I am but *that* I am; as such, this is the earliest step in the process of the unfolding of individuality."

Linda continues, "Online it can take longer to get to know the person for real. They can say all they want to on email and you feel like you have gotten to know them, but nothing is better than meeting face-to-face. You can perceive so much more in just one few minute's meeting than you can perceive through a computer screen. Someone's persona surrounds them in real life, and they can't hide it as well."

Some people engage in alias identities online. They are surprised to experience emotions they never anticipated. Because the Internet gives free rein to unlimited selves without bodies to anchor them in reality, it may allow previously unexplored parts of one's personality to appear. While exciting and enthralling at times, this freedom can also be confusing. Those people most likely to be confused or easily upset are individuals who are inexperienced at examining their psychological functioning. Often, individuals who previously denied or have hidden unacknowledged elements of their personality will see their behavior on the Internet as being not of themselves and not make anything of it.

An example of this comes from Natalie, a thirty-nine-year-old who has been married for twelve years. She speaks as if she knows herself, but reveals an uncertainty that comes through as bravado on one hand, and repeated questioning on the other. An indication that she is struggling to integrate this new behavior is evident by noticing that she is focused on the experience of her virtual-sex partners, and the opinion of whomever is reading her story.

"I like to pursue men online. I know that I'm there for them online for sex and there's nothing wrong with that, I don't think. They love it, too. Married or not you don't have to tell everything to your husband, now do ya?"

Interestingly, she does not express how she feels during sex with men online, or how she feels about it when she is offline and with her husband. Looking inward may be too painful for her. She may be struggling to integrate her aberrant behavior with whom ever she wants to be in the world.

Psychology theorists Eric Fromm, Ph.D, and James Bugental, Ph.D., called for a return to what Bugental described as, "the expression of one's whole being in relationship..." Finding such an expression on the Internet, in a medium where anonymity and the lack of a physical presence are the norm, makes it difficult to imagine developing that type of all-encompassing love.

These aliases become associated with the messages they post. This, in turn, helps individuals develop online "presences," reputations, and identities. Another person online can't know for sure if these reputations and identities are completely fabricated, partially true, or all true. This freedom can give people the opportunity to explore and recapture lost parts of themselves.

For example, Tina, a twenty-four-year-old restaurant hostess, wrote, "We did, however, have our first interactive cyber-sex experience a few weeks after meeting online. I wanted to do it and I think he wanted it, too. But then it was over. Somehow it felt like a form of closure. After that, we stopped writing, and I got heavily involved with another man online, one who didn't travel for business and who I had no expectation of ever meeting in person. I decided that I would not show this new guy my picture. I really wanted our minds to connect. He impressed me with his thoughts and sense of humor. Then I felt I could be sexual again."

Making matters yet more complicated, once a person has invested time and energy into a pseudonym or alias, their emotional attachment to these fabricated identities can sometimes take on powers that are surprising even to themselves.

As Rita, a thirty-six-year-old nurse wrote, "I was nervous about going online, but my social life was for all intents and purposes nonexistent. When I was online, I took the name of somebody I admired in college. I acted the way she would have, and in a way I did not have the courage for in real life. When I became her online, I noticed that I thought in a different way. I acted more confidently and spoke more freely. I didn't censor myself."

It is even more interesting to note that people often choose an alias that captures an aspect of their own personality which they admire, want to improve, or would like to have associated with their comments. These factors also add to the complexity and fall into the Internet enigma. An identification and loyalty to an alias, even if it only represents a part of one's personality, is similar to the Internet being considered a place. It feels real in some ways, and unreal in others.

Allison explained, "My alias on the screen was "Ravenly," and I picked this name because it was exotic and dark. And in some ways that is how I see myself."

However, she described how other parts of her personality were kept secret, despite questions she received, "When I was asked to describe myself, I was a little hesitant because I didn't see myself as attractive. But I more or less told them the truth. But instead of giving an honest description, I portray myself in an indirect sort of way. For instance, I told them I worked out in the gym daily, and they assumed I was in good shape."

The Internet provides individuals more freedom of choice to increase risk-taking, and to learn about their impact on others and themselves. Knowing that someone is one thousand miles away can make it safer to share some types of information, such as sexual preferences, without exposing one's emotional vulnerability. The Internet enigma complicates the picture, because it also creates situations where they make themselves more emotionally vulnerable.

Emotional Vulnerability in a Parallel World

When we are unsure of ourselves in a relationship, we unconsciously use a variety of techniques to keep ourselves feeling balanced. These are known as defense mechanisms. Several defense mechanisms can come into play in relationships, but email and chat rooms are particularly conducive to a commonly used mechanism: projection.

Projection makes someone particularly sensitive to those things in others which are difficult to recognize in oneself. Projection is likely to fill the gaps to the degree that information is lacking. Chat rooms and email, then, being void of visual and auditory cues, often give people too much room to imagine what might be meant by a phrase, an email, or an entire relationship.

Let's try an experiment. We'll give you a few sentences, and after each, close your eyes and notice what you imagine:

- ➲ I want you to...
- ➲ I want you to be with me...
- ➲ I want you to be with me forever...
- ➲ I want you to be with me forever so I can...
- ➲ I want you to be with me forever so I can...get your help taking care of these three screaming kids.

The lack of information in the first few lines allows you to fill in the blanks with your own fantasy. Your fantasies are typically based on your own emotional needs. If you happen to desperately want a relationship, and someone you have been flirting with in email said, "I want you to," you might find yourself automatically thinking, "fly to Denver to meet me this weekend." But as information is increasingly provided for you, your mind is forced to eliminate possibilities and focus on the needs of the other person.

In the absence of information, we fill in the blanks with our particular needs. Much like a good computer program that remembers the last file used, personal needs and preferences stay at the forefront of our minds and fill the gaps when there is uncertainty.

Because people have different degrees of skill in communication, filling in the gap is not as accurate for some people as it might be for others. Some people project more of their feelings than others, and some individuals are more accurate in their projections. Email and chat room interactions leave many more gaps in communication than do face-to-face communications, and so, projection has much more room to create havoc.

Chat rooms and email make users more vulnerable because they restrict the amount of information available about a person. When in doubt, it is far better to encourage the other person to complete the thought. For example, "What do you mean? Tell me more. I don't understand." Asking the unasked question helps avoid problems.

Relationships on the Internet can also be swiftly terminated. Some people can use this feature of email and chat rooms to their advantage if they are intending to be devious or deceptive. Seducers and Criminals revel in this characteristic of text-based environments.

The Internet also allows people to present only a very controlled part of themselves. It is easy to see how people can misrepresent themselves. In his book, *Bandits on the Information Superhighway*, Daniel Barrett, Ph.D., cautions us to check ourselves on how much we really know about people with whom we share our hearts. He encourages people to be wary of assumptions, and look for facts. If attempts to get facts only lead to vague answers, it's time to stop revealing information.

In this parallel world, many frames of reference are not available. In real life, when a person lives in your geographic area, you can confirm your impressions. You might have shared knowledge of the same neighborhoods, schools, and activities.

Jessica, a thirty-year-old elementary school teacher, wrote, "I finally visited him. I knew what he looked like, because I had seen a picture of him. He took me to his favorite 'haunts,' which, in truth, frightened me. I didn't like the crowd, the language, or the serious drinking I saw. There are places in my city like that. If he wanted to go to one of those places in my area, I wouldn't have gone. I would have ended the relationship because that would have told me that we don't have much in common. Just hearing names of 'haunts' didn't help. I should have asked more."

Online relationships can be rich if the participants take the time to evaluate what they are fleeing and doing, but caution must be used. In "Are You Ready For Virtual Love?," psychiatrist and sex therapist Avodah Offit, M.D., wrote the following about the need for self-examination. "But perhaps the most intriguing danger of email is its ability to foster relationships that are like the patient-to-therapist connection, with one person developing exaggerated erotic dependence on another. Women (and men too) often feel that they have 'fallen in love' with their psychotherapists; people who they imagine will forever take care of them emotionally, physically, and financially. This same phenomenon may occur on email if the distant correspondent comes to be perceived as an imaginary parent or caretaker."

If, for example, someone's face was cradled tenderly as a child or slapped cruelly by a parent, that person may read those different possibilities into in an email posting describing the desire to touch his or her face. Long forgotten words and experiences from childhood can easily trigger stronger emotional reactions than intended. The more emotionally needy or unstable the person, the less he or she might realize his or her own communications are unclear, or carry a negative tone. Overly sensitive people react too quickly, without clarifying their statements or asking for an explanation of what the other person is saying.

Basic writing skills, interpersonal dynamics, and defense mechanisms are often neglected when looking at text-based romance, yet these are the cornerstones of effective online communications. The amount of information assumed and projected in virtual romance is dependent upon the reader's ability to read and remain objective, as well as the writer's honesty and writing abilities. The amount of fantasy that occurs with projection can easily consume the cyber-romantic, especially when reminded of a cyber-lover several times a day through short love notes delivered through email or instant messaging. Before long, fantasy can become an obsession, a constant preoccupation to fill the gaps left by disembodied words on a screen.

Obsession

As noted by writers for centuries, "love is blind." If love is blind offline, love in email and a chat room is blind, deaf, and mute! Still, flirtations, love, and sex flourish in these environments. To more fully understand this phenomena, we must first understand obsession.

Obsession is the mind's way of bridging the anxiety that occurs when there is a discrepancy between one's desires and one's reality. It is a repetitive replay of the elements of the discrepancy in a search for a solution to reduce that anxiety. Obsession is often found in romance, intimacy, and sex—where people's desires are strong, motivated by instinctual drives. And it is especially true in people dealing with virtual romance, where:

- ❯ the amount of factual information received is severely limited to text on a page rather than a whole human being;
- ❯ you only know what the other person chooses to tell;
- ❯ the pace of exchange is faster, so essential details may be intentionally or unintentionally omitted;
- ❯ the effort to make contact requires minimal input, so commitment may not be the same in both people; and
- ❯ the impact of the written word is delivered immediately, privately, and directly.

Obsession causes people to see that which does not exist, as well as ignore what does exist. In *Soul Mates: Honoring the Mysteries of Love and Relationship,* Thomas Moore discusses love through correspondence as such: "Relationship at a distance can do things for the heart that a closer, day-to-day companionship cannot."

Moore discusses how the soul is allowed expression in obsession, how one's often unmet needs are given a voice through these passions. He also discusses how obsessions can give us valuable clues about who we are and where we need to go to reach inner peace during our lifetimes. While it is often said that the early phases of romance include projection of our needs onto the other person, the Internet seems to make this happen more quickly, frequently, and succinctly than previous forms of correspondence. Obsession can fill the gaps between the moments of connection, and thereby alleviate the anxiety caused by separation. It can give us relief from painful feelings of loneliness.

Relief from Loneliness

Humans are social beings. Individuals seek affiliation to form relationships with other people. It is perhaps the escape from loneliness that drives us to connect with other people. Loneliness hurts, and is frequently a reason people go online. Many psychology researchers such as Abraham Maslow identified the need for "belongingness."

The number of Americans who feel lonely is surprising. David Burns, M.D, writes in his book, *Intimate Connections,* "In one recent national study by *Psychology Today* magazine, more than 50 percent of the 40,000 people surveyed reported feeling lonely." Generalized to the entire population, this suggests that loneliness afflicts more than 100 million Americans. There are two kinds of loneliness—social and emotional. Social loneliness occurs because of isolation from others. It is experienced by people confined to their homes, or who for some reason have few interactions with others.

The second type, emotional loneliness, occurs when emotional needs are not being met, because there is not an intimate connection to someone else. Intimacy needs are very strong for most people and when they are not met by the significant others in one's life, a profound sense of loneliness can be experienced.

Psychologists Carin Rubenstein, Ph.D., and Philip, Ph.D., Shaver write in *In Search of Intimacy* about four typical responses to loneliness, which they identify as sad passivity, distraction, active solitude, and social action.

- ❯ Sad passivity occurs when no action is taken, or one indulges in self-defeating behavior such as drug or alcohol use, overeating, or gambling.
- ❯ Distraction is a temporary solution, like going for a drive or taking in a movie. It does nothing to resolve the problem, but makes you feel better for a while.
- ❯ Active solitude is doing something alone from which you benefit, such as cooking, playing the piano, listening to music, reading, or woodworking.
- ❯ Social action is reaching out to others to alleviate loneliness. This is done by meeting friends, volunteering, phone calling, writing letters, or connecting with friends.

For many people, the Internet is being used to alleviate social and emotional loneliness. Individuals can pursue active solitude by using the Internet for study, research, and finding information. They can cope with their emotional loneliness by using the Internet to reach out to a global network of people or support groups at anytime of the day or night. Emotional loneliness in marriage may cause individuals to look for companionship online. The problem with meeting these needs online is that the strong feelings of closeness that easily develop may quickly be misinterpreted as intimacy. This can lead down the slippery slope into a cyber-affair.

Because of the unique qualities of the Internet, which fosters quick relationships that may be experienced as "love," it is valuable to ask, "What is love?"

The Components of Love

We enter the world with the need to be loved. If we approach the Internet with this need, we naturally respond to people when they appear to offer it. If we feel loved by a stranger we have never met, is it real love?

We have chosen the work of psychologist Robert J. Sternberg, Ph.D., who wrote about love in his book, *The Triangle of Love: Intimacy, Passion and Commitment* to illustrate our understanding of the subject. Although published before the Internet became publicly available, applying his concept of love to what we know about the Internet can help us understand how people can come to believe they have fallen in love online. Dr. Sternberg says that the three components of love are passion, intimacy, and commitment. Each can reach high peaks, but at different times.

Passion

We know passion is the intoxication of love. It is the "love is blind" component of our strong emotions. At this stage, the lover has no flaws. Passion may be the first component to develop, but it is also the first to decline. It must be sustained with imagination and excitement, or it can fade quickly. When partners feel a decrease in the intensity of their passion, they feel they are falling out of love, that something is missing. Rather than working on the committed relationship, anxiety about losing something precious may cause them to look for an affair.

A person often looks to the affair to recreate passion in his or her life. It is exciting, and yes, it can be found online. In fact, after the initial attraction, passion is usually the first component of love that appears online, and can easily draw people into cyber-infidelity. Passion may draw someone every night with a pounding heart to log onto the Internet and be with their lover. It is a state of idolization of the lover and is purely emotional, and may intrude upon their thoughts day and night. But whether it is an affair or a committed relationship, passion alone has an elusive quality. Dr. Sternberg believes that passion alone, without intimacy and commitment, is fleeting infatuation. Passion is often amplified by idealized desires that are projected onto someone else. These projected feelings can lead to obsession in an unconscious effort to alleviate loneliness. However, when passion is the only emotion that binds a couple together, it can quickly feel empty, and feelings of love can disappear.

Passion can also fade in relationships that exhibit intimacy and commitment. After a while, the routines of life can dull passion. Couples need to find mutually romantic and erotic ways to keep their passion high. If they can work at maintaining passion, and pair it with intimacy and commitment, they have a chance at finding real love. Intimacy is the foundation of trust and a component of love in a relationship. Trust is built by repeatedly exposing one's true and vulnerable self. Taking a step toward the truth is actually taking a step toward intimacy.

Intimacy

Intimacy can also reach great heights, but develops more slowly. With intimacy, love moves from being blind to seeing and accepting. Intimacy requires the courage to confront oneself and reveal oneself to someone else.

In his book, *We: Understanding the Psychology of Romantic Love*, Robert A. Johnson writes, "Human love is the power within us which allows us to affirm and value a person for who they truly are, rather than an ideal or projection, which we would like them to be. With love we value the person as a total, individual self—accepting both the negative and positive about that person, the admirable qualities and imperfections."

Intimacy involves honesty. It means taking the risk to share at a deep level, and revealing fears and weaknesses. For many people who were hurt in their childhood attempts to love and be loved, achieving intimacy as an adult is an anxiety-ridden task. Such people are caught in an unenviable bind that is driven by the fear of loneliness on one hand, and restrained by the fear of connection on the other.

Harriet Lerner, Ph.D., writes in *The Dance of Intimacy*, "Working towards intimacy is nothing short of a lifelong task. The goal is to be in a relationship where the separate 'I-ness' of both parties can be appreciated and enhanced, and where neither competence nor vulnerability is lost sight of in the self or the other. Intimacy requires a clear self, relentless self-focus, open communication, and a profound respect for differences. It requires the capacity to stay emotionally connected to significant others during anxious times, while taking a clear position for self, based on one's values, beliefs, and principles."

People engaging in virtual romance report astonishingly strong feelings of intimacy. However, it is a paradox that people can bond so closely when they have never met one another, do not see one another, know only what has been selectively shared, and do nothing together in the real world. They have no common reference point, such as mutual friends, to verify observations and conclusions. They cannot visit each other's families, and therefore know only what the other has chosen to reveal. With such controlled exposure, the truth may not be known, and therefore, attaining true intimacy may not be possible.

David Schnarch, Ph.D., writing in *The Journal of Sex Education and Therapy,* concludes, "Email does seem capable of conveying some measure of intimacy that has been previously established between friends, lovers, and family. This shouldn't surprise us—Telephone contact often operates the same way and for good reason: The more salient the partner, the more the threat of rejection elicits anxiety, the greater the challenge to one's sense of self, and the higher the subjective intensity of intimacy. Moreover, the greater the preexisting knowledge users have about each other, the deeper the emotional meaningfulness of text messages sent back and forth." The optimal situation is for single online lovers to meet quickly in the real world, to dispel any false projections they may have of each other, and get to know one another in real contexts. Once they meet, such lovers can sustain their romance in email between offline meetings.

Individuals in committed relationships that lack intimacy in the real world are particularly prone to mistaking online closeness for real love. They can easily mistake the passion of a virtual relationship and the false feeling of intimacy for love, and therefore can seriously threaten the committed, offline relationship.

In the real world, passion and intimacy form romantic love, but romantic love can also be fleeting if a commitment is not established.

Commitment

The third component of real love described by Dr. Sternberg is commitment. Commitment is the slowest-developing component of real love. Over time, commitment can also achieve great heights. Commitment forms the "glue" of a relationship. At the basis of real love is a shared belief system that develops over years of giving support, working toward common goals, and helping each other to realize their dreams. It is the cognitive part of the relationship, based on common values, faith that each partner treasures the other, and availability to one another in good times and bad.

Passion alone is infatuation. Intimacy alone is friendship. Passion combined with intimacy forms romantic love. Commitment alone is "empty love."

Put passion, intimacy, and commitment together, and a full picture of love emerges. Once it is there, it must be nurtured. As Rona Subotnik, M.A., MFT, and Gloria Harris, Ph.D., write in *Surviving Infidelity,* "...love depends on enhancing the passion of the relationship, investing energy in developing intimacy, and making a commitment."

When these are not found in the committed relationship, a person may stumble upon them online. They may seem very real, but beware the power of the Internet on our emotions—it can distort the dynamics between people so that it becomes hard to know what is real and what is not.

Restless in Reston

It is Thursday night, eight o'clock in Reston, Virginia, and Elisa is speaking to her sister, Shelby, who lives in Seattle.

"You sound upset. What's wrong?" Shelby asks.

"I don't know where to begin," Elisa replies.

"Start anywhere."

"Okay. It was a Sunday afternoon and I was so lonely. The children were on a weekend trip with Bart's parents. Bart was playing golf and I didn't know what to do with myself.

"I went for a drive in Leesburg, but even Virginia is not pretty in February. 'Do I really want to drive on a day like today?' I asked myself, but I kept on. I saw those bumper stickers that say, 'Virginia is for lovers.' That's the problem. Bart and I have grown far apart. I feel desperate about it.

"Well, anyhow, I stopped in a coffee shop, and overheard a conversation between a group of people at the next table about chat rooms. They were laughing and talking about being addicted to the Internet and that it was fantastic for meeting people.

"I couldn't believe I did it, but I got up and walked over to their table, and asked if they could tell me where to get started on the Internet. They said that I must be an Internet 'virgin.' I had a very amusing conversation with them. They told me a lot about meeting people online. A few days later, I tried it.

"After logging on, I chose a chat room. I scrolled down and tried to decide what to say. I decided to open with "Anyone know how to make a good drink?" That's how I met this guy, Richie.

"We posted to each other a few more times before he had to go somewhere.

"As the weeks went by, my loneliness disappeared. Whenever I felt sorry for myself, I'd log on and people recognized me. I regularly talked with people who understood what I was going through.

"On a Saturday, when Bart was working, I went to a private chat room with Richie and talked for, oh, about four hours. I learned so much about myself. Under other circumstances, I would never do this—spill my guts to someone I had just met. Soon we were emailing each other a few times a day. Next thing I knew, we sent each other a picture and things started happening.

"What are you talking about?" Shelby asks.

"Well, we started becoming intimate."

"Intimate? How do you become intimate on a computer?"

"Well, you share things. I described my body, and he did the same."

"Described your body?" Shelby asked.

"It didn't happen overnight," Elisa insists. "But soon we were having cyber-sex."

"Elisa, you're married!"

"I'm lonely. Bart's never home, but he always wants me to be home. I have no life. I have no one to talk to. It's driving me crazy. Bart doesn't listen."

"How can you say you have no life?"

"Okay, we have a social life. What I really want is just to sit home by the fire and talk. Bart doesn't like that. He likes parties—excitement, activities that he says help him in his job to "network." I don't know—maybe I am a loner, or something is wrong with me. When I am at these parties, I feel so very lonely and yet I'm surrounded by people. So what if I found a man online to talk with? I feel a little guilty about it. When I think of stopping it, I think of my loneliness and just continue."

"OK, so what do you know about him?" Shelby asks.

"He's okay. He talks and he shares. I know all about him. He's a golf pro, and he's divorced. He works at a resort in Palm Springs out in California. He leaves me romantic emails: song lyrics and stories about hopes for what the future will hold for us.

"He is very sexy and his words stay in my mind for days. I can't remember any-one who pays attention to me like Richie does. He's a wonderful lover, always remembers what I like to hear, and I am walking on air. He wants me to join him in Palm Springs this summer when the kids are in camp."

"Are you really thinking of going?"

"I am. Richie is a golf pro and he's interested in me. More than interested! He's passionate about me. We may even be in love! He's a fantasy come true. I want to leave my life here."

Shelby cannot believe this. "Leave your life? Elisa, this isn't you. Aren't you hav-ing any doubts? Hasn't he done anything to make you wonder if he's legit?"

"Well, yes. But I handled it."

"What?"

"After having cyber-sex with him for three weeks, he wanted to take it to a new level that he said would be fun. He wanted to make it a foursome with another cou-ple in another chat room. He wanted me to pretend to be male and him female, and we would seduce them. He said he would take the lead and show me what to do. I told him I wouldn't do it and that it was against my moral principles. I thought he would break up with me. I have my limits. He left the chat room without as much as a good-bye. I was very upset, and sent him a few emails. Finally, he answered. He said maybe I'll change my mind one day."

"Something's wrong here. I don't get it, Elisa," Shelby says. "I think you ought to talk to a professional. You've got so much at stake, and the kids..."

Shelby's confusion stems from not realizing the power of the Internet to make people who have never met feel intimacy and passion, and to think they are in love.

The problems in Elisa's marriage can further be understood with knowl-edge of how people interact with each other in families.

Dynamics of Relationships

The late Murray Bowen, M.D., founder of the Georgetown Family Center, developed a comprehensive theory to explain people's behavior in families. This is known as the Bowen Family Systems Theory, and consists of nine separate concepts. Understanding some of these basic ideas will help us see the part that couples' dynamics play in the development of affairs. Dr. Bowen believed that basic to our relationships is the way we deal with anxiety or emotional tension. Managing anxiety is a function of the degree to which people are differentiated, and this is the cornerstone of his theory. People fall on a continuum of differentiation ranging from Low to High. Those on the lower part of the continuum are called "poorly differentiated," and are more vulnerable to stress.

Poorly differentiated people experience an increase in anxiety when pressured by others. Such a person often finds himself or herself unable to make decisions rationally, if they differ from what others expect of them. So they acquiesce to the desires of others, regardless of how it affects them. This happens because making such a decision against the wishes of others produces anxiety. When this occurs, it is referred to by therapists as "fusion," which is a difficulty with tolerating separateness or differences.

People who manage their anxiety by exerting control in a relationship or allow themselves to be controlled by another are considered to be fused. They believe that being loved and accepted is dependent on sameness. Fused individuals cannot exercise their own will or tolerate differences without stress.

Often, they become emotionally reactive, and this can be manifested in conflict with others, depression, anger, and other similar ways. This occurs because there is another type of fusion between their feelings and their thinking. They make decisions based on their emotions, rather than thinking things through. These people often make self-defeating decisions, such as giving in to the sexual impulses that can easily occur online. Elisa has made many such self-defeating decisions in her relationship with her husband, Bart. This is seen in her continued participation in activities that she finds almost unbearable. She cannot separate her needs from his demands. Bart also shows fusion in the relationship by his refusal to tolerate separation that would come from Elisa's not spending as much time in these "together activities." Dr. Bowen posits that individuals marry or form relationships with others who are at the same level of differentiation as they are. While this is clearly illustrated in this marriage, it is also seen in Elisa's new relationship with her cyber-lover, Richie, when he requests a sexual encounter that clearly is in opposition to her desire. Yet, we see that in this case Elisa refuses. How, then, can we explain what may seem like an inconsistency, when Elisa says, "I have my limits"?

The Internet provides a means by which some individuals find ways to cope with anxiety. Odd as it may seem, infidelity is often a misguided attempt to manage anxiety. Furthermore, difficulty in recovering from infidelity may be another result of the inability to separate feelings from thinking.

Solid Self

The discrepancy in Elisa's replies can be understood in terms of the solid self. Dr. Bowen described the solid self as that core part of you that is non-negotiable. In his early work, Dr. Bowen referred to "solid self" as "basic self," and wrote, "The basic self is not negotiable in the relationship system, in that it is not changed by coercion or pressure, or to gain approval or enhance one's standing with others."

In contrast to the solid self is the pseudo-self; that is the self that one presents to the world in an attempt to gain acceptance and therefore reduce anxiety. The pseudo-self is negotiable in the face of relationship pressure, and operates to reduce the stress in relationships. Elisa demonstrates a pseudo-self in relationship to the men in her life. She pretends to accept her husband's absences from her, and she expresses love for Richie, who rudely abandoned her in a chat room when she expressed discomfort with online group sex. The ability to operate out of a solid sense of self, to stand up to external pressures, can be considered acting with integrity, and is synonymous with differentiation.

Elisa's solid self was operating when she refused the sexual encounter that Richie proposed. That concept was non-negotiable for her, or as she put it, "I have limits." Her limits did not extend to the request made by her husband, Bart, because that affected only her pseudo-self. Although this caused her distress, she acquiesced to his demands, because the pseudo-self is that part of us that bends to pressure. We become more differentiated when our decisions are made with consideration of all the factors affecting each individual. If Elisa were to do this, she and Bart would have reached a compromise on this issue. To achieve such differentiation, both would need to be self-defining and self-validating.

While poorly differentiated people continue to acquiesce and distance themselves, the more differentiated individual can stay in emotional contact, resist pressures of fusion by others, and thus maintain a strong sense of self. This is done by self-validation.

Self-Validation

Self-validation is a step toward breaking emotional fusion because it is an honest and accurate representation of oneself. Dr. Schnarch describes self-validation in *Passionate Marriage*. He writes, "Self-validated intimacy relies on a person's maintaining his or her own sense of identity and self-worth when disclosing, with no expectation of acceptance or reciprocity from the partner. One's capacity for self-validated intimacy is directly related to one's level of differentiation; that is, one's ability to maintain a clear sense of one's self when loved ones are pressuring for conforming and sameness. Self-validated intimacy is the tangible product of one's 'relationship with oneself.'" To be self-validating, Elisa would need to speak to her husband about her dissatisfaction with their marriage. She would discontinue her online relationship with Richie, who already is showing a tendency to use coercion by leaving discussions in which she does not want to engage in activities that violate her ethical values.

"I" Statements

"I" statements are a way in which individuals can be both self-defining and self-validating because they can be used to they represent the solid self. They show integrity, honesty, and differentiation. Such a statement from Elisa might be, "I am not happy with our social life as it is. I want more balance. I want us to stay home more and talk. We seem to be drifting apart. I know you feel it is important for you to network at parties, but I want us to discuss this and come to a compromise we both can live with."

By saying this, Elisa validates herself while acknowledging Bart's needs. Hopefully, such interactions will lead to more differentiation for both. The anxiety of separateness is at the root of their acquiescing or pressuring behaviors.

Identifying Anxiety

Anxiety can manifest itself in relationships in many ways. Individuals with high degrees of anxiety can easily get into conflict with one other, distance from each other, or form a triangle, as when one of them has an affair. Elisa had a cyber-affair with Richie as a way to solve her problem of loneliness and lack of intimacy in her marriage, and thus formed such a triangle. According to Bowen Theory, triangles are formed to remedy an unstable relationship between two people. The Internet has provided Elisa a solution, but it is a maladaptive one. Basic to her problems are the dynamics of her relationship with Bart and their individual degree of differentiation.

People who are poorly differentiated in a fused relationship will try to get their partner to accept their anxiety. Dr. Schnarch writes in *Passionate Marriage*, "...differentiation is the ability to soothe your own anxiety and to resist being infected with other people's anxiety. Anxiety is contagious and poorly differentiated people pass it between them like a virus."

Such a person is blaming, anxious, and tries to downshift anxiety onto the other person usually by name calling, threatening, and attacking. This behavior leaves the respondent feeling demeaned, powerless, and probably angry. The blamer tries to maintain the fusion with the other, pass on the anxiety, and make the situation the fault of the respondent. Richie's way of reducing his own anxiety about Elisa's refusal to participate in group sex is to emotionally cut off from her. His anxiety is relieved only after receiving a few emails, and making the comment that perhaps she would change her mind one day. He does not recognize that Elisa is her own person and he continues trying to bind her into a fused relationship. It would not be surprising for him to try and coerce her into another sexually uncomfortable experience in the future. Given her lack of differentiation and lack of ability to see how he is passing his own anxiety onto her, she is at risk of succumbing to his pressure. Learning to manage anxiety is a step toward improving differentiation and resolving differences so that the relationship can be stabilized without creating a triangle through an affair.

Managing Anxiety

Finding ways to manage anxiety through self-soothing behaviors is a basis for strong and successful relationships. In her popular book, *The Dance of Intimacy*, Dr. Lerner wrote, "The degree of trouble we get into in a particular relationship rests on two factors. The first is the amount of stress and anxiety that is impinging on a relationship from multiple sources, past and present. The second is the amount of self that we bring to that relationship. To the extent that we have not carved out a clear and whole 'I' in our first family, we will always feel in some danger of being swallowed up by the 'togetherness force' with others. Seeking distance (or fighting) is an almost instinctual reaction to the anxiety over this fusion, this togetherness which threatens loss of self."

The challenge for couples is to stay emotionally connected to each other as they manage their anxiety. This is done by being self-soothing, self-validating, and thinking through their issues. By mismanaging these anxieties, Elisa and Bart have prevented intimacy from developing in their relationship, and have looked for validation from others rather than providing it for themselves.

Elisa and Bart illustrate how anxiety and differentiation prevents intimacy, one of the major components of love. This, in turn, threatens commitment. The Internet allows people to connect and to project their needs and fantasies onto each other. It can lead to blind passion without requiring anxiety management or self-definition. When one or both parties are involved in a monogamous relationship, this powerful mix provides fertile ground for cyber-infidelity.

In a lecture on intimacy at United States International University, San Diego, based on the work of Drs. Bowen and Schnarch, Sally LeBoy, professor of family therapy and a marriage and family therapist, said, "Intimacy is achieved by remaining both self-defined and connected. Pleasing our partners at the expense of self-definition will ultimately decrease intimacy."

Managing anxiety in the face of infidelity is difficult. The biggest step in learning to control anxiety is to separate thinking from feeling. When people are anxious, they often cannot think clearly. Sometimes, people witness an accident and cannot remember what they have seen because of the anxiety they experienced at that time. In subsequent chapters, we will present skills to help you manage anxiety. In the next chapter, we will demonstrate how anxiety can be easily misunderstood online

3

Cyber-Sex

Sex online! Cyber-sex. Fasten your seatbelt and come along for the ride as we explain the ups, the downs, and the unexpected twists in the cybersexual freeway of love.

Now that we have discussed the powers of virtual attraction, we must take a closer look at cyber-sex itself. The term "cyber-sex" covers so many different activities that it is often confusing. As stated in Chapter One, we offer this definition for our purposes in the book. *Cyber-sex occurs when people use computerized content (text, sounds, or images obtained from software or the Internet) for sexual stimulation.*

Researchers Freeman-Longo and Blanchard reported in 1998 that sex is the most frequently searched topic on the Internet, and that involvement with one of several different types of cyber-sex is a very common activity for Internet users. Estimates of the worldwide Internet population for January 2001 are around 375 million people, and commerce.net reports this number will rise to over 765 million by the year 2005. As discussed in Chapter One, Alvin Cooper, Ph.D., and colleagues reported in 1998 that approximately 20 percent of users engage in some kind of online sexual activity, and 8 percent of these people are estimated to have "sexually compulsive features." If such estimates are correct, more than seventy-five million users worldwide are currently engaging in sexual activity online, and 155 million users will be by the year 2005.

Because the Internet is open day and night, it offers the ultimate convenience to those interested in cyber-sex through a variety of sexually stimulating people and material. Psychologist Mark Griffiths, Ph.D., of the United Kingdom, writing in "Excessive Internet Use: Implications for Sexual Behavior," discusses the wide range of potential uses of the Internet for sexual interests and activities. He notes, in addition to good sources for sex education and sex therapist referrals, it is possible to buy and sell sexually-related goods such as books, videos, CDs, sex toys, and aphrodisiacs, and to visit cyber-sex shops on the Internet. Pornographic websites are available with visual offerings (strip shows, video streaming, and various Web-com devices), or written erotica (chat rooms, Usenet discussions, and similar sites). The Internet user will find dating services and sexual partners such as escorts, prostitutes, and swingers. People with various sexual disorders can find support for their activities in chat rooms, newsgroups, and bulletin boards. Criminals can also easily find victims online.

The 1998 survey from MSNBC.com indicated that approximately 50 percent of more than seventeen thousand respondents had visited sexual sites and 6 percent had shopped for sex materials. The Internet makes pornographic material exceedingly easy to obtain. Estimates are that the online adult entertainment industry has already reached one billion dollars.

The Immediacy of Cyber-Sex

The immediacy of cyber-sex provides instant gratification by reinforcing sexual behavior and fantasies that would otherwise be ignored. One form of cyber-sex occurs when people type erotic and stimulating material to one another through a chat room. Their purpose is to bring each other to orgasm as they exchange messages and masturbate together in real time. Let us see how this begins by looking in on Amy and Blue Eyes.

Bill, or "Blue Eyes," as he is known online, has just settled in after a long day at the office. His wife is preparing dinner, so he has a few private minutes to himself in the upstairs den. Bill's psychotherapist has suggested that he use this time to relax. However, he sees that his online lover, Amy, is logged on.

Amy: Oh, there you are! I was hoping you'd be here. Did I tell you that I love blue eyes? They are really sexy. Are yours more like Brad Pitt's or Paul Newman's?
Blue Eyes: I don't think you want Newman. He's too old for you. I'm ready for you. Let's find a private chat room.

Amy agrees, and they proceed to a private chat room to continue their conversation.

Blue Eyes: I've been thinking about you all day, and decided I really want to cyber with you tonight, rather than just talk around it.
Amy: Yep, I guess you're right. I tend to be a bit shy, and have been waiting for you to get me started. So how do we begin?

Bill's quick fingers broke the ice. They stimulated each other to orgasm by typing the details of their fantasies of being together and their physical reactions when typing. They both reached orgasm, and they decided to meet again the next night. "Blue Eyes" went down to dinner, and assuming his offline life as Bill, discussed his day at the office with his wife.

A few weeks later, when Bill went to his therapy session for his anxiety treatment, he mentioned that he had started visiting the dating website chat rooms, looking for a way to calm down after a high-pressure day at the office. He said, "I've been going into the chat rooms. I just join the ongoing conversations and start dropping little sexual innuendos. If someone responds, I Instant Message her and ask that we speak privately. I then come on to her by describing a sensual scene. It makes me feel really horny, and I forget everything else.

"Amy flirted with me for a few days in the chat room group before she decided to meet me privately. She was a challenge, because we always left the chat room without cybering. That really turned me on, and I just had to get her to cyber with me. All next day, I kept thinking about how I'd talk her into meeting me privately, and how I'd invite her to sit down, make herself comfortable, and get acquainted physically. But after we cybered a few times, we both lost interest and stopped meeting. After this last experience with Amy, I am worried that I might be getting hooked on this. I think I need help before this gets out of control."

Bill started with the goal of finding cyber-sex because he wanted to distract himself from his reluctance to turn to his wife when things were not going well. She already knew he was having anxiety attacks. He felt inadequate. He did not have the job he wanted, and they did not have the house they had been dreaming of for years. Bill learned that with an affair or two on the Internet, he could usually find a quick orgasm, feel more relaxed, and be ready to spend the evening with his wife. Whatever was bothering him about her would fade away. When his anxiety increased, he would just let his mind float to the last erotic email he received. Everything was fine, as long as he could keep his little secret.

With the help of his psychotherapist, he realized he was at risk for developing a cyber-sexual compulsion, and that cyber-sex only made him feel more anxious. The excitement of newly discovered cyber-sex made sex with his wife seem plain, ordinary, and even boring. He did not know how to tell his wife that he was frustrated with their sex life, or what to do to make it less monotonous. These added secrets only made him feel more anxious, thereby making the problem worse.

Bill was like millions of other people who go online for sexual gratification, only to find that they are distracting themselves from deeper needs. Luckily for him and for his marriage, he recognized that he was developing a problem and brought it to his psychotherapist.

Types of Cyber-Sexual Activities

The Internet is viewed by some as a "safe place" to relieve sexual tensions and experiment with new sexual behaviors that cover a wide spectrum of activities. Searching for cyber-sex can lead to forbidden surprises from around the world, served with anonymity in the comfort of your home. You can quickly and easily find almost anything you want. Psychologist Sandra Risa Leiblum, Ph.D., of the Robert Wood Johnson Medical School, in the article "Sex and the Net: Clinical Implications," puts it succinctly, "Net sex exists because people want it."

Cyber-sex can be either interactive or noninteractive. In a 1996 master's dissertation, Robin B. Hamman identified several types of cyber-sex. These are presented in the next section, along with a few others identified by the authors.

Chat Rooms

Dating chat rooms are text-based environments where people interact. (See Appendix A for a description of different types of chat rooms.) According to Drs. Cooper, Morahan-Martin, Maheu, and Mathy in the article "Random Sampling of User Demographics Related to Cybersex and Other Online Sexual Activity," chat rooms are preferred by 15 percent of the online population for online sexual activity. Chat rooms find their popularity by maximizing a person's ability to converse with people who have the same interests. They are appealing because of their constant accessibility, and the opinion of some that chat rooms are the ultimate in safe sex.

The action is described in words seen on the screen, to which the players respond synchronously. Chat rooms are interactive, virtual "places" where a number of people can erotically stimulate each other. Email can also be used in this way by people who are both online at the same time.

One of the more interesting aspects of the Internet is that the use of one such technology does not preclude the use of another. For example, people talking in email might decide to go to a dating website where they can Instant Message one another or go to a private chat room for a while. They might also decide to send a picture to each other, or a voice clip of themselves saying something sexy or having an orgasm. Participation in these written environments usually involves masturbation to descriptions of sexual activities. They can be play-by-play announcements of fantasies, events, feelings, and sensations, or after-the-event playback of how it went.

Erotic Stories

A noninteractive type of cyber-sex involves an erotic fantasy storyline published in a written environment, such as a bulletin board, a newsgroup, or a website. A variation of this type is emailing someone a sexually arousing story. Depending on the timing of the response to such a story, this can be interactive or noninteractive.

Online Pornography

No longer do people need to experience the flush of embarrassment at being discovered by a neighbor when buying the newest issue of *Hustler*. They can view online pornography from the privacy of their home. People's extreme fascination and preoccupation with sexuality has led to the most rapid growth of an industry ever recorded. Various types of pornography exist online. Personal pornography is sent through email for arousal. These are often pictures taken at home of an individual performing sexual acts, which are then sent through email as an attachment or posted on private websites.

Millions of websites are already devoted exclusively to sexuality—from all countries, cultures, and languages serviced by the Internet. Static picture websites offer audio-visual areas in which a person can see erotic pictures and hear erotic sounds. These websites offer many types of pornography, some of which is free of charge.

For a fee, recent and varied types of pornographic material are available from commercial websites. The viewer can enter a number of different bedrooms and engage with different scenes and sounds. Virtual pornography customers can also watch thousands of video clips of actors performing a wide variety of sexual acts.

The Internet also brings pornography to life by making it an interactive rather than a passive activity. For the consumer, pornography delivered by the Internet is better than dining in a tapas restaurant. Anything can be ordered, sampled, ingested, or rejected, and with a passing whim replaced by something new. Consumers can sample an unlimited menu while remaining completely anonymous and private. Anyone looking for sex on the Internet has only to type in their credit card number to enter one of millions of sites offering everything from sex toys to live, video-conferenced exchanges with an entire selection of potential and willing playmates.

The most significant shift brought to sexuality by the Internet is the capability of any user to become the producer, rather than simply the consumer, of pornographic software. For the first time, imagination is brought to life without immediately experiencing negative repercussions. Visiting Internet sex sites is like strolling through the red light district. As Dale Spender writes in *Nattering on the Net: Women, Power, and Cyberspace,* "It's the 'realness' of the new porn which makes it so different from anything that's been around before. As with every other type of information in cyberspace, the viewer/user becomes a participant; a 'doer' of pornography rather than an observer of it."

Furthermore, pornography has already proven to be a driving force in the development of the Internet. In some instances, the sex industry has even financed the early development of certain Internet services. In large part, it has financed the continued push for increased capabilities to bring both interactive and live-video services to our family rooms. Its enormous appeal helped pay for the delivery of sexual content and the mechanisms required for collecting related charges through electronic commerce. In *The Death of Distance,* Frances Cairncross writes, "The sex industry (or 'adult entertainment,' as its promoters primly call it) has helped to pay for and pioneer lots of techniques of electronic commerce."

Credit cards can be immediately accepted from users in nearly every industrialized nation in the world. Live sex-on-command websites require only a credit card and a few clicks to access one of several available playmates. In the privacy of a chat room, you can type your requests and have them enacted immediately by the model of your choice.

Moreover, with credit card companies marketing to a younger population, adult entertainment investors have targeted a group that most likely does not have the maturity or life experience to handle their cyber-sexual purchase. On the other hand, given the newness of these developments, one must wonder how many people have the "necessary" life experience to handle such a purchase, even as mature adults.

Email

We have mentioned that email can be used for many different types of online interactions, but surprisingly, it is rarely the favorite medium for sexual activity. According to the MSNBC.com study conducted by Dr. Cooper, slightly less than 4 percent of people who engage in online sexual activity prefer doing so over email. One explanation could be that the relative loss of anonymity in email proves too uncomfortable for one-on-one sexual communication.

In contrast, *ABC News* reported in the online articles "From E- to Eternity," and "The Virtual Breakup," that matchmaker.com, the largest online dating service, reports 73 percent of their five thousand users use email to flirt. These people may not be engaging in actual sexual activity, but instead often use email for courting. Some advantages to email contact are that it is low-pressure, casual, lighthearted, and controlled. It lets people be bolder. Ending relationships through email is also becoming popular. Much like leaving a breakup message on an answering machine, email provides a low-pressure alternative to a face-to-face separation.

Video Streaming

One also can purchase a private viewing of a video-streamed segment of someone behaving seductively or engaging in a preferred sexual act with a specific type of model. Popular types of models include "teen" girls, Asian women, blondes, lesbians, and women with large breasts. Specialized websites cater to customers with other preferences, such as gay men, large women, or women engaging in a specific type of sexual behavior, such as fellatio or bestiality.

Interactive Video-Based Websites

Interactive video-based websites allow people to watch each other in sexual activity. One-way video Web services enable customers to view a model performing erotic or sexual acts upon request. The customer sees the model through a video camera, but the model does not see the customer. The customer typically requests specific behaviors by using a keyboard that delivers a written message to the playmate. They never have physical contact, but the playmate responds within seconds of the customer's typed command.

Private, Two-Way Video Cameras
Another type of interactive, video-based cyber-sex involves the use of two-way video cameras. When used with commonly available software, such as Microsoft's NetMeeting or White Pine's CU-See-Me, video cameras also allow two people to see each other and interact sexually in real time. With such cameras, people can experiment with previously forbidden behaviors and never reveal their identity. By using anonymous servers, they can connect with others, point their cameras away from their face and to erotic parts of their anatomy, and stimulate each other without ever looking into each other's eyes.

Each of these many types of cyber-sex allows people to masturbate while being stimulated by material from the Internet. People can play out their favorite fantasies, create new ones in real time, explore deviant behavior, and never have physical contact with anyone but themselves.

Cooper and his latest research team found that while home computers are used by between 80 and 85 percent of people engaged in cyber-sex, some 4 to 6 percent use their work computer solely for their cyber-sexual playtime.

Fantasy vs. Reality
The Internet allows you to escape into countless worlds that give the impression of being safe. You can try on any number of personalities, experiment with being bold or shy, and present yourself to the world as a character in your own fantasy.

As Ken notes, "Cyber-sex provides an alternative way to satisfy sexual fantasies. Feelings of embarrassment and guilt are avoided with cyber-sex."

Greg adds, "Cyber-sex may fuel the imagination, and could perhaps enhance real sex, much in the way a pornographic magazine might."

Andrea says, "Cyber-sex can be a godsend in that it allows people who feel inhibited sexually in the real world to connect on the Internet. In fact, that's how I met my girlfriend."

As discussed earlier in this book, fantasy adds the power, glamour, and excitement to written or visual online relationships. Recognizing this essential element of such relationships can help people understand one of the strongest appeals of infidelity, because fantasy is often used to supply the unavailable. For some, the Internet can create a fantasy life that is unrivaled in real life. It is easier to create whatever they want online than to deal with the limitations and pressures of real-world encounters. Online lovers can appear to be devoted, sensitive, and interested because they aren't sharing the stresses of daily life. Escaping into an online sexual tryst can combine the powerfully reinforcing physical release of orgasm with the imagined comfort of a lover's understanding embrace.

Dr. Esther Gwinnell, in *Online Seductions*, reports that there are a number of bulletin boards and chat rooms which cater to the description of sexual fantasies. "Their underlying premises guarantee that one's inner erotic world will be accepted, even encouraged. They offer the possibility that your vivid fantasy life may somehow be shared with another person, even if you will never meet that person face-to-face."

People display a wide variety of sexual expressions. The sexual expressions of an affair run on a continuum from fantasy to real life. The same is true for cyber-sex. Cyber-sex starts with a predominant focus on fantasy, but can shift over time into reality.

The first step along the fantasy-reality continuum is pornography, which can be found in books, magazines, or online environments such as bulletin boards, newsgroups, still pictures, or video streaming. The goal of such fantasy is to envision the right anatomy, find the witty turn of a phrase, or think of having sex with a stranger, perhaps a celebrity. From there on the continuum, fantasy moves to sexual activity involving a known person in the real world. Sexual desires are then projected onto that person whom is actually known. Many people find this a difficult position. They may become self-conscious about their real-life interaction with the person, fearing that they might give away their secret fantasy—and sometimes, they do.

The next step along the continuum adds the dimension of interactivity, which moves the experience from pure fantasy to what might be best termed "pseudo-reality." The simplest form of sexual interactivity involves textual environments that allow real-time exchange through the Internet, such as email and chat rooms. As we move along the continuum, interactivity involves the sense of sound. People use the telephone or Internet phones to enhance sexual gratification. Previously, people have been able to engage in paid phone sex by dialing 900 numbers; now they can meet someone from the Internet and have relatively free phone sex.

Telephone contact heightens real-life aspects of arousal because there is a real, living, breathing, responding person providing enough cues to bring an added dimension to the exchange. Typically, reality does not intrude enough to shatter the direction of the desired fantasy. A further step along the continuum involves pictures in addition to sounds, found in two-way interactive video. The final step in the continuum is going offline and making fantasy a reality by having a real-life exchange with an eroticized individual.

The continuum does not necessarily define the cutoff point of infidelity. Nearly all would agree that meeting face-to-face would constitute infidelity, and occasionally looking at snapshots of naked models would not. But a gray area exists as each technology adds different aspects that bring it closer to real life. People must decide for themselves and with their partners what infidelity is, based on their promises to each other.

When partners do not agree, it is time to have an open discussion of each other's view of the acceptable and unacceptable types of erotic stimulation, and whether these constitute infidelity for the couple.

To show how this continuum works, let us share the story of a client we will name Eva. She is a twenty-six-year-old preschool teacher who told us how her behavior changed gradually from fantasy to reality.

"As a preschool teacher, it's been hard for me to meet men. I see many handsome guys, but they are the dads dropping off their kids at school. I could go out in the evening to singles' events, but I'm really tired at the end of the day. My weekends are spent doing chores, shopping, going to lunch with girlfriends, and going to church.

"At one point, I began to realize that I was very taken with our minister. He's nice to everyone and a really delightful person. I began to think about him frequently, and then I started to fantasize about his holding and kissing me. Although I knew he had a wife and three children, I couldn't seem to stop. One Sunday, when he was shaking hands with all the congregants as we were leaving, he asked if I would join with him and his wife at his home, with some other singles, for tea later in the day. I eagerly accepted. Too eagerly, and I nearly called him 'dear' as I do in my fantasy. I blushed terribly and stammered a bit.

"All afternoon, I debated with myself whether I should go. I realized that I had come close to stepping out of my fantasy into real life. Well, I went to the tea. I was really on edge and monitored my remarks carefully. During the afternoon, the subject of chat rooms came up. It seemed that a few people were meeting other singles that way. I learned that I could talk to others on my computer, so to speak.

"I made friends online, but it was very innocent. Although I stopped with my daydreaming about my minister, I still had not solved my problem about meeting someone. I decided to go to a more sexual chat room—well, talk about fast track, this was a shock!

"I met lots of men, and eventually I had cyber-sex with many of them. This did not seem promiscuous to me, for some reason I don't understand. I would never have sex with so many men in real life, but it did stop me from thinking about my minister. After three months of this, I met someone online who really intrigued me. We started having phone sex, and for me this seemed very real because I could hear his voice. I am very attracted to him. Now, if I had phone sex as often as I had cyber-sex, I think I would feel promiscuous because phone sex seems more real.

"My phone lover and I are talking about meeting each other when he manages to accumulate at least ten days' vacation time. I'm scared, but excited. It's all becoming very real."

Eva started by focusing her sexual energy on a fantasy with an unavailable man. Her activities entered pseudo-reality when she shifted that energy into online and telephone affairs. She is now on the threshold of stepping into the physical world by planning a face-to-face meeting with someone she has met online. As people move along the continuum from fantasy to face-to-face interaction, they may need added input to keep the exchange novel and stimulating. Clearly, many are reporting the ability to initiate sexual contact with strangers in chat rooms and email, and then trying to increase the intensity by moving onto phone sex.

We are beginning to see blends of reality and fantasy that some are having difficulty distinguishing. With pornography becoming increasingly interactive, how does a spouse deal with a partner who spends several hours a week masturbating to an interactive video-based website, while typing commands to a live playmate? What would be the reaction of a partner who knows his or her partner consistently spends time programming interactive software depicting a dream partner with artificial intelligence?

It is clear that a spouse's knowledge, consent, and participation of their partner's actions on the Internet would remove the elements of deceit and betrayal that characterize cyber-infidelity.

Telephone Sex

On the continuum of sexual experiences, phone sex moves away from the computer to real life. No longer do couples need to merely type descriptions of their experience. They can hear the other person's whispers, sighs, moans, groans, and other sexually arousing sounds. Orgasms are audible and more real.

Shauna said, "Phone sex happened spontaneously. It just seemed natural after having cybered so many times. Prior to that we wrote erotic poems and stories to each other."

Andrea stated, "The cyber-sex started with him asking me through email what I would do to him when we met, and how I would make love to him. As I would describe the things I would do, he would become excited and begin to masturbate to my words, as I would to his words. Then we moved to the phone—it was awesome. He loved hearing me breathe hard and pretend he was in bed with me. I would sometimes use a vibrator while I talked to him. I could hear him as he was masturbating and it excited me so much. Most of the time, I started the sexual conversations. I loved the thought of him getting excited thinking about me, and that I was able to make him erect by my words and fantasies. We became virtual lovers and phone lovers. We were just waiting for the day we could be together in person."

Phone sex offers accessibility and affordability, but if it involves the exchange of personal phone numbers, anonymity may be jeopardized.

However, the similarities of cyber-sex and phone sex are many: no fear of unwanted pregnancy, no sexually transmitted diseases, and no face-to-face rejection. Moreover, they both offer escape from immediate anxieties, including freedom from loneliness and social isolation. A *SelfhelpMagazine* Essay Contest respondent, who identified herself as Voluptuous, had this to say about how she began having phone sex:

> "My husband gave me a computer so I could do some freelance word processing and bring in a little money. I don't want to go out because I'm embarrassed about my weight. I'm not happy in my marriage, but I feel I'm stuck.
>
> "Well, the business didn't take off right away. It was slow starting. So I started going to the chat rooms. It was an uplifting experience for me, because I got to 'talk' with people. I have felt alone for years, despite my husband and children.
>
> "My confidence grew and I started flirting. I was treated like other women. I became a regular in one chat room. I didn't overdo it. I still had household and childcare responsibilities. I started having cyber-sex.
>
> "I was approached in a dungeon chat. Even though it was a sexual chat room, we discussed everything except my weight.
>
> "I told my husband and he got very jealous at someone being interested in me. But now he says it is okay with him. My virtual friend and I still don't have sex using the computer. We do have phone sex and we really like it. I am more comfortable on the phone because I have a better sense of what is happening."

The problem, of course, is that by offering such a quick sexualized alternative to anxiety, these technologies put people at risk for compulsive sexuality, and as with Voluptuous, for infidelity. These same individuals might not have been at risk had they no option but to go into the world and learn to develop new skills to manage anxiety, or make new friends.

On the other hand, phone sex is seen by some clinicians as being a safe decompression zone for those people who engage in high-risk sexual activity in the real world. They have decided to practice safer sex by limiting their encounters to the relative anonymity and physical safety of the phone. It is important to keep in mind that during anonymous phone sex, one's partner is unknown. A person can never be sure if he or she is dealing with a shy person who is venturing forth to experiment in new territory, or someone who is sexually compulsive or a criminal.

Cyber-Sex vs. Real Sex

When individuals engage in cyber-sex, their minds embellish and embroider the words of a virtual lover to meet the needs they bring to the interaction. Freed from the body, the imagination can loosen inhibitions and unleash passions in novel ways. People can also have a preference for how information is communicated. Some people prefer to be talkative, and others prefer silence. Indeed, sex therapists often hear complaints that some talkative partners are unable to focus on the sexual experience, and want more silence from the other. On the other hand, quiet lovers can have partners who report feeling ignored during sexual contact. Ruth, the wife of an attractive, yet noncommunicative man who sought counseling to improve their sex life, has a common problem. "When we make love, it isn't lovemaking at all. It feels sexual, but it is boring. The truth is, I am not there. I close my eyes, stop talking, and think of someone I saw at the mall, at the bank, or at work. Our love life leaves me feeling quite alone and quite unloved."

When operating in written environments, such as email and chat rooms, words are the only reality people can exchange. Often, it is enough to reach an orgasm. People make deliberate attempts to find words that will create feelings of arousal in their online partner. They develop exquisite sensitivity to those words or phrases that create the greatest response in their partner. Words are mixed with fantasy to produce erotic pleasure. Lovers rely on words and their individual fantasies to produce an emotional response that will unite them sexually.

Many researchers believe, however, that people need to be in each other's physical presence to experience real love, real passion. Psychologist and sex therapist Dr. David Schnarch writes in *Passionate Marriage,* "Humans have evolved the capacity for love; it's wired in our sexuality. The deeper and more meaningful the connection between two people and the more emotional energy you bring into your encounter, the greater the contribution to total stimulation. The important issue is passion. When you are exploring your sexual potential, you are no longer focusing on whether or not you have enough motivation to get started. This type of desire comes from maturation, not infatuation." As discussed in previous chapters, psychologists have based many notions of identity upon the presence of oneself in a body. The sharing of one's full presence, body, mind, and spirit, is seen as being the ultimate form of emotional connection between two people.

Where Do People Find Cyber-Sex?

Just as with real life, flirting online can happen anywhere. Sometimes just a business email can lead to flirting, and from there to cyber-sex. Such exchanges require the participants to look at nuances and to read between the lines. Consider the following exchange that a businesswoman received from a new customer. In the email, he was describing his need for her company's product, when he slipped in this comment:

> **He:** Hey, I was looking at your picture on your company's website and trying to figure out what that little smile of yours really means. I have some ideas of what it could be. It could be fun to find out—don't you think? It could be important for our work together. What do you think?

First Reply
She: I don't think it's important or relevant to our mutual goal. Let's get back to our real business.
He: OK. But you can't blame me for trying ;-)

Alternative Reply
She: Really? People do like my smile. I don't know what it means. What do you think?
He: It could mean anything. Why don't we get together in a chat room and explore the possibilities?

This exchange shows the two directions that a communication can take. In the first, the businesswoman realized her customer's intent to flirt, and tactfully directed him back to business. In the second reply, she senses his flirtation and plays along with it.

Other people look for cyber-sex directly. They go to dating websites such as swoon.com, match.com, or even aol.com and immediately find willing partners. Others use search engines, type in the word "sex," and surf the websites they find until they have met their goal. As described in Appendix A, still others go to the Internet's "underground" and search for interactions in MUDS, MOOS, talkies, and Internet Relay Chat. They can find pornography in newsgroups and bulletin boards.

Other websites cater specifically to the needs of well-defined subgroups of socially isolated people, including single mothers and widows, disabled, gay, lesbian, bisexual, or transgendered people, to name a few. The Internet provides something for everyone.

Who Is Having Cyber-Sex?
Research in this area has only begun. From an MSNBC survey of nearly thirty-eight thousand respondents, the largest Internet study to date, Dr. Cooper and colleagues identified a number of important findings:

- ➔ Almost 80 percent of people identified themselves as heterosexual, 7 percent as gay or lesbian, and 7 percent as bisexual.
- ➔ People who engage in online behavior have online sex about eleven hours per week.
- ➔ Less than 50 percent of women thought cyber-sex breaks marital vows, compared to 60 percent of men surveyed.
- ➔ Approximately 70 percent of respondents reported that they are not addicted to the Internet or sex.
- ➔ Almost 50 percent use cyber-sex for "distraction." Education and fantasy scored as other frequent examples.
- ➔ The average age of men and women taking the poll was thirty-six and thirty-two, respectively.

Other groups of people who are likely to hide while finding romantic and sexual satisfaction online include married or otherwise partnered adults, children and teenagers, as well as various types of sexual predators (sadists, pedophiles, etc.) and other types of criminals.

It is difficult to draw any conclusions about how many adults of any type are being unfaithful to their real-life relationships. Well-conducted research has not yet been reported in this area. Nonetheless, anecdotal reports from researchers, psychotherapists, and online consumers indicate that a great number of people from all occupations are committing infidelity because of their actions on the Internet, and experiencing the accompanying risks.

Gender Preferences in Cyber-Sexual Contact

On average, men spend more than twice as much time online investigating sexual material than women. This comes as no surprise to most, observing that men typically spend much more of their *entire lives* having sexual fantasies and fulfilling sexual urges than women do. Timothy Egan reported in the article, "Technology Sent Wall Street into Market for Pornography," that more than three-quarters of all pornographic movies were rented by males. Astutely, Web developers picked up on this trend and aimed the majority of their content at men.

But, don't think that women stay away from sexual material on the Internet. In fact, the female population of the cyber-sexual world has steadily risen in the last few years. Most women tend to avoid the solo flights into the hardcore cyber-sex world, and prefer a copilot to assist in the adventure. Chat rooms and other interactive areas are the favorite virtual hangout for many women, where the details of a secret *Top Gun* fantasy can be played out. Egan notes that, "women are more affiliative...the opportunities for the development of sexual relationships within online communities should be especially appealing to women as would be the support for sexual concerns."

Jenny, a thirty-year-old artist, wrote, "I think looking at pornographic material is more of a male thing. Women find cyber-sex more intimate because we can write about our deepest fantasies and thereby create greater sexual arousal."

On the Internet, both men and women are interacting in novel ways. Craig, a thirty-three-year-old chef, said, "Even though cyber-sex is a mutual act of self-exploration and masturbation, the women for the most part want to be asked. They don't usually initiate cyber-sex."

Brad, a thirty-three-year-old financial planner, said, "I like it because it is a big responsibility to constantly take leadership in a relationship—and that's what men are supposed to do. So this makes it easier on me. I have time to think before I type."

Women Experimenting with Sexuality

The anonymity offered by the Internet frees women from the traditional mores that for centuries have restrained open discussion of sexuality in the real world. It makes sense that given an anonymous, accessible, and affordable opportunity to break free of possible repercussions of expressing themselves sexually, women are taking advantage of the Internet to explore new experiences. Drs. Alvin Cooper, David L. Delmonico, and Ron Burg state in the article, "Cybersex Users, Abusers, and Compulsives: New Findings and Implications," "For women, the freedom to break from cultural expectations and to express themselves sexually with anonymity on the Internet may be potent lures to explore online sexual outlets."

Marci, a twenty-five-year-old dance teacher, said, "There are things I am interested in knowing about, like S&M. I wouldn't in a million years have anything to do with S&M offline. It's just something a 'nice girl' would not do. So I can do it in a virtual world and still be a 'nice girl' in the real world."

Thomas Moore, writing in *Soul Mates: Honoring the Mysteries of Love and Relationships*, says, "A woman who feels inhibited about presenting herself as sexual yet desires to be sexually attractive to men can experiment with being more flirtatious. She may find a way to describe herself online as attractive and sexually appealing, affording her the chance to incorporate this view into her self-image, off as well as online."

Although researchers are just beginning to examine how much actual changed behavior will take place due to experimentation with new behaviors online, the following descriptions of women's sexual experiences can give you a sense of the enthusiasm with which some women are approaching new opportunities provided by the Internet. They also give a sample of the variety of experiences available to women on the Internet.

Jamie, a twenty-seven-year-old computer programmer, said, "Cyber-sex has been a learning experience for me. I was always very passive and quiet in bed with a partner and this has helped me overcome this. I am now able to open up and show a side of myself that I never knew existed...it is very exciting to me and to my boyfriend as well! We have also engaged in phone sex with each other. Cyber-sex has added a definite 'spark' to our sex life."

Kelly, a thirty-two-year-old shop owner, said, "I always had a hard time talking about my sexuality and expressing it. I felt safer and more daring online, so I was able to share much more with my partner here than I have ever been able to do in real life. It has helped me talk about things and say things that I never ever thought I would ever be able to say to Ron."

Selena, a forty-six-year-old lesbian businesswoman, reported, "She approached me, and was rather aggressive in pursuing me. She carefully described some very erotic fantasies she has, which turned me on and made me think sexy things all day afterwards. She woke up my libido in ways that it had never been before. We talked a lot about other things before we ever made our way into a sexual conversation, but overall, it only took four days before we were both masturbating online together."

As you can see, women are experimenting and enjoying the discussion of such experimentation. These observations are in line with observations made by the Cooper, Morahan-Martin, Maheu, and Mathy research team: most women don't seem to be getting caught in the cyber-sex compulsion traps. They seem to be experimenting, and unlike our several *SelfhelpMagazine* Essay Contest respondents, if women do engage in direct cyber-sex, they typically report having orgasms after being on the Internet, rather than while being on the Internet. Most women are like Julie, a thirty-three-year-old interior design student:

"Before I experimented with the dating and sex websites, a friend suggested I get one of those freebie Web-access accounts that give you a gazillion free hours for the first month. So I did. I sorta decided the month was going to be like taking a class, like Sex 101! I spent an hour or two a day to look at my leisure, read about other people's interests, and get an eyeful of what is out there! To tell you the truth, some of what I found was shocking and really obscene—but I enjoyed the freedom of looking at newsgroups, IRC, MUDS, and, of course, dating and porn websites.

"I was so amazed that I even copied some things and showed them to my friends. We laughed a lot, but it led to a great discussion of their exploits and how they had handled some scary things with their sexual contacts. I think the Internet is great for learning about sexual things we'd never otherwise see. Then I closed the freebie account and stopped getting that weird mail those websites and newsgroups send you after you visit them."

Many women seem to be using and enjoying the Internet's access to sexual material for educational rather than erotic goals. Regardless of their goal, the Internet is freeing women from the popular requirements of a tiny waist, large breasts, and full lips to enjoy and experiment sexuality. Similarly, men can win affection without powerful biceps, chiseled chins, or a full head of hair. They need not prove prowess with expensive cars, important jobs, or prestigious titles.

Men Experimenting with Sexuality

Men are also experimenting with newfound freedoms provided by the Internet. Richard Booth and Dr. Marshall Jung wrote about online sexuality in *Romancing the Net: A 'Tell-All' Guide to Love Online*, "Men, who often feel pressure to be more assertive and 'getting somewhere,' may feel less responsible for setting the pace of the relationship. This also includes the pace of the sexual aspect of the relationship. Men can relax and let relationships develop in a more organic way, with sexuality emerging from an emotional connection rather than a physical one."

This type of experience was described by several men in the *Selfhelp Magazine* Essay Contest. Dan, a forty-year-old lawyer, wrote, "Cyber-sex is a safe outlet to imagine and experiment with how to stimulate your partner mentally as well as physically."

Larry, a twenty-six-year-old geographer, wrote, "Cyber-sex allows people to explore dormant corners of their own sexuality in a different environment away from the pressures of the real world."

Andy, a thirty-three-year-old mechanic, wrote, "I can explore my sexual fantasies on the Internet. It is sensational that there is no face-to-face contact, and therefore no embarrassment. I have not had a sexual partner for a while because I am shy and have a hard time meeting women in face-to-face situations."

Greg, a twenty-nine-year-old banker wrote, "Sometimes the girls I talked to would ask me right away if I wanted to cyber. But that was not the usual case. Most girls like to warm up to an orgasm, so I'd start off by asking if it was hot where she was, and then I would ask her what she had on. If she had anything on, I would ask her to take it off. It would go from there. If it's cold where she is, we crawl into a bed with lots of covers and share body warmth—without clothes, of course. I enjoy the slowed pace, but knowing from the start that the encounter will lead to orgasm."

As mentioned previously, men are also finding that to be attractive online, they need to demonstrate an entirely different set of skills, requiring the skilled use of the written word to communicate and to compete with each other for attention.

Other Cyber-Sexual Exploration
In deciding the appropriateness of cyber-sex, many factors must be considered. Given the diversity of the global community, couples can be expected to define fidelity as well as choose to experience sexuality in a variety of ways. With technology providing an increased ability to exercise freedom of choice, sexual activities are changing. Committed couples, then, must renegotiate their fidelity and sexuality agreements.

The potentially combustible mix of technology and sexuality is not only controversial, but fascinating in that new possibilities are emerging for couples who choose to be open about their cyber-sexual activities.

Cyber-Sex for Committed Couples
As identified in the *SelfhelpMagazine* Essay Contest, two types of open cyber-sexual arrangements are occurring with some frequency among couple's on the Internet: *overt cyber-sex*, in which one partner in a relationship knows of the other's affair, but doesn't voice a desire for it to stop; and *virtual ménage-a-trois*, in which the real-life couple engages with one or more people in romance and cyber-sex.

Overt Cyber-Sexual Relationships

Some spouses of partners who engage in cyber-sexual liaisons do not consider online sexual activity to be infidelity. When couples reach an agreement about participating in cyber-sex, many variations can take place, depending on the needs and preferences of the parties involved. Some people engage in cyber-sex with others with the full knowledge or participation of their real life partners. Because these arrangements are not deceptive, they are not considered infidelity by those who choose to include such sexual behavior in their definitions and promises of fidelity.

Chloe, a thirty-year-old reporter, explained to us, "My husband knows I have some kinky conversations on the Internet. So far, he brings it up during our lovemaking, and we both get very hot."

Armand, a fifty-eight-year-old dentist, confessed, "Frankly, I'm relieved that she gets satisfied online. I don't have a sex drive anymore, and she does. I'd rather she gets it at home than if she were to go outside our relationship in our small town."

This is similar to the open marriage of the sixties, in which couples were free to have other sexual liaisons while in a committed relationship. An open marriage is an agreement between committed partners to have other lovers, but their own relationship is considered primary. Living arrangements differ according to the agreements made by the couple. The open marriage of the sixties has generally fallen out of favor and has not been considered a success. Those engaged in such an arrangement need to carefully assess their relationship, their motivations, and whether other options are available to keep their sex life exciting and to solve their problems. While overt cyber-sexual contacts can be sexually stimulating for a couple, they also can be sought out by those who cannot tolerate intimacy. Couples that engage in these activities often strike a precarious balance between heightened excitement and heightened disappointment.

Virtual Ménage-a-Trois

Some people find that going online to meet a third party in real time heightens their sexual experience. Their exchanges are added fuel for sexual contact. Others find new partners to add to their committed relationships.

Rachael, a twenty-five-year-old fashion consultant, said, "Sex outside usual norms is a new frontier that awakens the pioneering spirit within marriage, as long as both people engage in the exchange together—at the same keyboard, at the same time. In fact, it can be quite pleasurable. Whether or not to tell the third party what's happening is a whole other issue...."

"Hotpeppers," a thirty-three-year-old sales rep, told us his story.

"I used to date a lot of women, but pretty much did one at a time. Now that I'm married, I have to admit feeling a little restless, even though I love my wife and the sex is good. You know what they say, 'Variety is the spice of life!' I got to thinking maybe she felt the same way. So I brought up the subject of maybe adding somebody else once in a while. I could see she was thinking about it, but wasn't comfortable with actually carrying through with it...So I figured out the perfect solution—a computer! I gave her one for her birthday and we both got online. I was thinking I'd get to have some hot tamales and my wife and I could get off on it.

"What I didn't figure on was how much she enjoyed doing it with other guys online. We got into some arguments over that one, I can tell you. But then she reminded me I was the one who brought it up. She said if we were going to do the threesome thing, then she got to choose first—the online guy she wanted, or no dice. Then I could choose a chick for the next go-around. It felt like playing with fire—fun. Now, just as you're maybe thinking this sounds like the perfect arrangement, I'm here to tell you it isn't. It's why I'm writing. I thought so, too. But things got out of hand. We—no, mostly me, I guess—couldn't handle the jealousy. She wanted to be with one guy in particular more and more. I discovered they met offline. I blew up and forced her to choose. She chose him. Now I am alone. I really miss that woman. So my advice is, you can't always have your cake and eat it too."

The Internet helps us understand that our planet is populated with people who live in different cultures and hold different beliefs. Whether they are American, African, Australian, or from any other continent on the globe, their beliefs are to be viewed as part of the diversity that makes us each unique and part of the human race. Our planetary diversity is our strength, and learning how other people experience and enjoy sexuality is one of the unique characteristics of the Internet. Nonetheless, some people get trapped in their exploration of sexuality on the Internet. They lose the ability to manage their own behavior toward themselves, those they love, and those they meet online. In the next chapter, we will have a more thorough discussion of sexual impulses gone haywire.

Cyber-Sexual Compulsivity: Impulses Gone Haywire

In an episode of the popular TV program *Law and Order*, a young man was accused of murdering a woman he had been involved with on the Internet. "Hotrocks," had been emotionally and financially involved in the relationship, so much so that he eventually maxed out his father's credit card just to spend time with his virtual lover. His parents testified that they did everything they could to stop him—they removed the computer, closed credit card accounts, and disconnected the cable lines, but none of it was effective. Hotrocks bought a laptop and continued his virtual infatuation. His mother told the jury that her son dropped his friends, his social activities, and his previous life. They sought therapy for him, but he would not go. She said, "It was as though he was addicted!"

Sexual Compulsivity

Could someone be "addicted" to sex on the Internet? We usually think of addiction as having to do with tobacco, alcohol, gambling, or drugs. Nevertheless, this young man was preoccupied with his Internet activities, just as if he were addicted to gambling. Was the mother correct in her assessment that he was "addicted"?

The world of cyber-sex becomes even more complicated if someone becomes cyber-sexually compulsive. In this chapter, we will discuss sexual compulsivity and its relationship to Internet-based infidelity. We will use the term "sexual compulsivity" to describe sexual behavior on the Internet that is beyond the user's control, progressive, and an interferes with normal life activities. However, when we refer to researchers who have contributed to this field, we will use whatever terms they use, which often includes the term "addiction."

Before we get started, we want to clarify an important point about our use of terms such as "sexual compulsive" or "sex addict." The terms we use in this chapter are not meant to cause shame or represent the totality of a person. Individuals are complex human beings, but often have specific behavior patterns that need to be addressed. These issues can be discussed without such judgment. If you or your loved one has a sexual compulsion, you both deserve respect for seeking assistance by reading and speaking with others about the issues. If you hear other people shaming or blaming you for trying to learn about sexual compulsivity, find other sources of information or support.

Scope of the Problem

The National Council on Sexual Addiction and Compulsivity estimated that 6 percent of Americans are sex addicts, bringing the population of sex addicts in the United States to approximately sixteen million people. The accuracy of such estimates is difficult to assess. People with sexual disorders are often ashamed of their behavior, and typically do not give accurate reports of their activities.

When researching sexual compulsivity related to the Internet, the picture becomes even more difficult to assess. Sexually addicted people can more easily operate online than anywhere else. They are difficult to find, because they do not congregate in public places where researchers could more easily study their characteristics. Unless they commit obvious crimes, sexually compulsive individuals also cannot be not tracked by legal officials. So far, many researchers have relied upon self-report measures, which are not the preferred methods of the research community, but they are still better than none at all.

Underlying Dynamics

Psychologist Patrick Carnes, Ph.D., has contributed to our understanding of sexual compulsivity through a number of publications in the general field of sexual compulsion. His research and writing has shed light on understanding the person, the course of the problem, and the interventions that help bring relief to the suffering individual and the surrounding family. Dr. Carnes writes that the sexual addict is a person in pain who typically believes he or she is bad and unworthy, someone who feels unlovable, whose wants will never be satisfied, and who thinks that sex is his or her most important need. According to Dr. Carnes, the sexual addictive cycle includes preoccupation, sexual compulsivity, and eventually, despair.

The following true or false quiz, based on Dr. Carnes's two books, *Don't Call It Love* and *Contrary To Love,* will increase your knowledge of this problem.

Sexual Compulsivity Quiz

	True	False
1. If a person used more self-control and self-discipline, the sexual addiction would end.	❏	❏
2. It is the fun and pleasure of sex that is the "hook" for the sexually addicted.	❏	❏
3. The sexual addict feels little or no remorse for his or her behavior.	❏	❏

	True	False
4. A complete change in sexually addictive behavior does not mean a spontaneous cure.	❏	❏
5. There is a progression of sexually compulsive behavior that could lead to endangering others.	❏	❏
6. Curing sexual addiction means immediately stopping all sexual behavior.	❏	❏
7. Overcoming defenses is one of the first steps in recovery.	❏	❏
8. A twelve-step program like those used by alcoholics can help.	❏	❏
9. Family history is important to review to gain an understanding of how addiction occurs and how to manage it.	❏	❏

Answers

1. **False.** The essence of any addiction is that the person has lost control over their ability to choose. Potential loss of family, work, and finances do not act as a deterrent, nor do the possibilities of public humiliation or arrest.
2. **False.** It is the relief from pain that draws the sexually addicted to compulsive sexual behavior. Sexual excitement masks the despair, shame, and self-loathing that can otherwise haunt the addict.
3. **False.** The addictive cycle includes despair, which initiates alternating feelings of shame and guilt. A desire to escape these feelings drives more behavior that is sexual.
4. **True.** Addictive behavior can stop suddenly in an attempt to get control over the addiction, but the sexual compulsivity can easily resume if left untreated. The behavior can be reversed or deescalated to normal levels if it is discovered, or if someone is hurt.
5. **True.** The severity of behavior can increase. A sexually compulsive person in the beginning of developing the addiction might start with frequent masturbation, pornography, or multiple sexual relationships. Behavior can escalate to making obscene phone calls, rubbing up against people in crowded public places, "accidentally" touching others inappropriately, and voyeurism. The highest level of sexual compulsivity includes prostitution, sexual behavior with children, rape, or indecent exposure. However, these behaviors are not always the result of sexual addiction. The history of an individual's sexual behavior must be considered when making such determinations.
6. **True.** Compulsive sexual behaviors need to stop, but there is a *caveat.* For example, when an alcoholic or gambler goes into recovery, he or she must completely abstain from alcohol or gambling. However, complete cessation cannot always be the first step to recovery. For example, a compulsive eater cannot stop eating, but can learn to make different choices regarding food. Similarly, the sexually compulsive individual will not be asked to permanently abstain from sexual behavior. Treatment usually begins with a period of complete abstinence. All sexual behaviors, such as visiting sexual websites and masturbation, are stopped. If there are

multiple relationships, the person is encouraged to stop sexual behavior in all relationships, and determine which is the primary relationship, if there is to be one. This primary relationship is then the one to be developed and maintained. Sex is gradually resumed with this primary partner.

7. **True.** The sexual addict is encouraged to reexamine behaviors in light of defense mechanisms common to addiction. These include denying the problem, rationalizing, and minimizing the effects of addiction on his or her life.

8. **True.** Twelve-step programs are successful if a person is committed to working through the program. Other cognitive behavior group programs are also effective. Smart Recovery and Rational Recovery are two such examples. Individual psychotherapy is often an important part of recovery.

9. **True.** Family and individual history are very important in understanding sexual compulsivity. A complete and objective review of the family and one's own pattern can also improve self-esteem and, more importantly, help give clues for recovery and self-forgiveness at a time when emotions are at a low.

Cyber-Sexual Compulsivity

In an article called "Initiation and Maintenance of Online Sexual Compulsivity: Implications for Assessment and Treatment," Dana Putnam, Ph.D., identifies a number of factors that increase cyber-sexual compulsivity. He states:

> ...sexual addiction and compulsivity may develop in response to physical, sexual, family, and social trauma. Family sexual behavior and attitudes have also been noted as contributing factors and it has been hypothesized that hypersexuality is caused, at least in part, by biological factors such as testosterone and serotonin levels. In addition, personality disorders, mood and anxiety disorders, and substance abuse and dependence have all been considered as conditions associated with sexual compulsivity. Although these factors have been discussed primarily in relation to compulsive sexual behavior in general, there is reason to believe that the same factors may apply to individuals who were not sexually compulsive prior to using the Internet.

Jose, a forty-three-year-old patient seeking treatment for cyber-sexual compulsivity, had this to say:

"My father was an alcoholic and so were his brothers. They were a rowdy group and often partied late into the night. I remember falling asleep to the sound of music mixed with a curious blend of fighting and laughing. My mother would often be upset after such evenings, because my dad and his brothers would leave the house and not return until the wee hours of the morning. As I grew older, I came to understand that they would be out having sex with other women. I swore to myself and to my mother that I would never do such things to my wife. Now that I'm an adult, I am both alcoholic and, since we've had an Internet connection, sexually compulsive. I have been in treatment, on and off, for over five years. My behavior has not only damaged my marriage, but also my children.

"I take antidepressant medication, attend Rational Recovery meetings, and see a therapist every other week. I understand my problem to be related to family of origin and a genetic makeup that makes me prone to anxiety. I have abused alcohol, drugs, and sex to numb out my anxiety and replace it with a cocky, know-it-all attitude that pushes people away. I also see how I need to take responsibility for my actions despite my history and biology."

The Powerful Orgasm

Various psychological factors may also maintain cyber-sexual behaviors once they have become compulsive. When online, the state of sexual arousal can lead to masturbation and its powerful reinforcer, orgasm. The most obvious factor contributing to online hypersexual behavior is the release of sexual tension.

For those people who have difficulty sustaining an offline sexual relationship, online sexual behavior is particularly reinforcing. When online sexuality is preferred to face-to-face sexuality, it is considered a serious impairment to normal functioning. Many psychologists believe sexual compulsivity is often the result of previous sexual trauma.

While such early experiences can lead to the development of sexual compulsions, other factors typically maintain them. Factors known as classical and operant conditioning can keep these behavior sequences in place. Classical conditioning occurs when a behavior is paired with a bodily response. When someone experiences sexual arousal by looking at pictures, playing with a program at a computer, or when using the Internet to find sexually stimulating material, the act of searching can be sexually stimulating in and of itself. For those who engage repeatedly in these activities, the mere act of thinking about sitting at the computer or logging on to the Internet can lead to sexual arousal (tingling, erection, lubrication).

John, a thirty-seven-year-old businessman, confessed, "I'm not sure how it happens, but when I'm in a hotel room, the only thing I can think about is plugging in my laptop and going to those Asian porn sites. I usually begin to get erection as I slip my hotel key into my hotel room door. I can't help it. The only way I can get relief is to log on, see what's new, and have an orgasm or two. Then I can relax and the rest of my life comes back into focus."

Operant conditioning occurs when behaviors are reinforced. For example, one type of operant conditioning occurs when individuals scan pornographic websites to find the right stimulation. They are not certain how long it will take to find an arousing picture that matches their particular preference.

Sexual relief can be one mouse click away, or might require several minutes of hyper-linking and scrolling. The individual never really knows when the right stimulus will be found, but one thing is certain, it will appear. When it does, it is reinforced by an orgasm.

Isaac, a thirty-nine-year-old gas station owner, explained, "I just hate myself. I'm completely out of control. I can't stop surfing until I find just the right picture. Sometimes it can take an hour, and other times it takes two minutes. I never really know, but when it happens, my whole body explodes."

Much like a gambler who keeps throwing the dice to get the winning combination, the cyber-sexually compulsive individual keeps clicking and linking to find the right stimulus for an orgasm.

Similarly, when cyber-sex involves two or more people arousing one another, the reinforcing orgasm can be reached at unpredictable rates. These types of situations are highly reinforcing, and tend to create compulsions that are very difficult to stop, despite an individual's discomfort with negative consequences. Unpredictable reinforcement schedules can lead to behaviors that feel out of control.

Cyber-sexually compulsive behavior is also highly rewarding because it alleviates negative feelings. Individuals who have difficulty coping with emotional states, such as anxiety, depression, or physical stress, can redirect their energies to finding the perfect sexual release.

Other circular behavior patterns can strengthen compulsive urges. For example, sexually compulsive individuals may have a high need for sensation-seeking or conflict. When they argue with others, they might feel the strong need to use sex to temporarily forget the situation. When online, they can experience the freedom of letting their fantasies run wild and objectifying their victims, while avoiding anxiety, rejection, or other negative consequences.

As you can see, when people develop patterns of online sexual arousal paired with the need to avoid negative emotions, the computer and Internet can become a safe harbor for them in almost any storm. Wherever they are, whatever stressful emotion they are experiencing, they can bridge their difficult moments by planning the next opportunity to escape into their fantasy world where they will be physically and emotionally aroused, yet safe.

Marta explained, "I live in a culture where women are trained to serve men. Having been trained in the U.K. to be a physician, I find it very difficult to live with my people and serve them according to our customs. I find freedom from this oppression when I can surf the Internet as 'Manhattan Rocks.' People can't tell if I'm a man or a woman, and, frankly, it doesn't matter. The real problem is that I can't wait to finish my workday and be alone with my computer at night. When I work with arrogant men or submissive women, I just tell myself, 'Ha! More fodder for my night games in the S&M chat room!'

"The sad truth is that I work with lots of arrogant men and submissive women, so I am constantly thinking about my S&M virtual games. By the time I get home, I am so turned on that I can hardly stand it. I spend several hours a night at these websites, and feel as if I can't get enough. I go to bed exhausted, only to face another day of the same thing."

As we can see with Marta, this safe harbor can soon become a trap, because it can compete with the outside world and interfere with normal functioning. People who are trapped by these activities are being studied by researchers from around the world. While much is yet to be learned, a few significant findings are beginning to emerge, and these findings are discussed in the next section.

Who Engages in Cyber-Sex?

Dr. Cooper and his teams of researchers published a number of papers in the area of cyber-sex and cyber-sexual compulsivity. In a paper called, "Online Sexual Compulsivity: Getting Tangled in the Net," Drs. Cooper, Putnam, Planchon, and Boies outline three types of people who engage in cyber-sex: recreational users, sexual compulsives, and at-risk users. We will discuss them at length to give you an opportunity to understand the specific characteristics and motivations of the range of people engaging in cyber-sex, and which ones are considered cyber-sexually compulsive.

Recreational Users

Recreational users seem to be the largest category of users, and seem to avoid harm from their cyber-sexual activities. Distraction, relaxation, and taking a break from the stresses of life tend to be their reasons for engaging in cyber-sex.

> Mary, a twenty-five-year-old financial adviser, and Diane, a twenty-six-year-old lawyer, are two friends from college who have met each other in Rehoboth Beach, Delaware for a vacation every August for six years. They are hammering away at their steamed crabs and laughing, as they have a blast trying master the mystery of opening them.
>
> "This is fun," Mary says.
>
> "It is," replies Diane. "But, Mary, I found another way to have fun."
>
> "Don't tell me! You're skydiving. Or are you rock climbing?"
>
> "No, it's better than that."
>
> "This sounds intriguing."
>
> "It is. I'm having cyber-sex on the Internet."
>
> "You're kidding!" Mary exclaimed.
>
> "No. It's no big deal. It's a lot of fun."

"Tell me."

"Oh, I've gone to some chat rooms every now and then," Diane began.

"And?"

"I meet someone interesting. We talk, joke, laugh, and then cyber."

"Really? How often?"

"Oh, once, maybe twice a week."

"Are you going to stop dating guys?"

"No, of course not. It's only a pastime, and I'm learning a lot about sex!"

Diane is typical of those initially intrigued by cyber-sex, and most likely will be one of the people who can easily walk away without developing a compulsion. They seem to have a healthy need for emotional connection and interactivity in a face-to-face relationship, and those connections sustain their interest over time. Women who engage in these activities also frequently report the educational benefits they get from online sexual activity. Women are less likely to feel that their online sexual activities are out of control, or use cyber-sex to cope with stress.

Sexually Compulsive Users

People in the second group, the sexually compulsive, are characterized by their denial, repeated efforts to reduce their online sexual activities, and repeated failure to discontinue these behaviors. Their self-talk will often contain phrases such as:

- ➲ "I can stop anytime I want."
- ➲ "I am not hurting anyone."
- ➲ "I'll go online for two hours instead of three."
- ➲ "This is the last time I'll do this."

Much like drug abusers, their tolerance increases over time, and they may require increasingly explicit stimulation to get the same "high." They spend too much time looking for sexual satisfaction online, despite the problems created. As a result, they may lose their marriages, lose their jobs, and find themselves in trouble with the law.

Some of these individuals are involved with "paraphilias," which include behaviors such as being preoccupied with pornography, having multiple affairs, engaging in sex with anonymous or multiple partners, obsession with phone sex, and paying prostitutes for sexual services. Compulsively masturbating to sexually explicit websites meets the traditional definition of paraphilia. With the arrival of the Internet, we see more people, women as well as men, caught in these traps than ever before.

More than twice as many men as women tend to be sexually compulsive, as reported by Drs. Cooper, Morahan-Martin, Maheu, and Mathy. Women reported being more sexually compulsive over the Internet than in the real world, with most preferring chat rooms. Cyber-sexually compulsive males, on the other hand, have no preference for any particular medium for their compulsions.

These behaviors can cause a significant degree of personal discomfort or other problems in basic areas of life, such as work performance or personal relationships in the real world. These individuals can easily find themselves in trouble with the law, as well.

Fred gives an example of how this can happen. "I've always been a bit horny. What can I say? I just like sex. When I got married to Penny, I swore that I'd give up the girlie magazine subscriptions. Within a month, Penny bought a computer, and I was out of control again. I've been able to keep it in check, but I really get turned on by a wide variety of pornography. I've even hidden a few pictures on my computer at work, and when I get uptight, I shut my office door...it terrifies me to think I might get caught, but I just can't help myself. I update those pics every week...."

Another group of sexual compulsive behaviors involve the "uncommon paraphilias." As would be suspected, these involve unusual sexual activities. However, "unusual" must be discussed within the context of cultural values. Some cultures are more accepting of variations in sexual practice than others.

In the United States, individuals who engage in the uncommon paraphilias can be at higher risk for crime, because they often involve a unwilling participant. Exhibitionism is a paraphilia in which people find it stimulating to expose their genitals and watch the reaction of others. Voyeurism is defined as sexual images or behavior that involve observing people who are undressing or engaged in sexual activity. Sexual sadism is an erotic preference for inflicting pain or hurting people. Pedophilia is a sexualized preference for children. Individuals with uncommon paraphilias can also focus on body parts, such as fingers or toes. They may also have a sexual preference for nonliving objects, such as shoes or undergarments.

The Internet has become a meeting place for people who are dependent upon unusual sexual behaviors or fantasies. The perception of anonymity on the Internet has fostered the growth of entire communities of people with paraphilias to supply each other with information, erotica, and support for a wide range of behavior that would be considered abnormal and sometimes criminal. Once an email address is picked up by those who intend to profit from such disorders, people suffering from paraphilias can find themselves plagued with unwanted email reminders of their compulsions. Individuals who are sent unwanted solicitations may need to completely change their email address or take more elaborate measures to stop receiving such mail.

At-Risk Users

Dr. Cooper's research team has also identified at-risk users. This is a new group, considered to have become cyber-sexually compulsive since using the Internet. They have no other history of sexual compulsivity, but their involvement with cyber-sex has caused problems in their lives. They may have had a vulnerability to sexual compulsivity before having access to the Internet. They may have had a tendency to deal with emotional issues with excessive sexuality offline, but never to the point of suffering serious consequences. Challenged by the accessibility and affordability of the Internet, their capacity to withstand temptation has crumbled.

It must also be mentioned that developers of adult entertainment sites make it easy for men in particular to become overly involved with cyber-sex, even when they aren't looking for it. Website owners can capture private email addresses from web browsers, so ads such as this one can be sent via email after a user visits adult entertainment websites.

These ads are written to entice the reader to impulsively click, and within seconds enter a playground of beautiful models posing, ready for sex. Regardless of how they find their way to the sex areas of the Internet, members of this at-risk group are further divided by researchers into two sub-groups. The first is the stress reactive type. People in this sub-group only seem to use cyber-sex at times of particularly high stress, and not as a frequent coping mechanism. Overall, they seem to have a higher level of coping skills and a wider social support system. Nonetheless, they occasionally have trouble being alone. Their level of anxiety rises dramatically when they have a serious fight with their spouse, or are left alone for a weekend. They have learned that having a cyber-sex-ual experience lowers their anxiety and confirms that they are not alone. When their stress has passed, they do not sustain their compulsive interest in cyber-sexual activities. They return to find comfort in their other social connections.

The second subgroup is considered depressive. They are at-risk users who may be depressed, anxious, or both, and seek cyber-sex to shake off their overall malaise. These individuals are likely to seek sexual gratification online in an escalating way, seeking new sources of stimulation as they get bored with the old. They might experiment with a wide variety of sexual formats and become involved with phone sex or live video streaming.

Let us look at one women's story to see her depressive, at-risk behavior. In actuality, she is a composite of a number of people who have shared their stories with us. We will call her Alma.

"I am fifty-three years old, a widow, and I am leading a wild life on the Internet. I've always been in control of my sexual activities, but since I got my connection to the Internet, I've gone over the edge. I think I've had cyber-sex with over two hundred men and I know I'm addicted to sex online. I don't want a relationship. After I've had sex online with someone, I don't want to meet him again.

"I also love phone sex, but only one time with each partner. I make the call and also have my phone blocked because I don't want any "*69s," or callbacks. I lurk and masturbate to chat room discussions in dating or pornography websites.

"Most of the guys I had sex with were young—some were as young as my son. It didn't matter because I was never going to get involved. I like them young. That's why the Internet is so great. They don't get to see me. They imagine I am what I tell them.

"However, about six months ago, I met a very interesting guy online. I decided to have a second meeting, then a third, and so on. I was really obsessed with him and he really liked my sexual ideas.

"We finally decided to meet. He was twenty-seven-years-old. I think I look young for my age. I decided not to tell him the truth. I was so nervous about our meeting. I did a whole makeover on myself. We met in Corpus Christi. I wore a big hat and dark glasses. He was as good looking as the picture he had sent me. It seemed to go okay, but he kept asking questions that I knew were eventually going to get to my age. He liked the sex and so on, but something was not right. He was very turned on, but after his orgasm, he was cold and detached. At the end of our few days together, I asked when he wanted to meet again. He told me I was old enough to be his mother and he didn't want to see me any more. I tried to contact him, but he doesn't respond. I cry a lot and am taking an antidepressant. I never thought this would happen to me."

This story illustrates how overly involved Alma has become since she gained access to the Internet. She has no history of sexually compulsive behavior. She had been able to restrain herself in the past, but given the accessibility and anonymity of the Internet, Alma now finds herself out of control. She is compulsive and cannot stop herself, although she knows her behavior is problematic. Alma needs a self-help program, and if that does not work, she needs the help of a trained professional.

Who Is Cyber-Sexually Compulsive?

How would you know if you or your loved one was cyber-sexually compulsive? What is the difference between healthy curiosity and a problem with cyber-sexual compulsivity?

Men and women who are not sexually compulsive typically report a feeling of emptiness and loneliness after the initial thrill of experiencing cyber-sex. Their curiosity is satisfied, they learn something they wanted to know, and they move on with their lives. In her June 1997 article, "Sex and the Net: Clinical Implications," Sandra Risa Leiblum, Ph.D., writes, "However, even the most luscious fruits become routine after repeated sampling and the lack of real nutrition usually becomes apparent. After a while, what was titillating becomes trite, and sheer repetition engenders staleness."

Dr. Leiblum continues, "For individuals who are not true sexual obsessives, the repetitiveness of the images and the unreality of the activity are doomed to eventual disappointment." If you have tried cyber-sex, and the excitement wears off for any variety of reasons, you probably are not cyber-sexually compulsive. The lack of actual physical contact in cyber-sex, the anonymity allowed by the Internet, and the sense of false intimacy makes it impossible to have a truly intimate relationship. Eventually, these experiences become meaningless and empty, and driven by a healthy need for connection, people become dissatisfied.

People who are caught in the trap of cyber-sexual compulsion do not report disinterest. On the contrary, they cannot stop themselves from being interested. They often do not understand their loss of control. In a 1998 article, "Sexuality and the Internet: Surfing into the New Millennium," Dr. Cooper defined sexually compulsive behavior as "an irresistible urge to perform an irrational sexual act."

Byron's story shows the emotions felt by someone who is cyber-sexually compulsive.

Byron, is a thirty-three-year-old venture capitalist. He came into therapy because he was worried that he was developing a serious sex-related problem. He started a dot-com company when he was only twenty-seven years old, made a fortune, and now is an angel investor for other start-up companies. Byron told us about an important night in his life. It was a celebration in a private room at the glamorous Hilton Hotel in Scottsdale, Arizona. The celebration was arranged by his staff to celebrate the fifth year of the success of his business.

Byron told his therapist, "We had a lot of laughs that night. I know I come to life with that kind of excitement. I often felt that excitement when I built my business. But when I'm alone and the buzz of my business day is over, I hate to go home. Sure, it's beautiful, but I can't stand being there. So I settle in with a bourbon and ice, log on to my computer, and feel the excitement come back.

"I like the Married Only chat rooms, because there's no responsibility. They're all cheaters, and they know it. That's what I like.

"I can usually find someone to cyber with me within a few minutes. Sometimes three or four of us meet together and have group sex. Or someone will suggest a porn site to visit, and we can then all go the the same site and get off on the same pictures or videos."

Here are eight questions to gauge cyber-sexual compulsivity:

1. Did you find that your need for virtual sex did not diminish after a period of experimentation?
2. Are you devoting an increasing amount of time to cyber-sexual pursuits?
3. Do you find yourself denying or minimizing the negative consequences of your time spent having cyber-sex?
4. Have you made repeated, unsuccessful attempts at limiting or stopping your cyber-sexual behavior?
5. Are your loved ones complaining that you are increasingly unavailable to them because you are spending more time online?
6. Are your cyber-sexual activities replacing social, academic, occupational, or recreational activities?
7. Are you obsessed with cyber-sex when you are off the computer?
8. Do you feel a loss of control in choosing whether you will spend time engaging in cyber-sex?

As you can see, the questions are a way for you to assess the irresistibility and irrationality of cyber-sexual activity. If you answer yes to some of these questions, there may be a problem with cyber-sexual compulsivity.

Breaking the Cycle through Self-Help
If you feel that you are, or are becoming, sexually compulsive online, the following self-help steps may help you break this cycle. Give them a solid effort. Buy a notebook to record information about yourself and follow these instructions precisely. You might surprise yourself with how much you can do on your own if you follow these specific directions. If you do not find success immediately, make specific note of where you did not stick with the plan. This information will be invaluable to you if you try again later.

Self-Monitoring
Developing an increased awareness of your harmful behaviors can help give you clues about triggers and solutions. Keep a log of the time you spend online, and note what was happening just before you go online for sex. If you are unable to avoid the chat rooms, keep track of the events, feelings, and thoughts just before logging on to those rooms. Note the number of hours that you spend online. Also, if you find yourself getting sexually aroused, keep track of the number of times that you bring yourself to orgasm, how many minutes it took, and your level of anxiety before and after your orgasm.

You may find that you are anxious before going online, and that your anxiety is reduced after experiencing an orgasm. You may discover that you seek to cyber when you are alone for long periods, or if you feel rejection or anger. You can gain a lot of information by tracking your own behavior for a week. Your added knowledge of your behavior patterns can also help you identify possible relapse cues, once you have managed to quit.

Melanie, a thirty-year-old dental hygienist, is typical of someone trying to break off a cycle of sexual compulsivity. This is how Melanie kept a record of her progress to gain control of her sexual compulsivity. The following entries are from the first week:

> Saturday: I'm not going to go to the chat room tonight, but I feel so anxious. I know I'll feel good for a while if I go, but then I'll feel such shame. It's Saturday night, and Frank is at work. It's the perfect time for me to work on this.

> Sunday: Somehow I got through it last night, but I thought about the chat rooms all evening. Today was a better day. Frank and I played tennis and went to dinner. I'm getting ready for tomorrow. It's a busy week at work. I'm shutting down the computer now.

> Monday: I'm thinking about cyber-sex all evening. I'll call my neighbor, Jane, and talk to her instead.

> Tuesday: I need to go online. I can't help it. It is 6:30 P.M. and I am feeling lonely because Frank is working late tonight. I go straight to the chat rooms and find someone to cyber with me. OK, it is now 7:38, and I just had an orgasm with some guy named "HornDog." I am spent and relaxed, but I feel empty and a bit sad, too.

> Wednesday: I've been feeling badly all day for having no will power last night. I need to quit again. I'm starting to tell Jane a little about my problem.

> Thursday: I'm not shutting down the computer, but tomorrow I will look around for some other activity group.

> Friday: The desire for online sex hasn't gone away, but I did find a group for weavers. I haven't worked on a loom for years. I'm getting excited about that. It's a fight to stay away from my old hangouts online, but I am trying.

Lowering Your Defenses

Changing self-destructive behavior is not easy, and is usually time-consuming. When you decide you are ready, take the time to write out the ways in which you are harming yourself and those you love.

If you indulge yourself by believing that you are not harming anyone, examine how you might be deceiving yourself with distorted thinking. If you are avoiding the pain of working through a problem with your partner, make a list of the potential benefits and dangers. When you speak of your concerns, be honest, but kind. If you are not certain of how to be honest and kind at the same time, write about the things that you would need to do to learn those skills. Look at the ways in which you are avoiding a fully honest relationship offline.

Consider other instances in which your cyber-sexual pursuits have made your life unmanageable. Write about the activities you have missed because of excessive time online, the feelings you have carried after your activities, and the consequences you would face if someone bothered to track your online activities.

Consider the others involved. People minimize the infidelity they commit by their actions on the Internet by saying they are not connecting with a "flesh and blood" person. They fool themselves into believing that they are just dealing with a computer screen and keyboard, and that their cyber-lover does not have feelings. Being the victim of martial infidelity through a cyber-affair hurts deeply.

Two weeks later, Melanie writes, "I am glad I am dealing with this problem now, before I get married. I don't think a marriage can handle this. Sometimes I think I should tell Frank about my sexual compulsivity. But I'm afraid I'll lose the best man I've ever known."

If you need a reality-check about whether or not your anonymity can be compromised, take a visit to websites such as Sexinvestigations.com or Cyberaffairbusters.com.

Complete Cessation

Now that you understand your patterns, try to abstain for a specified amount of time. A month is reasonable. Stop contact with everyone you have been meeting for cyber-sex. Refrain from visiting any sexually oriented websites. If in the past you have been sexually compulsive in ways that do not involve the Internet, *do not go back* to any such previous activity.

Support

Share your struggle with a friend and ask for support. You can tell your friend that being supportive means not being judgmental. It means you need someone to listen and to help you through the time you feel the urge to cyber. Another way to find support is to find a twelve-step or other program for sexual compulsivity. This can be found through your phone book or community counseling centers in your area.

Three weeks later, Melanie writes in her diary, "I've found a twelve-step group online. Jane suggested it. It was a relief to know there are others like me. They were so welcoming. My heart was breaking. Maybe I'll survive this."

If you are unable to control yourself and Web time turns into flirtation or sex, restrict your online time to activities that are required as part of your job. Seek the help of an online support group or read information about cyber-sexual compulsivity.

Consider these websites:

- ➲ Online Sexual Addiction: Education, Support, and Resources: www.onlinesexaddict.com
- ➲ Sex Addicts Anonymous: www.sexaa.org/index.htm
- ➲ Sex and Love Addicts Anonymous: www.slaafws.org/
- ➲ Sexual Addiction Recovery Resources: home.rmi.net/~slg/sarr
- ➲ Sexual Compulsives Anonymous: www.sca-recovery.org
- ➲ SexHelp: www.sexhelp.com
- ➲ The National Council on Sexual Addiction and Compulsivity: www.ncsac.org
- ➲ The Sexual Recovery Institute: www.sexualrecovery.com
- ➲ *SelfhelpMagazine* Cyber-Affairs Email Discussion List: www.selfhelpmagazine.com/subscrib.html

These communities can help you understand your behaviors by allowing you to communicate with people who share your situation and want to find solutions to the complications caused by their behaviors, or those of the people they love.

It is also possible to prevent visiting sexual communities with the help of an Internet Service Provider (ISP) that will block these sites. Software is available that will do the same. These options are not fail-safe, in that you can always start an account with another ISP or use a friend's computer, and you can disable any software you might have installed on your computer. However, these measures can serve as a self-imposed roadblock, as a way for you to stop from proceeding if your impulses overtake your better judgment. By the time you sign up with a new ISP, or disable software, you will remember that you created this roadblock to prevent yourself from engaging in activities you want to avoid. The roadblocks cannot stop you, but they can delay you long enough to rethink your decision.

Going Online

When you are ready to go online, make a list of acceptable websites and chat rooms to prevent the possibility of deceiving yourself later. People often start with the best of intentions, but find that they slowly move toward online sexual activities. If you cannot adhere to your own list, take yourself offline completely for at least one week. Before allowing yourself to go back online for anything other than work, decide where you will go and what your maximum amount of leisure time will be. If need be, use computers in public places, such as libraries, coffee shops, and public workspaces, in order to restrict your ability to go to sexually oriented websites.

If you are in a committed relationship, move your desk or install your computer in a shared room. Remove the possibility of secrecy.

Two months later, Melanie writes in her diary, "I love going online, but I've been able to be more discriminating in which chat rooms I choose to visit. Thank heavens for the people in the twelve-step program and for Jane. I am looking for a face-to-face twelve-step program in this area. I think I can handle that now."

If these self-help techniques do not work, you may need the help of a professional with expertise in sexual compulsivity. A well-trained professional can help you understand the source of your dependency, teach you to identify and correct the distorted thinking that leads to anxiety and depression, help you understand the reinforcement mechanisms that maintain your compulsivity, and can guide you into a satisfying lifestyle that raises your self-esteem. If you give yourself the opportunity to get help, you can find direction for living your life in peace, rather than quiet despair.

Three months later, Melanie makes this entry in her diary, "I told Frank. It was a terrible scene, but when he calmed down, I asked for his help. He was pleased, at least, that I was trying to find a solution and had stopped. On Friday we have an appointment with an addiction therapist recommended by a woman in my twelve-step program."

Frank did not suspect that Melanie was using their computer to have a cyber-affair or that she was sexually compulsive. However, when a partner has such suspicions, he or she does not know where to turn, or what to do. Whether the problem is deep-rooted cyber-sexual compulsivity or recently developed at-risk behavior, almost all problems that result from sexual compulsivity touch loved ones, especially family members.

Family Issues with Compulsive Cyber-Sex and Cyber-Infidelity

Jennifer Schneider, M.D., Ph.D., reported in the article, "Effects of Cybersex Addiction on the Family: Results of a Survey," that of the ninety-one women and three men aged twenty-four to fifty-seven who had experienced serious negative consequences from their partner's cyber-sex involvement, over 60 percent of their partners did not pursue offline sex.

The results showed that the effects of cyber-infidelity were similar to traditional affairs, such as "hurt, betrayal, rejection, abandonment, devastation, loneliness, shame, isolation, humiliation, anger...loss of self-esteem. The online sexual activities were the cause of separation and divorce in over 22 percent of those surveyed."

Children and Young Adults

The effect of parental cyber-sexual compulsivity and resulting infidelity can be harmful in a number of ways. As children mature, they will look to the Internet to solve their informational and entertainment needs. This section will look at both parental and societal roles in teaching children to use the Internet properly.

Parents who siphon their energies into their extramarital virtual lover may be damaging their children in a number of ways by:

- ⊙ portraying infidelity as an acceptable behavior;
- ⊙ exposing children to parental discord due to the discovery of infidelity; and
- ⊙ neglecting parental responsibilities because of over-involvement with the Internet, including exposing children to virtual pornography.

Parental Cyber-Infidelity

Children are secondary victims of parents using the Internet for pornography and contacting an extramarital, virtual lover. The first and most serious problem is the modeling children obtain when exposed to parental infidelity through the Internet. If children learn that it is acceptable for a parent to solve emotional problems through sexual gratification or infidelity online, children can learn that cyber-infidelity can be a quick and easy option for handling stress or family problems. By following a parent's example, children can learn to satisfy their emotional and sexual needs online, and thereby add fuel to the already burning problem of using the Internet to break vows of fidelity.

Parental Discord Regarding Cyber-Infidelity

A second risk is for children who witness their parents arguing and threatening divorce upon discovery of cyber-infidelity. As we have discussed, children must be shielded from as much information as possible to spare them undue anxiety. When parents are emotionally reactive, they can be out of control with their words and actions. Witnessing distraught parents threaten divorce can put the child in a highly emotionally charged, yet helpless, state. This can raise anxiety levels to the point of acting out, or other self-destructive behaviors. Another issue is how children will be taught to handle evidence of their own parents' indiscretions inadvertently left on a home computer.

Parental Neglect

A parent's emotional absence due to over-involvement with the Internet, whether based in Internet addiction, cyber-sexual compulsivity, or cyber-infidelity, can have profound influence upon children. To have a parent present in the home, but unwilling to give a child the time and attention needed for proper emotional development, can be confusing as well as damaging. When parents are physically present but emotionally unavailable for prolonged and repeated periods, children suffer. They often cannot understand why the parent is unwilling to engage with them, and they often develop lowered self-esteem and self-confidence. The most obvious antidote to this problem is for parents to seek treatment for their compulsivity or infidelity, and thereby free their energies for the duties of child-rearing.

It is also crucial for parents to become aware of the hazards of allowing their children to spend unmonitored time on the Internet. For some children and adolescents, the fascination with technology does not decline, but increases until they are living in a parallel world. The parallel world can become a haven from the real world.

Herb Brody, in an online document of an interview called, "Session With a Cybershrink," said that Sherry Turkle, Ph.D., spoke of her concern for the young people who were turning away from society in favor of online communities. When she spoke to them of the many social problems in the real world which could benefit from their attention, they felt that there was more satisfaction in a commitment to building community and friendship in the parallel world.

Turkle said, "I talked with one young man of twenty-two or twenty-three, who told me how involved he is in political activity within one of the Internet's parallel worlds—a multi-user domain (or MUD) where people create characters and build their own virtual living and working spaces as a backdrop for their online social lives. He just loved the grassroots feel of the involvement. Since this was right before the last Congressional elections, and some key seats in his home state were up for grabs, I said, 'Well, what about real-life politics?' He said, no, that was of no interest to him: politicians were all cynics and liars. Part of me wanted to cry."

Young people who have unsupervised Internet access are also at risk for failing important skill-development challenges. The harm is in allowing them to avoid the typical lessons involved with being socially included and excluded. Withdrawal into the parallel world at the expense of real life can occur when parents are neglectful for any number of reasons, including their own over-involvement with the Internet. If parents are watching their children and young adults, they will notice when too much time on the Internet becomes a warning sign that something may be amiss with their child's social development.

Another aspect of parental neglect is a youth's exposure to parental files containing transcripts of writings to a virtual lover, cyber-pornography, or cyber-sex software. In these circumstances, children are often at a loss, and can be overwhelmed with embarrassment and anxiety. Ways to handle such situations will be discussed at length in Chapters Eight and Nine.

Partners
Most people are very upset by the suspicion of a partner's cyber-sexual compulsivity and related infidelity. They feel that not only are they coping

with out-of-control behavior, but also with a frightening third party they cannot understand or control. Faithful partners may need to vent their feelings, but directing such emotions at a sexually compulsive or unfaithful partner is rarely constructive. If you are concerned that your partner may be sexually compulsive, and you want to gain more understanding of these disorders before proceeding, consider these resources:

- ⊙ S-Anon: www.sanon.org/
- ⊙ Codependents of Sexual Addiction (COSA): www2.shore.net/~cosa/
- ⊙ Recovering Couples Anonymous: www.recovering-couples.org/
- ⊙ Family Members/Friends Affected by Sexual Addiction: members.nbci.com/SxA_recovery/SxA_recovery.htm

Cyber-Compulsivity Complicates Cyber-Infidelity

When infidelity is complicated by cyber-sexual compulsivity, few people can decide where to begin healing as a couple. Medical evaluation may be part of the intervention. It may be that medication is needed to help curb obsessive thinking. Antidepressants can be used to deal with the despair and depression that accompany sexual compulsivity. For some people, medication can mean the difference between freedom from cyber-compulsivity and the nightmare of recurring relapse.

When living with a person who compulsively uses the Internet for sexual gratification, check your own behavior. It is often surprising for faithful partners to realize that they have unintentionally been helping to maintain the compulsive behavior. Such behavior can fall into the realm of codependency, which will also be discussed in Chapter Six.

The following is the story of Marci and Jake, and how they dealt with the cyber-compulsivity leading to infidelity.

Jake called for an appointment for couples counseling. He came in with his wife, Marci. The forty-year-old couple sat straight in their chairs, but Jake's face was torn with anguish. Marci was aloof, pretending that nothing was wrong.

When asked what brought them to counseling, Jake said, "I think it's infidelity, but I am not really sure. All I know is I am very upset." Jake said that while he was looking for something in his filing cabinet, he came across pornographic pictures from a man, which had been sent to his wife on the computer. "Marci won't talk about it. She's having an affair.'"

Marci had been listening quietly. Finally, she spoke. "It's not an affair. I don't know him. He just sends me pictures. I've only masturbated, we've never actually had sex. It's not a big deal."

Marci and Jake were confused, as many people are, because it is hard to grasp the idea of an affair with an unmet person or masturbation with such a person as being infidelity. The therapist explained cyber-sex, and that it was a "virtual affair," as painful for a partner as traditional offline infidelity. Marci used a defense mechanism called "minimizing," when she made light of the situation.

The initial therapy was to help both Marcie and Jake cope with their strong emotions. Jake wanted to know more about what they said to each other on the computer, and how Marci felt about "The Rod," the online name of her virtual lover. She reluctantly agreed to let him read a few email messages she had saved. It was very painful for him to see how another man could sexually excite his wife, and to know that she had saved these messages for later masturbation. He was devastated to see how Marci tried to turn him on with descriptions of her body.

"I just needed to know the details," Jake explained, "no matter how much it hurt. Then I could stop imagining a hundred different scenarios. Once I knew what happened, I could stop my mind from going any further." Jake sighed, "But that name really pisses me off."

Jake was feeling badly about himself, and powerless to compete with a "stud," as Jake referred to him. Marci, on the other hand, felt guilty and very ashamed of her behavior. Jake said, "I would think he is really full of himself to pick that name, except that it fits. I saw his picture, or at least the picture he said was his. For all she knows, he's some smarmy little creep."

"Oh, honey," Marci broke in defensively, "it's only a picture. It doesn't really matter online, anyway. I didn't touch him or anything. I only touch you."

"Yeah," Jake sniped with anger, "me and the other ten guys."

The therapist asked what Jake meant. After a long silence, Marci began to cry and to tell her story. Her history of infidelity started unraveling. "I thought it wouldn't hurt you so much this time, Jake, because it was on the computer," she cried.

"I haven't done it for a while and we promised each other not to mention it, so that's why we didn't say anything. It's all in the past," Marci said.

"That's right," Jake added.

Marci has been unfaithful to Jake several times in their ten years of marriage. Their promise not to talk about it was, of course, counterproductive, and an indication of how pained they were. They had hoped that their silence would put an end to it. Unfortunately, denial is not a solution. Underlying reasons for infidelity must be identified and addressed to be resolved.

Their therapy continued, with Marci telling the story of her infidelities, including the cyber-infidelity. They both came to accept the fact that the online relationship was infidelity. However, the causes of the affair had not yet been revealed.

The therapist took a history of the family-of-origin of both Marci and Jake. In the middle of the history taking, Marci was quiet as she remembered something. She stared at Jake, glanced at the therapist, and her slowly eyes welled with tears. She took a deep breath and revealed a secret she had kept for years, telling the story as if it were being read to an audience, with no affect and no voice modulation.

The therapist softly asked to start again from the beginning, and identify her feelings as she relayed the same information. She started again, but broke into deep sobs within the first three minutes. Until now, she had managed to forget the traumatic events of her childhood, and the feelings she buried as a little girl.

Jake was in shock. The therapist signaled him to hold his wife. He rocked her and smoothed her hair. Jake's emotions alternated between tears and anger. He cried with her, and promised he would be more understanding. Marci needed several sessions before the entire story was aired. This is the essence of Marci's secret.

"When I was six years old, my father took off—just left my mother and me. I remember the shock when my mother told me. I loved him! I thought I was Daddy's little girl, and so I couldn't get over how he left without even a good-bye. A few months later, a new man came to live with us. My mother told me he was going to be like a new Daddy for me.

"At first, I hated him, but he kept hugging me and trying to be my friend. He rubbed my body and kissed my face—something that no one ever did. Even though I hated him, it felt good. Then, one day when my mother was at work, he said he had a toy to show me. He showed me his penis. I was so scared. Mother was never home to see any of this. He told me if I told anyone, especially my mother, he would leave us and I would live with strangers."

As the sessions progressed, Marci told us how she met the men with whom she had affairs over the years. She would typically dress in a provocative outfit and go into dangerous neighborhoods to pick up strange men. She would have a room reserved at the nearest motel, so that she would maintain a sense of control over the situation. The clerks at the motels were often supportive, and assured her they would keep an eye on her.

"I had no children. Jake's job called for him to travel extensively. I felt so anxious. I knew what would make me feel better—being held. Afterwards, I was so ashamed I sometimes wanted to kill myself."

Jake said, "I was attracted to her first, her sweetness and her need for me. I come from a family in which we all pretty much went our own way. So, meeting Marci was like a new experience. She wanted so much to be with me. Now I know she is like two people."

Jake was right. Marci was usually sweet and loyal, until her sexual compulsivity overcame her. When she felt lonely, her anxiety became unmanageable, and she had to prowl the streets to find someone to hold her. She was always frightened that Jake would leave her if he ever found out. Her fears of abandonment were constantly present, even as an adult. While she would have weeks and even months without anxiety attacks, they would always return, accompanied by feelings of shame and desperation about how she was cheating on Jake, and putting him in physical danger of catching a sexually transmitted disease.

The source of her sexual compulsivity was in the sexual abuse she had experienced from her stepfather shortly after her biological father abandoned the family. Marci's sexual abuse as a child was frightening, but it was also comforting to be held. It was also confusing, but she did not dare talk to anyone about it. Her stepfather threatened to walk out the door and never come back if she did not cooperate and keep the secret. She did not want to lose a second father.

In the course of therapy, she revealed her degree of sexual activity in high school, and her hopes that she would regain control of her behavior after marrying Jake. Her sexual urges were strongest when he was away, and she felt compelled to act upon them. When she discovered the Internet, she learned that masturbating to the comforting words of a stranger would help relieve her anxiety. She thought she had found a safe answer for dealing with Jake's time away from home. She was relieved to avoid the unsafe neighborhoods, frightening men, and serious possibilities of catching or giving a sexually transmitted disease.

Of course, living in the parallel world of the Internet was not a solution. It only deepened her situation. Rather than visit those neighborhoods, she went online more often and stayed longer. When Jake was away, she would come home early from work and spend ten to twelve hours seeking one man after another. She felt completely out of control, but told herself she was physically safer. Deep inside, she knew her behavior was still deceptive and unfaithful to Jake and that something was wrong with her.

Marci was emotionally unstable because of her own personal history, but she had an excellent chance of recovery. Not only was she remorseful, but also she loved Jake and did not want to hurt him. Once Jake understood the roots of her sexual compulsivity, he was more easily coached into being compassionate and patient.

This story of Marci and Jake demonstrates that infidelity does not always lead to divorce. Clearly, Marci's infidelity can be traced back to sexual compulsivity, with roots reaching back to her childhood trauma. With that information in its proper perspective, both Marci and Jake could heal from their pain and build a new sense of trust in their relationship.

The first therapeutic step was for Marci, in Jake's presence, to email "The Rod" to permanently end their relationship. She then changed her email address to a joint address with Jake. Marci promised not to use the computer for a month. She agreed that when she would use it again, she would completely avoid sexual meeting places. She also promised to regularly tell Jake how she used the Internet.

The course of this therapy was complex because treatment included exposing and resolving the childhood abuse, fear of abandonment, the sexual compulsivity, the infidelity, and rebuilding trust in the marriage. Many interventions helped Marci in her recovery, including psychotherapy and antidepressant medication. She found a twelve-step support group called Sex and Love Addicts Anonymous, where she felt comfortable anonymously discussing the details of her secret life. The group gave Marci some peace in knowing that other people had struggled with sexual urges and had done things for which they were remorseful.

Marci said, "It was really helpful to learn that other people had been as low as I, but had made good progress. One woman told me that I helped her see how far she had come. That stung when I heard it, but it also gave me hope that I could make the type of progress she had."

When Jake's work took him out of town, Marci now had friends to help her with her fears of abandonment and sexual urges. Marci kept a diary in which she expressed her thoughts and feelings. She began to see the progress she had made by comparing her journal entries over time. She also exercised and learned meditation as ways to relax. Marci found she could soothe herself.

Some of Marci's most significant changes came in her therapy, in which she learned to recognize the distortions in her thinking. She understood that it was not helpful to jump to conclusions, to overgeneralize, to speak in absolutes like "never" and "always," and to label herself. She was assigned books to read on this subject, including *Mind over Mood* by Dennis Greenberger, Ph.D., and Christine A. Padesky, Ph.D.

Emotional reasoning had been one of her primary distortions in thinking. She began to understand from *Mind over Mood* that emotional reasoning is believing that something is true because you feel it. Marci had felt badly about herself because of her sexual compulsivity. She came to realize that she was indeed a good person, and her disordered sexual needs resulted from her attempts to cope with childhood trauma. She would seek high-risk situations to reduce her abandonment anxiety. Marci found this was only a temporary solution. She would feel remorse for her sexual behavior, and then seek more partners to cope with the resulting anxiety. She was caught in a cycle of behavior common to most sexually compulsive individuals.

Realizing her patterns of ineffective behavior, Marci made daily attempts to soothe herself and become less emotionally reactive. She began to identify her anxiety-ridden thinking. Marci learned to block her compulsive actions when she realized that she was anxious. She would take breaks to soothe herself with slow, regular breathing throughout the day.

Marci and Jake had a lot of work to do, because their issues were not only Marci's childhood sexual abuse and her sexual compulsivity, but also recovery from repeated infidelity, including cyber-infidelity. Jake's feelings of betrayal were significantly reduced when he understood her history and how it drove her emotions, her thinking, and her actions. Jake's self-esteem issues were addressed in their joint sessions.

The course of therapy was positive because of Jake's capacity to be supportive, understanding, and avoid blame when he was upset. It was also successful because of Marci's remorse and her desire to resolve past issues, as well as learn to manage her life as an adult. Most importantly, Marci learned that she could safely reveal her true self to her husband and he would not leave her. As a couple, Marci and Jake went through a transformation that was extremely painful, but successful. Their intimacy grew deeper and their commitment to themselves and to each other became much stronger.

The lesson to be learned from Marci and Jake is that cyber-sexual compulsivity and resulting infidelity are not necessarily fatal to a marriage, if the couple is willing to work hard on their issues.

Conclusion

The Internet provides people with a new and unlimited access to various types of sexual stimulation, in a setting where the difference between reality and fantasy is difficult to define. This new world is having a profound effect on people and relationships, which can open the doors to infidelity. The following chapters look at how and why infidelity occurs on the Internet, and how a couple can take steps to recover from the hurt that betrayal causes.

The Shock of Infidelity on the Internet

5

Infidelity: Virtual or Real?

It is 9:30 on Thursday night in Cumberland, Maryland. Pam, a thirty-year-old mother of two, is in a private chat room with her friend, Gordon, whom she met online in a square-dancing discussion group.

Gordon: Hi! How's your day been?
Pam: Hey-hey!! There you are. :-) I was looking forward to talking with you. You know, last night was really great.
Gordon: You mean, talking about your going back to school?
Pam: Yeah. You are a great listener.
Gordon: Well, I've had a lot of practice. I grew up with five sisters. I learned to shut up and listen—LOL!
Pam: Well, you're good at it. So five sisters, eh? What was that like?
Gordon: I teased them a lot, and they squealed—you know, the usual. But they were all pretty good. Big plus was that I was the only one with a room of my own.
Pam: And now?
Gordon: Well, I share a room with my wife.
Pam: Yeah, I think about that a lot.
Gordon: So do I.
Pam: What do you think about? ::::head turned slightly, waiting::::
[silence]
Pam: C'mon. Do you think about our nightly chats?
Gordon: And more.
Pam: What more?
Gordon: You're flirting with me!! It really doesn't matter what I think.
Pam: It matters to me. How long have you been married?
Gordon: Ten years. And you?
Pam: Eight. And if you're thinking what I'm thinking, you want us to be more than friends.
Gordon: Yes, but...it's complicated.
Pam: It's only as complicated as we make it. C'mon, say what you want. We're thousands of miles apart.

> **Gordon:** OK, I think about you often during the day. That picture you showed me on your website. Your flowing hair, your soft shoulders. I just want to take you in my arms, hold you, brush your hair back, and kiss you tenderly.
> **Pam:** Hmmmm. I'd like that too. A lot...

Pam and Gordon are sliding down the slippery slope to infidelity. Their hesitancy reveals their ambivalence about breaking their vows to their partners. *Cyber-infidelity occurs when a partner in a committed relationship uses the computer or the Internet to violate promises, vows, or agreements concerning his or her sexual exclusivity.* We believe couples need to extend their relationship agreements to include more precise definitions and agreements related to fidelity to accommodate everyday life and assumptions in a world turbocharged by technology; and extend their current assumptions by discussing intent and use of technology as it relates to fidelity.

We are currently at a significant point in our cultural development due to the advances in communication and social networking technology represented most globally by the Internet. Even as you read this, profound changes are continuing to alter our social mores. Current communication technologies are forming a new, global culture. This new culture will change relationships worldwide within the decade. It's only just begun. We cannot stop it, nor can we slow it down. However, we must understand the power of these advances and prepare to meet their challenge. This chapter is written to help you communicate more effectively with your partner about fidelity in response to these technological advances, and improve your relationship. We need to develop a vocabulary with definitions and agreements about values, intent, and fidelity to meet individual personal beliefs, understand each other's expectations, and resolve differences. Such a discussion may protect us from the pain of deceit and betrayal that are characteristics of infidelity and now, infidelity on the Internet.

Fidelity—Past, Present, and Future

Traditional marriage vows have included the basic concept of fidelity. Such sacred vows are usually interpreted to mean sexual exclusivity.

With the increased use of the Internet, the definition of this promise is being challenged by some. In a June 2000 study of over seven thousand randomly selected visitors to MSNBC.com, Drs. Alvin Cooper, Janet Morahan-Martin, Marlene Maheu, and Robin Mathy found that 45 percent of women view cyber-sex as infidelity, while 40 percent of men are likely to share that opinion.

As mentioned previously, of greater interest is that in a corresponding measure in the same survey, these researchers found that 60 percent of people who had already engaged in cyber-sex *did not* think cyber-sex "violates a person's marital vows." While we do not have reports from a wide range of empirical studies, it is becoming clear that the meaning of infidelity on the Internet is controversial. These findings should be of no surprise when we stop to consider the research we mentioned in Chapter One. These statistics are high, especially when one thinks of them being translated into the human pain and suffering that ensues from infidelity. Surely, the chance of being caught in cyber-infidelity is decreased, and the chance of catching a sexually transmitted disease is zero.

Once again, we run into the Internet enigma, where we can exercise free choice in more than one direction, we can meet, but not really meet, we can appear in a new place and interact with new people, and yet, really be right at home, with our families. We can have intimacy, but it isn't real intimacy. We can have sex with someone, but it isn't real sex, or is it?

The Internet makes infidelity possible, but people make the choices. Infidelity happens when two people have a commitment and that commitment is broken—regardless of where, how, or with whom it happens. Infidelity is the breaking of a promise with a real person, whether the sexual stimulation is derived from the virtual or the real world. This chapter is written in the hope of awakening couples who have been lulled into believing that a cyber-sexual relationship does not constitute infidelity. It may or it may not, depending on your agreement with your partner. This chapter then, is written with the goal of bringing to light the crucial need for couples to discuss their values and their decisions regarding technology, sexuality, and fidelity.

As we proceed, we want to reiterate once again that definitions of fidelity cover a broad spectrum in the global community accessed by the Internet. As we embrace diversity and a global community in the twenty-first century, we intentionally include all couples, regardless of their specific culture, geographic location, race, age, physical ability, religious background, and gender. World diversity allows for many types of commitment ceremonies, from the white bridal gown to the breaking of the wineglass to the exchange of farm animals for a dowry. It is understood that the views and customs of a couple in Norway will differ from those of a couple in Egypt.

Regardless of traditional customs, couples with access to technology will do well to be aware of the Internet enigma, which pulls us in many different directions at once. Prompted by the right virtual lover at the right moment in time, people can use the Internet to spin a web of self-betrayal and infidelity. All couples, then, could benefit from an agreement about the use of such technology and increased specificity in their fidelity agreements.

A Model for Successful Discussions

Couples must understand what the promise of fidelity actually means to each of them before they commit to a relationship. A model is available from premarital counseling which has shown to be effective in reducing the divorce rate for couples. This process involves a thorough review of topics that often cause problems in relationships. These issues are typically explored with a trained professional, usually a group leader or marriage counselor. The purpose is to explore issues that often go unnoticed or unquestioned when couples decide to make a commitment to one another.

A session is usually devoted to each of these topics: spirituality, including such training of children; educational and career goals of each partner; number of children and child-rearing preferences; financial management and lifestyle preferences; household management and weekly chores; sexual practices and fidelity; and management of friendships and relationships with extended family. The couple reaches an understanding of each other's views, and a mutual agreement about how they will resolve their differences. In these often-difficult discussions, some couples come to the disheartening realization that they are incompatible and choose not to make the commitment they intended. All couples contemplating a commitment would be wise to have such a review of values, attitudes, and expectations.

Tanya, a thirty-year-old dietitian, wrote us the following, "I know that the Internet can be like a bar. If my fiancé drank a lot before we were married, I know I would discuss that with him before I married him. So when Glen and I became engaged, I was worried about his frequent use of the computer to meet women. I know he spends a lot of time on it for work, and it is easy for him to flirt with women and then get sexy emails from them. I ask him to promise me that he would end these flirtatious relationships, not go to chat rooms, or start friendships with any other women. He agreed, and I feel much happier and secure about his use of the computer."

The Internet has quickly become part of contemporary life. Although cyber-infidelity may never before have been part of premarital discussions, this topic should now be included. Couples could benefit from asking specific questions of each other about their use of the computer and the Internet. Possible questions for discussion are:

- ◯ How do you handle stress?
- ◯ How do you handle loneliness?
- ◯ How do you feel about friendships with people online?
- ◯ What are your thoughts on fidelity in general?
- ◯ What are your general thoughts about masturbation?
- ◯ How much time do you spend on the computer?
- ◯ How do you feel about sexual websites?
- ◯ Do you consider cyber-sex to be infidelity?
- ◯ Do you consider visiting pornography sites and masturbating to visual stimuli to be infidelity?
- ◯ Do you want to watch others having sex or being sexual online?
- ◯ If you want to have such online sexual experiences, will they be secret or open?

◯ What happens if we have differences on these questions now and what happens if we have differences in the future?

These are penetrating and explicit questions. Yet, early exploration of these often-unaddressed issues can spare much heartache later. An important component is the last question, which refers to a plan for revising agreements as each member of the relationship changes values over time. Life changes and transitions, expected or unexpected, can add stress. Relationship agreements made at an earlier time can seem irrelevant later. Agreements need to be renewed on an ongoing basis. Relationships, then, do best if the couple has developed an agreed-upon mechanism for renegotiation of feelings and concerns that arise through the years.

As Bobbie told us, "I thought I would be OK with Suzanne having a relationship with another woman, but over time I started to brood about it. It was part of our understanding that we were both free to have other relationships. Now I'm not so sure I like that agreement."

It is at this point that Bobbie and Suzanne need to use good communication and problem-solving skills to resolve their conflict. They need to show empathy for the other's viewpoint, and will probably need to renegotiate their contract.

Jennifer, who has been married for seven years, spoke with anger about her husband, Hank, "I feel humiliated. We took our vows in church, with family and friends, and now they all know the sad truth that Hank had a secret love life online. And I have a broken heart." Hank and Jennifer would benefit from a renewed agreement to address their expectations concerning monogamy.

Cyber-Infidelity Understood
People are often bewildered when they first discover that infidelity can occur through the Internet. The common thought is, "How can people have an affair when they've never touched?" As we define cyber-infidelity, we'd like to specify that it often involves a desire of romantic intent and behavior that is supposedly reserved for a committed partner. If a couple has failed to fully communicate the range of behavior considered acceptable within the relationship, it is to be expected that one of them will feel betrayed when romantic energy has been diverted from the relationship through technology. Whether cyber-infidelity is mindless repartee, impulsive bravado, or a planned escape from one's committed relationship, it can nonetheless lead to unpleasant consequences.

Intent
To begin to understand infidelity, let us follow a couple as they go to a cocktail party in real life.

A man meets a woman with whom he flirts, smiles, and makes repeated sexual innuendos. She understands that the message is very sexual, and she has only to reciprocate his advances. However, there are limits imposed upon them, because this exchange is occurring in a crowded room. The only reason nothing happens physically is because of the situation. Is he cheating because of his intent?

If flirting at a real-life party led to a secret, erotic liaison, then it would typically be considered an affair. Let us take this example further, and watch this same man in a "Married but Horny" chat room, where the purpose is clearly to encourage infidelity.

A man enters the chat room and quickly strikes up a conversation. The couple feels the sexual tension, they move to a private chat room, and have an erotic conversation. Both of them masturbate. It is intimate, erotic, secret, and the intent to find erotic connection was present.

We see the similarity of these interactions in the two scenarios. The similarity is that the intent in both cases to have erotic connection with a reciprocating partner. Even if the chat room exchange did not lead to a face-to-face sexual affair, the intent to have a secretive erotic connection was still present. Therefore, we must conclude that intent is a significant part of infidelity.

More importantly, most couples have an unstated understanding that if one partner has a sexual liaison with another person, it constitutes infidelity. The possibilities created by technology are forcing couples to have previously unneeded conversations about the use of technology in their relationship, as it pertains to fidelity. If further defined to include technology-mediated behavior, the issue of intent will resurface as a central one.

Many people are surprised to learn that happily married people can have erotic attractions to other people. These attractions can be normal and healthy. Sexual attractions can often be purely physical, chemical reactions. They are not necessarily indicative of anything but a healthy libido.

Choice
The choices people make in response to these attractions challenge concepts of intent and commitment. Just as someone may salivate when looking at a dessert on a neighboring table in a restaurant, there is a difference between having a physical reaction and indulging it. People in restaurants, no matter how hungry, do not typically reach into their neighbor's plate and expect the world to understand that it was an impulse.

Similarly, engaging in a cyber-affair is a choice. People who engage in these activities cannot expect that upon discovery, their partners will look the other way or understand that it was a meaningless impulse. Circumstances on the Internet may make the decision to engage in romance a fleeting one, but infidelity always involves a choice. Infidelity always involves the decision to take romance beyond one's relationship's definition of fidelity.

Jenny, a twenty-seven-year-old advertising copywriter, said, "Yes, infidelity is a choice. It's a decision. I was very attracted to this guy in my computer class. We even went for coffee and he made a pass at me. He was married and I was single, but I didn't take it any further. You know, being in a relationship doesn't mean you're dead. You can still be attracted to someone. After all, people are married for a long time and feel attractions to other people, but you don't have to act on it."

If you are in a committed relationship in which you promised fidelity to your partner, do not expect him or her to accept your infidelity without further discussion. You may not be responsible for your attractions, but you are responsible for your actions.

Betrayal

Upon hearing the news of infidelity, most partners experience a profound sense of betrayal. When this occurs on the Internet, it is still betrayal, even though the cyber-couple may never physically meet.

For many wounded partners, the lack of physical contact does not seem as important as the betrayal of their sacred promise, their vow of exclusivity. The special, committed relationship is changed forever. The emotional weight of the betrayal often feels unbearable.

Secrecy and Deception

Acts of infidelity are typically characterized by secrecy and deception. Depending on the nature of the actions on the Internet that caused infidelity, some clients report that the experience of being deceived online is as devastating as traditional infidelity. Deception and subsequent feelings of betrayal make it difficult to reestablish trust in the primary relationship. Promises of future fidelity are doubted.

To the surprise of some people, cyber-affairs cannot be justified by simply informing a partner that such activities are occurring and then disregarding the partner's reactions and requests. As in the restaurant situation, if someone reached into a neighbor's plate and stole their dessert, consequences would most assuredly follow. Explanations of one's appetite being out of control would not suffice. Retribution would be in order. Until then, the wounded party would be justified in reviewing the events and trying to make sense of them. Similarly, one result of infidelity is the obsessive review of the deceptive events surrounding the cyber-affair.

Sexuality

Understanding infidelity involves recognizing that eroticism and sexuality are components of the online interaction, regardless of whether a couple is in actual physical contact. Lovers speak to each other in erotic ways, often with the purpose of sexually stimulating each other. They respond with heightened sexual sensations, and probably with orgasm, reporting how they felt during their moments of sexual excitement and then engaging in pillow talk. They report an afterglow and a feeling of satisfaction, as though they were sharing the same bed.

Emotional Closeness

In *Surviving Infidelity,* Rona Subotnik, M.A., MFT, and Gloria Harris, Ph.D., identify four types of traditional affairs in terms of the emotional closeness felt by the lovers. These types also apply to cyber-infidelity. The first type of affair is the serial affair, in which the unfaithful partner feels no emotional closeness to the virtual lover. In fact, the serial lover has one affair after another. There is no closeness because of an inability to tolerate intimacy. This type of affair is seen often on the Internet.

Offline, some serial lovers visit prostitutes and massage parlors, where they need not offer commitment or intimacy. Online, serial lovers can also find situations lacking emotional closeness by having cyber-sex with many partners in chat rooms, using interactive pornography, and visiting sites where sex is expected. This type of person can fit the description of the Cheater or the Criminal.

The second type of affair described in *Surviving Infidelity* also can be found on the Internet, and that is the fling. This is a casual type of affair, with no commitment and very little intimacy. Two people may find themselves attracted to each other, even though they might have been online for other purposes. The fling ends shortly, and typifies many of the cyber-affairs that are seen online. Some of the virtual lovers engaging in cyber-flings are the Escapist, the Dumper, and the Romanticizer.

The third type of affair increases in the degree of emotional connection to the virtual lover. It is a romantic love affair and poses a serious threat to the emotional life of a committed relationship. The virtual lovers feel very much in love, and they believe a decision must be made as to how they will handle their relationship. They cannot tolerate the situation as it is, and feel compelled to make a decision between real-life divorce and ending their cyber-affair. This type of affair can be seen in the next section, with Emily and Joshua.

In the few cases where a romantic affair does not resolve in one of these two ways, it becomes a long-term affair. If this sort of affair develops, it may be similar to the "parallel world" discussed in Chapter One, where one person can lead two separate lives, one online and one offline.

Listening To Cyber-Infidelity

The following are excerpts from several Instant Messages that a couple sent to *SelfhelpMagazine*. They give an example of one of the outcomes of cyber-infidelity. This Instant Message occurred after Emily and Joshua had their first phone contact:

> **Joshua:** :-) So how are you doing tonight?
> **Emily:** I am doing very well! :-) I am happy to see you! How are you tonight?
> **Joshua:** Fine, now that you're here :-)
> **Emily:** :-* [kiss]
> **Joshua:** So, did you go back online after we hung up last night?
> **Emily:** No. I went to bed...with a big smile...and had great dreams.
> **Joshua:** Me too.
> **Emily:** God...when I signed on just now...and saw you, my heart skipped!

Their contact took the usual course of online romance—playfulness, joking, and soon, hinting at sexuality. Joshua had to greet a visitor at his door, so the playful Instant Message conversation was interrupted, but it resumed thereafter with a more serious topic:

> **Joshua:** I want to know all about you. Do you have a religion?
> **Emily:** I am glad you want to know about me! I want to know about you too.
> I guess I am Lutheran, from childhood. But I just believe in God...and in
> being a good person. I'm really not into organized religion at the moment.
> **Joshua:** Sounds like me. I actually just started going to church again. Have
> you ever heard of the Unitarian Universalists?
> **Emily:** No, I have never heard of that group. Tell me about it.

In real life, this type of conversation would not likely occur on a first meeting because the rhythm and pace of romance is slower. But online, turbocharged by the "Triple A Engine," sexual innuendo and personal information can enter a relationship much more quickly, and playfulness rules. The next communication, which occurred on their second meeting, once again shows how rapidly this can happen:

> **Joshua:** So oranges turn you on, huh?
> **Emily:** um..yeah...so wet..so juicy..mmmmmmm LOL um...you turn me on too
> **Joshua:** I'll have to remember to bring LOTS of Oranges the first time we
> meet in person:-)

Many Internet users enjoy the lack of inhibition typically found in text-based environments, where people do not see each other. This feeling of freedom allows them to slip into sexual innuendo more quickly than they would if they were face-to-face. It also allows other important information to be shared openly and honestly, or withheld.

About three weeks into their daily meetings, a serious topic surfaced:

Emily: Joshua, I need to tell you something important.
Joshua: This sounds serious.
Emily: It is.
Joshua: Sounds really serious. I don't know if I want to hear this. Is this an 'it's not you, it's me' kind of thing?
Emily: No.
Joshua: O.k. I'm ready.
Emily: I'm married.
[Moment of silence]
Emily: Joshua?
Joshua: I'm here.
Emily: I'm really sorry.
Joshua: I can't believe this!
Emily: I'm sorry.
Joshua: I don't know what to say.
Emily: I should have told you sooner.
Joshua: So you are just fooling around.
Emily: Not really. I was sort of fooling around, but then I met you. I just wanted to be with younger people.
Joshua: What does your husband think?
Emily: He doesn't know yet. I don't think he cares. We have a bad marriage. We haven't had sex for two years.
Joshua: Do you have kids?
Emily: No.
Joshua: So what are you going to do about your marriage?
Emily: I'm thinking of divorcing him.
Joshua: Because of me?
Emily: Well, I mean, how could that be? I just met you. It's only that talking to you makes me realize how unhappy I am and that I could be happy.
Joshua: What's wrong with your marriage?
Emily: Marvin is much older than I am, by 27 years.
Joshua: Wow! Why did you marry him?
Emily: I think, to get away from my family.
Joshua: Wasn't there another way?
Emily: Sure, but I was so young, I couldn't do it.
Joshua: How does he treat you?
Emily: He's nice to me. He's not around much. He works hard. We've been married ten years.
Joshua: I see

Emily: ...are you still OK with all of this? With me...being married? I don't want this to be...a bad thing for you....

Joshua: I don't know. I'm more concerned about you. I REALLY don't want to be a homewrecker....

Emily: You aren't. My marriage was wrecked before I met you.

Joshua: Have you and your husband tried to work things out?

Emily: Lots of times. We had therapy, but it didn't work. The age difference is too much to overcome. I want to have fun. I'm young. He's settled.

Emily and Joshua struggled with her marital status. Eventually, Emily broke off her relationship with her husband and moved into an apartment. Her move helped Joshua resolve his indecision, and he decided to pursue this relationship. She obviously was serious about him.

Joshua: Ok, ok!! You win. :-) Now that you've moved out, I think this might actually work. I finally feel happy inside...and I have been so lonely.

Emily: You are so different from anyone I've ever met.

Joshua: Now that you'd done what you said you would do, I know I can trust you.

Emily: I am still worried about what you will think about my weight, my obesity.

Joshua: I just want a chance to get to know you—all of you. Let's meet face-to-face.

Emily: Oh, my God! My heart is pounding. Ok, how?

Emily and Joshua are using the Internet to find an escape from unhappiness and loneliness. In the discussion above, we see that they have dealt with the underlying issues that led to Emily's infidelity.

This couple kept in touch with us and Joshua wrote:

"Great news! Emily and I have moved in together! I went to get her and her belongings this past weekend. It has been two years since we met, and we've spent a lot of time together, both online and offline. Living in separate cities also gave us the time to focus on ourselves and work on fully preparing ourselves for this relationship.

"We were both concerned that issues from Emily's previous marriage might interfere with our new relationship, so we both got into therapy and sorted things out. Emily realized that she was trying to run from her marriage without fully communicating with her husband. So she took the time to do that.

"It got her nowhere, except to realize that he was unwilling (or unable) to be emotionally available for her. He shut her out and put her down, as he had done throughout their marriage. She learned why she married him, and why those very reasons led to her unhappiness with him. She was right to leave, but wishes she would have had the courage to separate without cheating on him first.

"She's gotten a lot stronger emotionally since then, and is more able to voice her feelings. In fact, sometimes I wish she weren't quite so willing to tell me what she thinks. No, seriously, we've been through many difficult moments, and for the first time in my life, I feel like this is really right.

"At first, I was worried that she would cheat on me, too. But our communication is sometimes painfully honest, and we both have learned to risk it all in the name of honesty. I've learned to be more patient and understanding than ever before, and to try to calm down when I'm not sure what's happening. I've learned to let go and support a woman as she makes decisions for herself, not for me.

"We've both proven to each other that we can set firm boundaries to take care of ourselves individually, and still love one another. Our relationship only grows stronger with every challenge. As it turns out, I let go and she came back to me. And...she's agreed to be my wife!"

These young people sought psychotherapy to help resolve the issues of Emily's infidelity. Equipped with new understandings of herself, she may be ready to move into this relationship with Joshua, who has also completed much of the emotional work.

Gray-Area Confusion

Emotional affairs are ones that are non-sexual and may or may not be secretive. In these situations, there is no intent to be sexual, but intimacy is present. The concern is that the intimacy felt in an emotional affair may plant seeds of eroticism. Studies show that women who have developed such intimacy in an offline relationship will be inclined to end their committed relationship if it does not satisfy their need for intimacy. The emotional affair can be dangerous because the sense of closeness can lead to a sexual affair.

Similarly, when cyber-friendships that begin innocently in chat rooms develop into emotional affairs, the possibility exists that the couple may begin to feel this closeness and spark a cyber-affair. This is what has happened with Pam and Gordon in the first story of this chapter, who met in a square-dance discussion chat room. They developed strong feelings of closeness which became eroticized. As we have noted, they started down the path of infidelity. The potential for serious consequences is high in an emotional affair. Individuals do not readily admit the potential for infidelity in these affairs, because participants do not voice their eroticized feelings.

Shirley Glass, Ph.D., ABPP who has written and spoken about cyber-infidelity, writes that, "Internet relationships can threaten the stability and intimacy of a committed relationship. Time spent online can be a harmless distraction or can be dangerously distracting. However, research has shown that even moderate Internet usage interferes with family relationships, particularly when an individual spends more and more time online and begins ignoring work, friends, and loved ones. Furthermore, online relationships can shift from an intellectually stimulating friendship to a romantically charged relationship. Secrecy, emotional attachment, and sexual intimacy are the hallmarks of an online relationship which has crossed over the line of a platonic friendship and drifted into an emotional affair."

Emotional affairs lead to what Dr. Glass calls the "slippery slope." The slippery slope involves married people who believe they have fallen in love online and "...do so gradually, and often don't realize how far they have gone until they are hopelessly attached."

Clients in group therapy often ask questions about the behavior of a spouse that on a "gut level" feels like infidelity, but which they want to deny. Some describe online sexual activities as a "gray area," where online behaviors do not exactly fit their traditional definitions of infidelity. The following comments illustrate the confusion.

Bethany said, "Neal downloads video-streamed pornography and masturbates. I want him to make love to *me*. His masturbating to online pornography feels strange, because Neal says it isn't infidelity. I don't know what it is, or what to think."

Hilda responded, "I used to have a similar problem with 900 numbers, but now it is the Internet. I could tell what Kevin was doing by the phone bills. Now, I can tell by the hours he is away from me and in that upstairs den."

Neal believes his behavior is not infidelity because he is not touching anyone. However, Bethany's desire for his sexual contact and his choice to invest his sexual energy elsewhere creates a problem. He is cheating Bethany of the passion and intimacy that leads to commitment in true love. As a couple, they are not in agreement about their use of sexual energy and intent. This couple needs to examine the use of power in their relationship and the lack of agreement about the role technology will play in their lives.

On the other hand, Hilda's husband makes his extramarital preoccupation more evident by masturbating to people available through 900 numbers. He interacts with another person for the purpose of eroticism and orgasm, despite the lack of any other relationship with the person on the telephone line. Like Neal, Kevin is in a gray area on the way to the danger zone. When Kevin has cyber-sex in his room with someone online and Hilda objects, he is fooling himself by thinking he is not hurting his relationship. He is entering a danger zone, which we shall describe shortly. Hilda and Kevin need to communicate with each other about their relationship, their individual concerns, and their needs as a couple.

Carol listened carefully, but said, "My case is a little different because it takes place in a group, and my husband, Gene, tells me about it. He says there is no one special. He just gets in the chat room, talks to a few people, and masturbates to orgasm. He says he's not cheating, and I should relax. The problem is that he does this almost every night before dinner, then comes to bed with me, and often wants to have sex. He is very different with me in bed, and likes to talk rough and wants me to do unusual things with and to him. He tells me, 'It's just a stress reliever.' I wish I could believe him, but it feels like I'm losing him to these strangers. I can't stop thinking about it, and I cry a lot. There's no one I can discuss this with. He won't see a marriage counselor. My friends and family would think this whole situation is crazy. What's happening? I feel like my marriage is falling apart!"

Carol's husband is redefining "cheating." She is allowing him to confuse her sense of sexual exclusivity. Carol's understanding of her marriage vows is that they would be sexually faithful to each other. She feels Gene is cheating on her, despite his lack of a specific individual as a partner, and despite his openness with her about it. She thinks the chat room group has become his lover, and he intentionally meets with them to experience an interactive sexual connection outside of their marriage.

Although he is not being secretive, he is acting against his wife's wishes and betraying her sense of security. He is dismissing her feelings, despite the fact that he is causing emotional strain on her and their marriage. This suggests that two problems are present. The first problem is their differing views of masturbation, and the second and perhaps most important is his disregard for her concerns.

Some couples have integrated masturbation into their marriage agreement. How is this different? Couples who do so successfully have clearly defined limits that are openly discussed, understood, and renegotiated as new possibilities emerge. However, this is not the case with Carol and Gene. An underlying issue here is the use of power in a relationship. When Kevin continues a behavior that seriously disturbs Carol, he is exerting unfair power and control. This couple needs to explore two fundamental issues: sexual behavior with people outside their relationship, and decision-making mechanisms used to determine behaviors that impact both partners in this relationship.

Many of our *SelfhelpMagazine* Essay Contest respondents had something to say about these situations. Hank, a forty-two-year-old architect, wrote: "People are people, and just because you meet online doesn't mean that you won't get emotionally invested. Actually, emotional investment is more likely because the only way you interact with your lover is through that fantasy filter...which will never show pimples or greasy hair or dirty fingernails."

Bianca warned, "This is a serious threat to marriages, it has affected mine tremendously."

Cyber-affairs can wreak havoc in a relationship. Writing in the *Journal of Sex Education and Therapy* in June 1997, Dr. Leiblum explains, "The most common complaint arises when one partner is heavily involved with Net-sex, and the other partner finds this behavior objectionable." She explains that while complaints take many forms, "The simplest complaint is the amount of time men spend with their computers. People will complain that their partners closet themselves away with their machines in inaccessible places for hours at a time under the guise of 'working.' These people feel shut out, ignored, and deprived of time alone with their mates."

The gray area surrounding definitions of infidelity on the Internet can quickly lead people to ignore the consequences of betraying the intent of their commitments of fidelity. Trying to slide between unspoken words is rarely successful, especially when it involves reciprocated eroticism and sexuality with people outside the relationship. If careful attention is not paid to the gray area, an individual can find that he or she has slipped into the "Danger Zone."

Danger Zone
What is the problem with cyber-infidelity? Ms. Subotnik and Dr. Harris write in *Surviving Infidelity* that infidelity, whether resulting in divorce or reconciliation, has a ripple effect that reaches far from the center and disturbs the security, peace of mind, and self-esteem of all family members.

Cyber-infidelity creates conscious or unconscious intrusions on the committed relationship, and people carry the emotional intensity from these experiences into daily life. If your spouse pretends to be dominated by an online dominatrix after you go to bed, memories of that experience could easily fill his or her mind throughout the day. Those memories could cloud your interactions with him or her today.

Your partner may experience you differently, but not understand why. An emotional distance can begin to change the trust and intimacy you once shared. It will most likely affect the relationship negatively, even if not discovered.

Therapists often hear couples talk about feeling that something was "off" and that they were drifting apart, even though there was no tangible information exchanged about an affair. Discovery of this type of deceit can leave the faithful partner with feelings of rage, depression, despair, and a painful loss of self-esteem.

As reported in *USA Today*, anthropologist Helen Fisher of Rutgers University notes that damage to primary relationships can be severe when people engage in cyber-infidelity. "They can be just as time-consuming and disruptive as a regular adulterous affair. You are very secretive, you hide information, and you can—and these people do—use self-stimulation to reach orgasm."

Peggy and James Vaughn, a husband and wife team who write, speak, and teach about infidelity, summarize the similarities in online and offline affairs by stating, "This new arena for affairs, although not initially involving physical contact, is highly charged sexually. It involves the same kinds of thinking and emotions as other affairs—including the secrecy, fantasy, and excitement, as well as the denial and rationalization—and has the same potential for being devastating to the primary relationship."

If you are in a monogamous relationship offline and are making contact with someone online, you are in the Danger Zone. Check yourself to see if you are doing the following:

- Visiting and meeting people in areas of the Internet that are developed for dating, romance, or sexual contact.
- Intentionally avoiding online romance, but responding when it appears in other types of discussions with someone.
- Feeling sexual tension and innuendo repeatedly directed to or from you.
- Interacting with someone online to the extent that you discuss sexual details—that is, not within the context of a group discussion for educational purposes.
- Having erotic fantasies or daydreams involving this person.
- Sharing the details of your emotional or sexual fantasies with and about them.
- Being secretive with your partner about the nature of your online sexual activities.
- Experiencing shame, guilt, or fear about this online contact to the extent that you would not want your partner to see the details of your activities.
- Spending more time talking to this new individual about personal matters than you do with your partner.
- When making love to your partner, repeatedly getting thoughts of your online partner.

If any of these statements describes you, you have entered the Danger Zone. It is time to take stock of what is happening in your life and remove yourself from danger. If you have an agreement with your partner about fidelity, discuss your activities with your partner. If you find yourself to be in violation of that agreement, correct your behavior.

Cyber-Affairs and Traditional Affairs
Cyber-affairs differ from traditional offline affairs in a number of respects. While deception and betrayal are common to both types of affairs, cyber-affairs are more easily hidden. Partners, neighbors, and friends have a minimal chance of discovering a cyber-affair. Contact does not involve an absence from home, the risk of being seen in public, or unaccounted expenses. An eager virtual lover can secretly find a partner, any partner, in a matter of seconds and at any time, day or night.

As we have noted, while people report that a sense of intimacy develops quickly online, virtual romance does not allow full development of passion, intimacy, and commitment, the essential ingredients of true love. Despite the intoxifying effects of infatuation on the Internet, love cannot develop without true passion, intimacy, and commitment in the real world.

Offline meetings, even if only occasional, allow couples to reveal themselves more completely. Being truly intimate requires face-to-face meetings with a partner. Showing up physically requires courage, because it increases one's vulnerability, without the cloak of secrecy so easily provided by a computer screen. Virtual couples may feel as if they have true love, but a virtual kiss is a virtual kiss. It might be better or might be worse, but it is different from a real kiss. The level of passion, intimacy, and commitment needed to sustain a successful long-term partnership requires sustained contact in the real world, even if only intermittently. Many people are finding they can start this process on the Internet, but eventually they need face-to-face time to ground their fantasies in reality.

Unfortunately, many couples engaging in cyber infidelity do not achieve true love in their real relationships, either. Without ever having experienced true love offline, they can quickly imagine it to exist online. To the dismay of many cyber-cheaters, their face-to-face meetings are a great disappointment. Their self-deception and self-betrayal become immediately apparent. The reality of another human being can be so discrepant with fantasy that the cyber-affair is often quickly terminated. Realizing this risk, many people who engage in cyber-infidelity do not want to meet their virtual lovers.

Another important difference between traditional infidelity and infidelity that occurs as the result of interactions over the Internet is that while faithful partners have similar levels of rage upon the discovery of a cyber-affair, they seem to focus on slightly different questions. Partners of individuals having a traditional affair usually ask these types of questions:

- Do you love him/her?
- What did he/she wear? Was he/she attractive?
- Was he/she a good lover?
- Did you like it better with him/her?
- How often did you meet? How long did it go on? Where did you meet?
- How long could he/she do it? What were his/her kisses like?

These questions do not apply to online affairs. Partners of individuals who have cyber-affairs often ask:

- Do you think you love him/her?
- How did you meet?
- How often did you meet?
- When did you meet?

- What did you say?
- Did you have an orgasm?
- How many times?
- How did it feel?
- Did you ever meet in person?

Faithful partners often want to call, write, or visit the third person and confront them with their anger. With cyber-affairs, partners feel frustrated and powerless, as if a phantom has captured their partner. In some ways, this may be true. The phantom could be infatuation, lust, and intoxication with the virtual lover. In traditional affairs, the wounded partner has the strong feeling that someone else exists, whereas in cyber-affairs, individuals can never really know if their competition exists or is simply a figment of their partner's imagination.

They also do not know if their partner would have wandered so easily if the Internet had not been available. Temptation and impulse become more complicated in a world where talk can shift from hardware production schedules to light-hearted flirtation to cyber-sex in virtually no time.

Some people are all too easily trapped by the electrically charged impulse to send quick one-liners to a faceless stranger—especially someone who responds within the time it takes to pour another cup of coffee. They can soon be sharing preferences for types of edible body lotions and other secret fantasies that have never been shared with a partner. They may not have the levels of self-differentiation and maturity to stop and think of the repercussions of their actions.

Many people find themselves involved a little too quickly and too deeply. Their afternoon virtual playmate soon becomes their cyber-obsession—with demands and temptations that are difficult to ignore and can quickly lose the appeal over time. Psychologist Dr. Leiblum reports in the *Journal of Sex Education and Therapy*, that, "Net sex follows a predictable pattern of initial infatuation and high involvement, usually followed by a gradual decline into more modulated and less intense activity, followed, for some, by indifference and only occasional involvement."

For people who are anxious, impulsive, and socially unskilled, such quick exchanges can excite the imagination and lead to lack of inhibition, without adequate forethought for consequences. In this way, emotional skill deficits in self-control become readily apparent on the Internet.

At-Risk for Cyber-Infidelity?

As discussed in Chapter Four, Dr. Cooper and his colleagues have identified an at-risk population for cyber-sexual compulsivity. These people otherwise may not act on their impulses, but given the accessible, affordable, and anonymous convenience of the Internet, they readily engage strangers with sexual fantasies and cyber-sex or regularly spend time admiring cyber-pornography.

It is likely that the Internet is also developing an at-risk group for cyber-infidelity. While they may be tempted in the real world to flirt with a customer, a colleague, or someone seeking advice about how to reconfigure their hard drive, their social training has taught them to restrain themselves. For these at-risk people, the Internet adds yet another level of complication to an already difficult set of impulses. Indeed, increased access to sexual materials on the Internet may account for an increase in infidelity. The faithful partner of today has a difficult task discerning if his or her partner is a philanderer, or has lost control because the Internet is giving free rein to behavior that otherwise would never have occurred. He or she may lack the personal skills to cope effectively with the general malaise that is the hallmark of low levels of depression, anxiety, stress, and loneliness.

Meanwhile, their behavior will most likely prove unacceptable to their partners, employers, families, and friends. Confronted with the facts of cyber-infidelity, faithful partners have few models to follow and are likely to respond with outrage and fury, along with underlying feelings of disbelief, hurt, betrayal, and mistrust. As with offline affairs, there are consequences. Regardless of the events, something is amiss in the relationship and/or the individual, and needs to be addressed if there is any hope of recovery.

Public Feelings about Cyber-Infidelity
Infidelity is a subject that can rivet the attention of any group, especially when the focus is cyber-infidelity. Many people express fascination with this topic, and have stories to tell to illustrate their strong views. Let us consider some of them.

General Public View
Polls taken over the years indicate that most Americans disapprove of infidelity. This was seen after President Clinton's affair with Monica Lewinsky, when polls repeatedly showed the American public disapproved of the president's personal conduct. The results did not reflect a political bias, because the overwhelming majority approved of his performance as president. Interestingly, the statistics showed the sentiment held true until the day he left office. On January 20, 2001, Inauguration Day, CNN reported a recent public opinion poll, which showed an approval rating of 68 percent. This is an astonishingly high approval rating for any outgoing president, especially one that had oral sex and phone sex with a young intern.

Hollywood's View
The plot of two recent films, *Sleepless in Seattle* and *You've Got Mail,* both directed by Nora Ephron, deal with infidelity. The first concerns an offline

affair and the second a cyber-affair. There are many similarities in these films in addition to the artful performance and charm of the leading characters, played by Meg Ryan and Tom Hanks in both movies. In fact, the charm and romanticized environments are so effective that most audiences are anesthetized to the underlying issue present in both films—infidelity.

In *Sleepless in Seattle*, the opening scene involves preparations for Christmas, and reveals fun-filled holiday activities of Annie Reed and her then-fiancé. We see them enjoying the festivities during a traditional family dinner. As Annie drives through the snow past the Kennedy Center in Washington, D.C., she hears a radio announcement from a child in Seattle who is concerned that his widowed father is lonely and needs a wife. She becomes obsessed with the child's father, even though she is living with her fiancé and planning their wedding.

Meg breaks off the relationship with her fiancé because of the possibility of finally meeting Sam Baldwin. Her fiancé graciously accepts her decision as Annie rushes off to meet the stranger. After many failed attempts, Annie and Sam finally meet and it is clear that they will fall in love. This portrayal of both the breakup with Annie's fiancé and her successful meeting and courtship with Sam are not accurate depictions of what occurs in real life. Welcome to Hollywood!

In the second film, *You've Got Mail,* the environment also exudes charm and romance. The film unfolds in Manhattan's Upper West Side, with enticing cinematic scenes. Kathleen Kelly is filmed in her New York apartment (which is decorated to convey sweetness and innocence), or in her charming little bookstore. Kathleen is worried that a large bookstore chain, managed by Joe Fox, will open a megastore nearby and cause her financial ruin.

Kathleen and Joe, then, are in competition for economic survival. They fear and dislike one another. Both characters are in committed relationships with other people. Unbeknownst to her boyfriend, Kathleen begins an email correspondence with a virtual friend. The friendship quickly takes on the hue of a virtual romance. Kathleen does not realize that her cyber-interest is Joe. The film ends as they fall in love offline, and (we presume) live happily ever after. Infidelity is never addressed, and their respective partners amicably agree to end their relationships. In fact, the end of the movie shows not only Kathleen and Joe as a happy couple, but their partners happily involved in other relationships as well.

We are anesthetized by the film's atmosphere, the Hollywood touch, and the chemistry of the leading characters. The viewers, like the films' producer, ignore the fact that the movie is based on cyber-infidelity. The pain of discovering infidelity is not presented.

Viewers are led to focus on the magic of the Internet to positively transform a distrustful and competitive real-world relationship. With the successful conclusion, they are invited to leave the theater content and thinking benign thoughts, oblivious to the reality of the typical repercussions of infidelity.

Are these films merely the expression of a myopic view of infidelity, or are they a statement of a taboo against looking at the painful issues underlying infidelity? We suggest the latter, and that technology has forced the issue upon us, into our discussions, and into our bedrooms.

Self-Deception

Self-deception can take many forms. Just as in offline affairs, some people report that a secret cyber-affair actually improved their primary relationship. They report that their sexual enjoyment with their offline partner increases, and they become more playful and creative in bed. They conclude that affairs must be beneficial. Loretta, a twenty-seven-year-old woman who has been married for four years, explained, "It has been a learning experience for me, I was always very passive and quiet in bed with my husband and previous partners. This has helped me open up and show a side of myself that I never knew existed...it's been very exciting to both me and my husband."

Janna, a twenty-two-year-old medical assistant, told us, "I think that it is a healthier form of sexual expression and it allows people to try things that they normally wouldn't (like homosexual sex, S&M, etc.). People can experiment and learn aspects of themselves they never could share with a close-minded spouse."

Even though Loretta reports advantages, the odds are that her marriage will suffer from secrecy. Janna is looking at experimentation as an advantage, and does not see it as the threat it is to her relationship. As previously discussed, even in these experimental situations, the secrecy can erode the trust in the relationship in many small but powerful ways.

If there is a need to try something new, one might question why you do not discuss your need with your primary partner. If such a discussion feels impossible, it may be wiser to see a relationship counselor to explore your communication impasse before indulging your impulses on the Internet. Your impulses may be a healthy indicator that you are growing, and you may need to stretch your relationship to fit your needs. Effort is well spent in this direction, rather than in deceit and its possible consequences.

Most psychotherapists discourage infidelity, because the consequences can be fatal to the primary relationship. Therapists will focus on the reason an individual wants to have an affair, and help that person resolve the issues that fuel this desire.

Lee, a fifty-one-year-old bricklayer, reported, "I would have thought that this would improve my relations with my wife, but this is not so at all. I can't stop thinking of my email love, and my wife doesn't interest me."

As is often the case, attempts to enrich one's repertoire and bring new passion to a failing relationship often lead to fantasies of the other person when making love to one's partner. "Aphrodite," a twenty-nine-year-old hairdresser, explained, "I got married really young. Guess I didn't know my husband very well. He's older and doesn't like to go out or do the things I like to do. I've been really unhappy in my marriage, even though I've been faithful. I went to the chat rooms because I was lonely. I've had cyber-sex and it has brought excitement into my life—and a feeling of power. I was just looking for fun and got it. But then this one guy seemed to be interested in me as a person—he didn't want to do the cyber thing. He would ask me questions about me. It made me cry to think someone cared. Now it's hard because I want to be with him and not with my husband...and I don't know what will or won't happen. I find myself constantly dreaming of being with my cyber-lover."

While these attempts to bring new energy to a failing relationship may seem transparent to the outside observer, people can easily deny the reasons for their escape into a virtual relationship, and convince themselves to indulge a secret passion. Jose, a thirty-five-year-old pharmacist, wrote: "I think online affairs can be beneficial, can spice up a boring marriage if the partner knows about it, but they are not without risk...."

The trickiest form of deceit is self-deceit. Psychologist Jeanne Shaw, Ph.D., writing on cyber-infidelity in the *Journal of Sex Education and Therapy*, explains, "Although people often think of infidelity as being characterized by lack of faith, trust, or loyalty to a partner, the irony is that the primary disloyalty is to oneself. Infidelity is primarily a self-wound in need of healing."

Although self-deception looms heavily when sexual excitement confuses the senses, most people report an inner voice that speaks the truth. Nagging thoughts, prickly shame, a queasy stomach—these are signs that one has betrayed one's own values. Then when the deception is uncovered, the unfaithful partner often feels debilitating guilt because his or her fears are confirmed and voiced by an angry partner, often repeatedly.

Self-deceit ultimately leads to self-betrayal. Dr. Shaw continues, "One may repent and focus on repairing the consequences of betraying a partner, but self-betrayal is more insidiously devastating." The lack of self-respect that one typically feels after infidelity is difficult to overcome. Knowing that one's word is not sacred, that it can be broken when prompted by a passing anxious moment, can destroy one's self-esteem. In part, building self-esteem is the systematic task of keeping commitments to others and to oneself. Avoiding lies of omission are another way to build self-esteem.

Lies of Omission
Deception can take many forms. To the surprise of many people in denial, lies of omission are violations of monogamy. When people willfully enter into a committed relationship, they typically make a promise of monogamy. While some couples do not make this agreement, the vast majority do.

A lack of communication leaves an area fraught with confusion and heartbreak, as well as manipulation. For example, some offending partners believe that they do not need to reveal sexual liaisons with their partners because, "If they wanted to know, they would ask." Whether such a position is blissful ignorance or outright manipulation, the non-offending party is not responsible for asking direct questions about whether an affair exists. Rather, the responsibility lies with the individual having the affair to report the infidelity.

Lies of omission are a form of deception. Deception is difficult to maintain, even online. It can be uncovered at unexpected times, even when the couple lives miles apart. As we can see in the story below, deception and betrayal related to cyber-infidelity can have more impact than initially intended.

Nicole and Ari

In an apartment on Gordon Street in Tel Aviv, not far from the Mediterranean, a handsome young man with dark, curly hair puts aside his painting. He pours himself a glass of wine, turns on his laptop, and gets comfortable. He starts typing, and smiles because he knows she is there.

In Montreal, an attractive blond woman sits down at her computer on the desk near the window that looks out over the busy la Rue Sherbrooke. She is a professor of art at nearby McGill University. The words come across the screen.

> **Ari:** Shalom, Nicole. :-) :*
> **Nicole:** Bon soir, Ari, mon ami. I couldn't wait for this evening. :-)
> **Ari:** Me 2.
> **Nicole:** I thought about u and the things u told me. I can't believe the difficult life u have had.
> **Ari:** I never told anyone else.
> **Nicole:** Why?
> **Ari:** I feel so close to u. You've told me about your father.
> **Nicole:** I'm so ashamed.
> **Ari:** Don't be.
> **Nicole:** You make me feel better.
> **Ari:** I dreamed about your body again. I picture you perfectly. You are perfect. I encircled my body about yours.
> **Nicole:** These weeks have been wonderful. u are a great lover, mon ami.
> **Ari:** LOL
> **Nicole:** No, don't laugh!
> **Ari:** I want to be your lover.
> **Nicole:** U R.
> **Ari:** 4 real.
> **Nicole:** What do u mean? %-) [confused]

Ari: I'm going to be in London in 2 weeks.
Nicole: u R?
Ari: I met a guy online & we are exchanging apartments. I get his flat in Chelsea.
Nicole: &?
Ari: u and I can stay together. u will be in London for your conference. That's Y I am doing it. We will meet. u can stay with me.
Nicole: Oh.
Air: Something wrong?
Nicole: No.
Ari: Are u afraid to meet me?
Nicole: No, not at all.
Ari: Nicole, say yes.
Nicole: (no reply)
Ari: What is it? %) [confused]

Nicole doesn't hear her two little girls come in the door, followed by her husband. He says, "Nicole, what are you doing? The children are..." Henri stops in mid-sentence. He sees Nicole press a button to minimize the computer screen. Puzzled, he walks over to the computer and reads the word as they come across the screen.

Ari: Nicole, answer me.
[silence]
Ari: Nicole, I thought u wanted to b with me. We talked about what real life luv would b like. Nicole? Nicole, are u there?

Henri turns to her and says, "Turn this off. We will speak later. The children are waiting." Nicole shudders as she puts on her coat.
"Mama, is something wrong?"
"No, dear. I just felt a chill in the air."
In Tel Aviv, Ari sits looking at the screen. "What is wrong?" he wonders. He scrolls through his past Instant Messages for a clue. One exchange seems to jump out.

Ari: When we meet, the world will b ours. There will be no one but us. Nicole? Nicole? Nicole? Are u there?
Nicole: Oui. But Ari, there R others in our lives.
Ari: They won't b important.
Nicole: Maybe, Ari, maybe. BTW [by the way] tell me about your hike. Was it fun?
Ari: Great, but it was sooooo hot.

Ari rereads this exchange repeatedly. "That's it," he thought. "There are others. She must be married. I can't believe what a fool I've been." He sinks into a chair. His face, his body, his posture, speak eloquently of the betrayal.

In Tel Aviv, Ari is feeling the beginning of the powerful effects that cyber-infidelity will have on his life. In Montreal, Nicole's husband, Henri—and probably their children as well—will be experiencing the pain that follows betrayal through lies of omission in cyber-infidelity.

Henri's emotional reaction to the discovery of his wife's cyber-infidelity is controlled. Most likely, this control is for the benefit of the children. Reactions to the discovery of cyber-infidelity are typically strong and often are reported as overwhelming.

In the next chapter, we will explore the ways in which infidelity is discovered and the reactions to it.

6

Discovery: Real Betrayal from the Virtual World

The discovery of a partner's secret romantic involvement with another person usually ignites feelings of betrayal, rage, hurt, and bewilderment. Because many cyber-relationships are emotional but not physical, they fall into the gray area of confusion discussed in Chapter Five. A lack of face-to-face contact with cyber-relationships can fool those involved, as well as their real-life partners. Of most concern are those people who know they are cheating on their monogamous partners, but try to convince everyone to the contrary.

The problem will always be that more people will deny rather than admit infidelity of either type—offline or cyber-infidelity. This chapter will attempt to clarify different responses to discovering cyber-infidelity, tempered by the fact that we are probably looking at not only the typical people who engage in affairs, but also a new group of "at-risk" people who otherwise would not have stepped outside their promise of fidelity. That was the case with Jordan's wife, Shannon.

"Shannon always loved computers and was staying up later and later 'to finish work.' I missed her when I went to sleep. I couldn't sleep one night, and I shuffled down to the study. When I saw what she was doing, I stopped breathing. She was masturbating with one hand, and typing furiously with the other. She was telling another woman what she wanted to have done to her sexually. I asked her if she always worked this hard, and she turned white. She also turned off the computer.

"It took several weeks, but I eventually talked her into telling me what she was writing to that woman. I knew she had an interest in other women before we married, but I never imagined that she'd ever given it a second thought after we were married. I'm not sure why I didn't ask if she'd have secret fantasies. I would imagine her with another woman, and found it to be very hot. But we never talked about it, so I figured her attraction to women went away. I guess that was pretty naïve of me, people just do not turn off those kinds of feelings. The Internet gave her the chance to explore her attraction to women again.

"I was worried that this meant she wanted a relationship with a woman, but we talked about it a lot, and she made it clear that she didn't. Our relationship was losing its passion, and the convenience of the computer made it easy for her to live out her secret fantasies online. Now she reassures me by sharing her thoughts, and I feel more a part of her world. I eventually came to understand that I had stopped seducing her long ago, and she had stopped back then sometime, too. It's taken a long time, but we have revitalized our love life, and we are truly interested in each other. But that is only after many months of heartache and talking it out."

Finding your partner engaging in cyber-sex can be not only upsetting, but bring into question the values upon which the relationship stands. However painful it may be, discovery of cyber-infidelity can be the opportunity to ultimately learn more about your relationship. Discovery of infidelity can lead to a healthy exploration of previously unexpressed desires and needs. Of course, this exploration is typically very difficult and time consuming. Some relationships are strengthened, and others are destroyed.

Signs of a Cyber-Affair
How do you find out if your partner is having secret, steamy discussions with an online sex kitten or cyber-stud? These following sections describe some of the signs reported by some of our *SelfhelpMagazine* Essay Contest respondents. Many of these signs can exist without the presence of infidelity. Often, a combination of different signs will be present if your partner is being deceitful about a cyber-affair.

Preoccupation and Distance
Your partner seems more preoccupied with getting to the computer than spending time with you after work. When away from the computer, you get the sense your partner is distant or daydreaming, and not quite "with" you in the same way. You speak, but are not heard. In response to your questions, you may get head nods and grunts. While being distant and preoccupied is a sign that something is up, the sense of urgency to privately get to the computer is a clue that there is a cyber-affair brewing.

Changing Sleep Schedule
Look for a regular change in sleep schedule, with new awake times being spent at the computer. An occasional late night is normal, but regular late nights or very early mornings are abnormal times to be at the computer. A corresponding sign is the desire to skip activities with you and the children, and to stay home and work on the computer alone for an hour or more at a time. There are times when disturbed sleep is due to depression or anxiety, so these possibilities must also be considered in your assessment.

Insistence upon More Privacy
You walk into the room, and suddenly the computer is shut off, a screen saver appears suddenly, or the screen being viewed is quickly minimized. Your

partner demands more privacy by closing the door, complaining when you enter the room, or locking you out. Your questions about online activities are met with irritability, jokes, sarcasm, or other noninformative answers. This is a more serious indicator of a secretive Internet life.

Moodiness

Your partner is less tolerant, irritable, easily distracted, or anxious when kept away from the computer, and shows other personality changes. Their mood is noticeably different after time is spent on the computer.

Lying

Things do not add up, but when you directly question specific events, expenses, or behaviors, you receive an answer that continues to raise questions. He or she hesitates, stutters, stumbles with an explanation, looks away, or gives other signs of avoiding the truth. Lies include repeated promises that time at the computer will soon end, but it does not. These people may be stalling.

Overreacting

Overreaction is a variation of the lying response. Your partner may fly off the handle when you question their Internet activities. Drama is often used to cover the truth because the threat of discovery causes anxiety to rise. Your partner may also use anger to intimidate you, and thereby prevent any further confrontation. Overreaction is a very powerful technique, and many people do not realize when it is being used as a distraction from the truth. If you get an overly emotional response to a polite question, trust yourself.

Stonewalling

Stonewalling is yet another form of lying; it is lying by omission. Simple, innocent conversation, such as "You really have taken to the computer" or "Have you found anything interesting on the computer?" will be answered with short responses. Instead of saying, "Yeah, I never thought I would get into the Internet this much," or "I found this great website," the answer will be a simple "No," which effectively ends the conversation. On the other hand, you might find your questions lead immediately to an abrupt change of topic. Often, the unfaithful partner will feel guilty or uncomfortable talking about the subject that is brought up, and will use this technique to avoid the conversation. While this type of response is common, when it is used when the subject of computer use comes up there is cause for concern.

Decreasing Interest in Responsibilities

You might notice signs of disinterest in shared relationship responsibilities, such as children's activities, extended family visits, household chores, or hobbies that had previously been interesting. This could be due to several reasons. Your partner may be too preoccupied with fantasies about online activities to remember that Junior has a softball game this afternoon, or the grass needs cutting. He or she may also be investing less in your relationship, and see less of a future with you.

Decreasing Interest in You

You notice a sudden decrease in activities that were previously enjoyed by both of you. Couples may gradually develop differing interests over years of shared living, but the sudden decrease in shared interests is an important clue. Other signs include decreased interest in making vacation or holiday plans; or in long-term planning for large expenses such as buying an automobile, looking for a home, or discussing retirement together. You might also notice your partner spending less time talking about work opportunities and events, extended family, or future goals.

Differing Sexual Contact

Look for a refusal to have sexual contact. This may also be a sign of physical disorder. If in doubt, ask your spouse to get a physical exam to rule out possible physical reasons for the lack of sexual desire. If he or she refuses to be examined, ask about the unwillingness to seek professional help, and see if you can understand the motivation.

Other indicators that can point to a cyber-affair include an absence of your partner's emotional presence when making love. You may feel your partner is preoccupied or not emotionally connected to you when having sexual contact. The pain of getting only sex when you are hungry for emotional connection is very real. This type of sex can feel like being used—quite the opposite of making love.

Any change in sexual activity with you, including an interest in trying new sexual behaviors and speaking differently to you during lovemaking, may be an indicator of an outside source of sexuality, especially if you cannot identify the reason for the change.

Signs of Sexual Activity without You

You may want to pay attention to whether your partner looks flushed, or is consistently wearing "easy access clothing" while in the computer room, making masturbation simple to hide. You may also observe if your partner gets sexually aroused when approaching, or is at, the computer. Much like Pavlov's dogs, a person may become aroused simply by being around a computer because of the many orgasms they've previously experienced using that computer. They may also become easily aroused simply by thinking of what might happen at that computer or by remembering past online sexual encounters.

Sudden Changes in Appearance

Changing a hairstyle, growing a goatee, using more makeup, or dressing differently are forms of experimentation that are common to people who are engaging in some form of infidelity. Whether the change occurs unconsciously or intentionally, sudden changes in appearance may occur because of influences from outside a relationship. An online lover may remark that he or she is attracted to a certain line of clothing or color of hair. To make himself or herself more attractive to the virtual lover, your partner may change physical appearance to accommodate the suggestion.

New Expenses

You might notice unexplained expenses on your credit cards or your phone bills. When you look at the phone bill, you may see calls placed at odd times to unfamiliar numbers.

Investigating

If you are thinking of investigating your own partner, you must think carefully and weigh the advantages and disadvantages. Review our discussions of codependency further in this chapter. If you are spending an excessive amount of time and energy tracking your partner's activities, you may need to look at your own life to see if your preoccupation is reasonable, or if it is a sign of your own emotional problems. Ultimately, you will need to find your own comfort zone. Stop investigating when you feel uncomfortable or think you are being unreasonable. Ask the advice of others, including a professional, if you are unsure of how far to go.

Over the last few years, people have used various methods to uncover whether their partner is having a cyber-affair. Some of the approaches they took involve deviousness, and others are illegal. For any of the following ideas that involve a computer, remember that the courts have been ruling that you could be violating your lover's or spouse's privacy if you do not have shared ownership of the equipment you investigate. The following examples are being given for informational purposes. You should not follow any of these techniques in a way that violates the law, and if you do, you must be willing to accept responsibility for your own actions.

Checking the Hard Drive

People who are computer-savvy have been able to check their partner's computer hard drive. They look for cute or odd names for folders. Some Web browsers, like Internet Explorer and Netscape Navigator, have a history function that records the webpages visited. This allows them to view the webpages recently visited by their partner.

If the web browser used is Internet Explorer, a graphics viewer program, such as ACDSee, will go through the following folders in the WINDOWS folder: TEMPORARY INTERNET FILES and CONTENT.IE5. These folders contain the cached graphics from visiting websites via Internet Explorer. Pornography is commonly found here.

Forwarding a Message

Another questionable and illegal practice that has been used, as described by Richard Smith of the University of Denver's Privacy Foundation, involves forwarding an email message to one's partner with a "web bug wiretap" embedded. If the partner then forwarded the message on to a virtual lover, the wiretap would cause the email to bounce back to the investigator who would then have the email address of the virtual lover, along with any comments written by their partner. The wiretap only works in certain email programs, and can be easily shielded. More sophisticated wire taps are created regularly.

Accessing the Partner's Account

Some people have gone so far as to find their partner's password and use it to log on to and check the email program, looking for hidden files. By doing this, they can run a search command for specific days and times when they think something suspicious occurred. Such commands will automatically sift through the entire email program for files created within specific time parameters selected.

Technical Surveillance Techniques

A number of different software programs have been developed to spy on spouses. Some are hidden programs that record any activity on a computer. Much like a camcorder, the program takes "snap shots" of the pages displayed on the screen and saves them for later retrieval. All websites visited, text typed, emails read, or programs run are saved indefinitely. Other programs are similar, but have additional capabilities. Some can record an entire chat room conversation and send a report to any email address. These reports can be accessed from any computer and can be read only moments after they happen.

The KeyKatcher is a device that plugs into keyboard port of a computer. It will record all the keystrokes typed on the computer, catching the email notes and addresses, passwords to websites, and chat room conversations. The KeyKatcher can be installed on any computer, even if the computer is protected by a password. The information can be recorded from one computer and sent to another. Someone could be typing email to a virtual lover, while their partner reads right along.

These programs are being used by more people than imagined. The president of a corporation that develops detective software was quoted in *Newsweek* magazine. He reported that after posting an ad on eBay reading,

"Husband cheating online? Catch him with this," sales of his software went "through the roof." Others involved in the production and sale of the surveillance system report heartbreaking stories from those who find a partner involved in cyber-infidelity.

Asking Online

People have even used the simple method of going online and inquiring if anyone has recently heard from their partner. If he or she frequents the area, someone will know of the partner. While this method is direct, it also runs a high risk of discovery by the cheating partner.

A variation of this approach is to run a search through Usenet's Newsgroups. By going to www.deja.com and entering an email address to search, someone's postings in their entirety can be found.

Writing a Sex Note

Some crafty people have typed a sexy note and sent it to their partner through a service that allows for aliases, to see what kind of mail they get in return.

Calling Telephone Numbers

If you have noticed increased expenses or strange numbers on your telephone bills, consider calling the unfamiliar numbers that appear frequently, at particularly odd times of the day, or when you know you were away from home. If someone answers, ask if he or she knows anyone from your city. Remember that an unfaithful partner is not likely to have used a real name. Interestingly enough, though, people often are honest about revealing their city or state of residence. If the person you have called is willing to converse with you, ask other questions, such as when they had the last contact. Be ready for some questions in return.

AT&T also offers a service whereby you can obtain the name and street address of a listing. Also, remember that many people currently have a *69 feature with their telephone service, whereby if you ring through to their telephone number, they can return your call by simply dialing *69. If they also have Caller ID service, they can obtain your telephone number.

Ask Directly and Watch

Remember, there is a fine line between investigating and codependency. Investigation can lift the shadow of deceit and secrecy from your relationship, but only you can decide how much secrecy and deceit you will use to uncover an affair. The most honest and preferred way to investigate a possible affair is to ask your partner directly.

If you decide to ask directly, watch your partner carefully for any signs of lying. Look for fumbling, twitching, blushing, dropping things, mumbling words, holding one's breath, and/or shifting eyes. Remain calm and gather facts. Storming, berating, or name calling will not change anything, except to make you more upset and unapproachable, and probably make the truth harder to find.

If you suspect that your partner is having a cyber-affair, or if you know, it is not easy to be sure what to do. These issues are complicated, and each case is different. What applies to another person may not apply to you. There are a variety of reactions to discovering a cyber-affair.

Hildie's Story

Hildie's story is representative of stories from people who have participated in support groups for partners of those involved in cyber-infidelity.

"I can see it all now. In fact, I can almost feel the shock and despair I felt three months ago when I knew for sure that Joey was having an affair.

"I was practicing working on the computer. I had been taking a class and wanted to impress Joey because it was a joke between us about how 'low-tech' I was.

"Well, at any rate, while I was experimenting with my computer skills, I stumbled onto a file labeled 'For Your Eyes Only.' I remember laughing and thinking, 'What's he, a secret CIA agent?' Well, Joey was keeping a secret. I read the files. I thought I would die! He might as well have been a secret agent, he was living a secret life online!

"I called him at work several times, but he was in meetings. I couldn't wait until he got home. I cried off and on all day. I slammed doors. It felt like a nightmare. I didn't know this man, and here I was, married to him for over fourteen years!

"When Joey came in, I hit him with it right away. 'You S.O.B.! You damned hypocrite! You liar! Who the hell do you think you are? You and your Sexy Sue! Funny? Well, I don't think so. How could you do this to me? How could you? How could you?

"Joey was stunned. He finally said, 'It's not what you think, Hildie. It sounds bad, but it was just play—just a game.'

"It's not what I think? You want to run your tongue all over her body. I may not know my way around the computer, but I know a lying, cheating dirt bag when I see one, and that's what you are! I just read four months of sex talk. Four months of reading about your longing for her. Four months of what she was doing to you. Joey the Stud! You're a real piece of work. And the whole time, you let me do your laundry for you, shop and cook for you, wait on you hand and foot. I hate you!

"I went on like this for almost a week. I could not calm down to discuss anything. Sometimes I cried, sometimes I lay in bed, unable to move, and other times I wanted to tear the house apart. I couldn't stop thinking about it."

Hildie's reaction was highly emotional but common. She let off steam, and that may have provided immediate relief, but it was short lasting. There are effective ways to confront and to deal with such pain. Since there is significant anxiety associated with confrontation, we suggest a combination of relaxation and mental rehearsal to prepare you for the task.

Preparing Yourself

Relaxation is the opposite of anxiety. When people are anxious, they often cannot remember what they had intended to say, or are unable to answer questions. In general, they find they are not thinking clearly. If they learn the technique we are going to describe, they can be less anxious and think more clearly. These general suggestions for relaxation may help you.

Slow, Rhythmical Breathing

1. Select a time to practice slow, rhythmical breathing when you will not be interrupted.
2. Sit in a comfortable chair or recline on a sofa or bed.
3. Breathe in for three to four seconds.
4. Exhale slowly for about three to four seconds.
5. Establish a rhythm of in and out breathing for three to four minutes
6. Allow your body to grow heavy and sink into your chair or bed.
7. Put your hand on your lower abdomen and try to make it move more than your upper chest. This will help you breathe deep into your abdomen and maximize your benefits.
8. Do not push or force your breath. If you cannot sustain the rhythm and need to take a few short breathes, that's OK. Resume your rhythm when you can.

If this makes you feel lightheaded, stop. Practice this exercise a few times a day, especially when you feel upset. You may find yourself tearing up, and that is OK.

If you cannot stop crying when you want to, that is another story. If you are crying in awkward places, such as in public or when trying to accomplish other tasks, give yourself some time. If these episodes do not stop after a few weeks, consult your psychotherapist or physician. You may be experiencing the physical signs of depression. If you have experienced depression in the past, make note of these episodes and consult your professional as soon as you get worried about a relapse.

Progressive Muscle Relaxation

Progressive muscle relaxation can be combined with deep breathing or achieved alone. This time-tested exercise is described by Edmund Jacobson, M.D., in his book *Progressive Relaxation*, and its purpose is to tighten four major muscle groups, then relax them while breathing regularly.

1. Start by tightening the neck, face, and shoulder muscles. Hold for a few seconds, then relax with your out-breath.
2. Next, move to the arms, hands, chest, and upper back. Repeat tightening, holding, and relaxing as you breathe out as in Step 1.

3. Next, move to your abdominal and buttock muscles. Repeat tightening, holding, and relaxing as you breathe out.

4. Lastly, tighten thigh, leg, calf, and feet muscles. Repeat tightening, holding, and relaxing as you breathe out.

It is important to be aware of how relaxation feels in your muscles. They may tingle, feel warm, or feel heavy. Some people individualize these techniques by imagining themselves in a beautiful garden, gazing at a mountaintop, or lying on a beach.

Mental Rehearsal

Anxiety is reduced through these relaxation skills, and you can now proceed with "mental rehearsal," which author Maxwell Maltz, M.D., discussed in his book, *Psycho-Cybernetics*. Mental rehearsal allows you to review in your imagination the confrontation you are anticipating. After you have practiced some type of relaxation, visualize the direct discussion you want to have with your partner.

By rehearsing in a relaxed state, you are able to practice and correct your mistakes, until you say what you really want to communicate. If you should become anxious while rehearsing, simply take a step back and start the relaxation process again. By using relaxation and mental rehearsal, you may avoid a highly emotional and chaotic scene. Remember that your feelings of betrayal, anger, guilt, and disbelief will still be with you, but may not overwhelm you in your confrontation if you practice remaining calm and saying exactly what you want.

With these skills in place, let us look at how the exchange could go between Hildie and Joey.

When Hildie finds the "For Your Eyes Only" file on the computer hard drive, she says to herself, "My God, I can't believe it. That jerk. He's sending these damned emails to Sexy Sue. Who is she? How dare he?" Hildie reads the email over and over again.

Then she thinks, "I can't call him now. I'm too angry, and he's at work. I need to think this through. I don't see any problem in our marriage, other than the usual ones about car pools and staying within the budget. No change in our sex life, both of us seem to have the same interest. I need to do something. I'll go for a long walk, and I'll think about what I want to say. I feel like I'm jumping out of my skin. I better start walking now.

When Joey comes home, Hildie says, "We have to talk."

"Sure. What's up?" Joey says.

"I know about Sexy Sue."

Joey is stunned. "Oh, no. Oh, my God, Hildie."

"I'm so angry at you, Joey. How could you do it? You betrayed me, big time."

"I never thought you would find out."

"You think that makes it OK?"

"No, no! Of course not!" Joey answers. "I want to end it. I've been trying. I can't stand the guilt. What I did was wrong. I just thought I could end it and you wouldn't need to find out."

"Is that why you saved the files on our computer?" Hildie replies. "No, I think you wanted me to find out. And I did find out. I am trying, really hard, Joey, to try to understand and not go ballistic. You need to tell me about this."

"OK, OK. It's no excuse, but I sort of slid into this. I went online into that chat room for amateur photographers. I met Sue there. We started talking privately and one thing led to another."

"You had cyber-sex with her! I read all about it on your emails."

"I'm sorry I did this. You can see that I talk to her very little now."

"Do you love her?"

"Of course not."

"Have you met her?"

"No. You saw the email."

"I am exhausted with all this. I thought things were OK with us."

"They are! I made a mistake. It's on a computer screen. I didn't think it was any worse than reading *Playboy*. It is, I can see that now. I love you."

Hildie calmly lays down her demands. "I want you off the computer. And I want you to go with me to a marriage therapist, soon! Tomorrow, maybe!"

"OK," Joey replies, "if it will keep us together."

This exchange was not easy for Hildie. She first had to control the way she was reacting. It meant not screaming, but trying to calm herself. She did this by taking a brisk walk which she found relaxing. If Hildie had known how to use deep breathing and mental rehearsal, she would have been helped even more. This confrontation would not be recommended for everyone. For example, if Joey had been a violent man, this confrontation might have triggered a physical response toward Hildie or any children who might be home.

In this conversation, we learn that Joey wanted to tell Hildie about his cyber-affair and was unable to do so. This is common. Joey needed to think carefully about what he wanted to say, to reduce his anxiety, and to tell Hildie at an appropriate time. Here is how such a disclosure could unfold:

After dinner, Joey says, "Hildie, I want to talk to you about something serious. Is this a good time for you?"

"Yes, of course. Anything wrong? Are you sick?"

"No, but I've done something that I feel badly about that is going to hurt you. But I've got to tell you about this."

"Don't tell me you're having an affair."

"Sort of."

"What are you saying?"

"Hildie, in the last four months, I've been involved with a woman I never met. It's been on the Internet."

"Oh, my God! I can't believe this!"

"I'm sorry, Hildie. I love you. It was a terrible thing to do."

Hildie and Joey would continue their discussions, and hopefully begin the task of reconciliation. As you can see, discovering or revealing cyber-infidelity is indeed a difficult experience. It brings up many uncomfortable feelings. However, in most cases, it is better to communicate rationally and honestly to make it possible for the underlying causes of infidelity to surface.

Emotional Reactions

Kimberly Young, Ph.D., stated, The most difficult moments in my study emerged from witnessing the anger, frustration, confusion, and pain of the women and men whose spouses' online habits had threatened or destroyed long and apparently stable relationships....Something new and frightening had crept silently into their lives, and they did not know what to make of it or do about it. Through simple words on the computer screen, another man or woman had invaded their homes and their lives. Within weeks of breezy Internet chatting, terminal love had struck with the force of a tornado, leaving cyber-widows trying to dig out from under the real-life rubble."

Early reactions to learning of cyber-infidelity are disbelief, rage, fear, anger, shock, and sorrow. One may react by screaming, crying, storming about, or becoming immobilized. There are many reactions reported by betrayed partners.

Disbelief

An early reaction to cyber-infidelity is disbelief, even when it has been suspected for a while. It can take a while for your thoughts to clear enough to make sense of the discovery. Gary told us his story.

"I can't believe she actually did it. She said she would find someone else if I didn't get out of the Navy and get a job that kept me around. She said she gets too lonely, and I knew she wouldn't go out and cheat on me, but I never thought of the Internet.

"When I came back from my latest West-PAC, she wasn't the same. She didn't hug on me like she always did before. When we got home, she helped me put away my things, but things weren't the same. We had sex, but she wasn't there. That weekend, I saw her go to the den to 'work on some school things.' When I snuck up on her an hour later to kiss her behind the neck, I noticed her hand was in her crotch, and she was typing with the other.

"I knew I needed to do something, because if I stayed there, I might lose control. So I told her I was going to the club to see my friends. I can't believe she actually did it. I was out at sea for six months, thinking of nothing but her. Then I come home and she throws this in my face. I just can't believe it."

The feeling of disbelief is closely tied to the feeling of betrayal. It can create violent feelings in many. For people like Gary, who have learned to control and manage their feelings with the help of a support system, these feelings can be diffused by confiding in people, seeking direction, and taking constructive action.

Shame

Shame can be experienced by both partners. It is a combination of feelings of guilt and disgrace about something that has happened. Another client, Dionne, whose husband discovered her secret life, put it well. "While it was happening, it seemed so cool. I was so good at being secretive, and no one was getting hurt. But now I feel humiliated. Don is crushed. He told me that some guy invaded our lives, just as though he had slept with me in our bed. Don won't touch me. I am so ashamed."

Yet Don, her husband, said, "That's right. I'm crushed. But I also feel this terrible sense of shame, because my wife not only had an affair, but it was with a stranger, using a computer. I feel there is something very wrong when a person has an affair, but strangely I feel a sense of disgrace that my wife was masturbating with someone she didn't even know, and using the Internet to do it."

Shame is present for many in both online and offline affairs. Some people report that they believe the use of the Internet for an affair makes it more disgraceful and shameful, and others report feeling less shame because of it.

Jealousy

Many people report preoccupation with jealous thoughts and a need to know as much as possible about their partner's virtual lover. When carried to extremes, some people keep a constant check on the activities of their partner, not trusting them to be alone.

Annette spoke to us in tears, "The pipes burst in our building at work soon after we opened. So we got the day off. I hurried home to Karen, thinking we could have a great day together. When I came home, the house seemed quiet. I knew she was probably at work on her computer, but when she didn't answer, I charged up the stairs and flung open the door. I was shocked. She didn't answer because she was in some kind of daydream. She was at the keyboard, and at the end of a powerful orgasm. I was speechless. She didn't hear me at first. Then she turned and saw me.

"Having seen how enthralled she was at the computer has stirred terrible feelings of jealousy within me. I want to know all about this other woman and why she was so attractive to my lover."

Discovering a secret life of a partner is very shocking, but even more so when it involves an attachment to the virtual lover or a fascination with pornography. It is distressing and dismaying to learn that clandestine meetings have been taking place, that such a secret has been fostered by your partner. Feelings of betrayal can rock the foundation of your relationship. It is even more wrenching if your partner is reluctant to give up the virtual lover or interactive pornography. When this happens, the relationship as a whole must be evaluated and individual issues be clarified and resolved. If the virtual romance is not ended, the emotional well-being of the family is jeopardized, which may extend to future generations as well.

Because infidelity results in a severe breakdown of trust on the part of the faithful partner, he or she will want to know about the partner's activities. While it is natural for some jealousy and vigilance to continue as a couple recovers from cyber-infidelity, the jealousy and vigilance can be minimized if the unfaithful partner maintains complete honesty and volunteers information about his or her activities. Knowing your partner's activities and whereabouts is a step toward building trust.

Codependency

However, if the faithful partner becomes obsessed with these activities, then another problem arises. That person can become codependent. He or she makes the partner the priority and forgets about his or her own self-care. An obsessive preoccupation with the activities of a partner can prove unhealthy. Constant suspicion and checking will not only keep the faithful partner upset, but also take its toll on an already stressed relationship. Suspicion may arise in the recovery process. If the unfaithful partner agrees to be completely honest in the way in which he or she is using the computer, much of the obsession will subside.

Once the facts are uncovered and an agreement is made to end contact with the virtual lover, the faithful partner needs to decide when to stop investigating possible clues. If this decision proves too hard, that partner may benefit from attending support group meetings or finding professional help. If the unfaithful partner cheats again, the aid of a therapist is now crucial for the couple.

Denial and Minimizing

Minimizing or denying the impact of infidelity on your partner usually leads to an increase in anger, rather than a decrease. The offending partner may be saying that it was of no emotional consequence, but the infidelity was packed with meaning to the partner.

"It wasn't for real," our client Dave told his wife, Jane. "She was on the other side of a monitor. I don't even know what the hell she looks like."

Jane wasn't convinced, "Damn you! How could you do it? You had orgasms with her. You're only supposed to do that with me! You spoke to her in sexy, loving ways, like you're supposed to talk to me. I can't believe this is happening. She came into our lives, and you invited her. You chose her over me."

When the unfaithful partner denies or minimizes the effect of cyber-infidelity, it may temporarily be helpful to him or her. However, the denial by the faithful partner is like a second wound. Although denial serves as a defense mechanism to protect the unfaithful partner from feeling guilty, it is detrimental to resolving the situation. Dave's surprise soon turned to shame and to guilt as he became more aware of the impact his infidelity had on Jane. He realized that she had taken their promise of fidelity as a sacred vow, and she had honored it. His disregard for their vow was painful for her, and he was able to acknowledge his betrayal of that vow, and her resulting pain. This pain must be acknowledged, not minimized as a first step toward resolving the infidelity issue.

Ending the deceit, acknowledging the pain, and understanding the faithful partner's perspective are imperative. Continued lies and deceit, even if the attempt is to minimize wounding the faithful partner, only make the situation worse.

Guilt

Cyber-affairs are generally more difficult to deny when evidence is found on a computer. Technology provides evidence of entire dialogues.

Once the denial has been broken, the unfaithful partner usually feels guilty about the cyber-infidelity and the resulting distress it causes. The degree of guilt experienced by the unfaithful partner can vary along a continuum, from denial and minimization to suicidal thoughts and actions. When people express a desire to hurt or kill themselves, professional help is not only warranted but also crucial and needed immediately.

There is also reason to be concerned when there is no remorse on the part of the unfaithful partner. It could be signs of a more serious personality disorder. Psychologist Jeanne Shaw, Ph.D., acknowledges the damage done by cyber-infidelity to both partners and the personality problems that might be present in the unfaithful partner. She writes, in the *Journal of Sex Education and Therapy*, "There is no question that infidelity is a severe betrayal of self that can damage both partners....The wanderer, ironically may be desperately trying to become whole in a way that assures failure....Internet infidelity might indicate that an individual is developed enough emotionally to find a partner but not developed enough to be openly, compassionately oneself in a relationship with that partner." Individual counseling is often helpful for people with personality disorders of this nature. They often don't see the need for it, however.

Contingencies set by the faithful spouse might be needed for a reluctant cheater to continue attending psychotherapy long enough for changes to occur. For more specifics on treatment, see our chapters on recovery.

Recrimination

At some point, the unfaithful partner usually wonders if the recriminations will ever end, but eventually they will. Infidelity is such a strong blow to the relationship that the anger over the betrayal is expressed repeatedly. The recriminations often diminish for a while, only to recur when not expected. When recriminations recur, the couple usually has made enough progress to cope more directly with the anger and continue to mend their relationship together.

Anger

Anger is by far the strongest emotion reported by the faithful partner. Both men and women can experience enormous rage upon discovering a cyber-affair. When Jackie heard a strange man's voice on the phone, telling her that their spouses were having cyber-sex, she confronted her husband with anger that scared them both. She told us, "I hardly knew what to do with this anger. I wanted to beat on him, to hurt him. I wanted to call her, but who is she? I wanted to smash the computer."

Whatever the differences that exist between the infidelity in the real world or the virtual world, its impact occurs in the real world. Its victims suffer psychological pain and despair. Coping skills depend upon background, resources, and emotional strength. Such skills can be learned in treatment.

Losses

When people experience the betrayal of cyber-infidelity, they report the emotional and physical losses described in this next section.

Innocence

The most poignant loss people report as the result of cyber-infidelity, is the loss of innocence in the relationship. Shocking to both partners, the loss of innocence involves loss of trust as well. As Sarah put it, "I lost all I believed in. I believed in him. I believed in our marriage vows. I feel as though someone or something has died. I think it is my marriage."

People often mourn the death of innocence and trust in their relationship. While the innocence is not likely to return, trust can, and most often does return, if the couple has the courage to examine the current stressors and underlying relationship dynamics that have contributed to the infidelity. It is important to note that when the sense of grief persists, it can become clinical depression. If you are concerned that this is happening to you or your partner, monitoring by a professional may be warranted.

Commitment

The experience of loss of commitment can prove crushing. For most, the reaction to a loss of commitment is a feeling of betrayal. As John said, "It is as though I had to shift all the things I believed in. I thought of us as a team, working together. He was my partner. He has broken his commitment to me. That is hard to take."

Janet said, "She was the first woman that I ever loved. Living a lesbian life is hard enough, but then this happens to me. This makes me want to never love again."

The desire to ward off the sadness of a lost commitment can propel faithful partners into seeking a retaliatory affair. Such behavior is an indication of emotional reactivity. Seeking revenge can lead to permanent damage, and most likely, destruction of the entire relationship.

When Susan, a twenty-four-year-old dog trainer, told us her story, she was in tears. "I'm here because I had a cyber-affair with some guy in Omaha. I've never seen him, and I never want to see him! But after I found out that my husband, Keith, had an affair online, I was so furious. I thought, what's good for the goose is good for the gander, and I went about finding 'HornyInOmaha.' I really hated what I was doing, but I went about it in a way that I could say sexy things that I knew would hurt Keith. I wanted to write really hot stuff and show it to Keith. I did, and Keith has now left me. I'm heartbroken and I need help."

Specialness

The once-cherished feeling of exclusivity evaporates with astonishing speed when a partner learns of an affair. Commitment brings this feeling of being special, and when commitment vanishes, so does that precious feeling.

When a person discovers that a trusted partner has experienced an intimate relationship with another person, the partner feels that his or her special place has been lost. Jay wrote, "Look, I'm not the emotional type, but, wow, this really hit hard! I know Cindy adored me once. I was that 'special guy' for her. I no longer feel special. She fell for someone who sounded wonderful. She showed me her email and his picture. He evidently did more for her through a damned computer than I did in person. I can't believe she really cares about me."

Confidence

Self-esteem plummets in people who have experienced cyber-infidelity. Men suffer because they think they were not manly enough, so their partner had to find someone else who could turn them on. Women feel they were not attractive or sexy enough. They might secretly wonder if their past mistakes, personality shortcomings, or failures led to an erosion of the attraction their partner once had for them. Even when reminded that their partner never saw the other person, their concern that they do not measure up does not change.

Helene, a thirty-three-year-old dental hygienist, wrote, "I am coloring my hair and getting liposuction for my thunder thighs, even though I know that is not the problem. He once loved me with brown hair and solid thighs. I need him to care about me. But truthfully, I know I fell from my No. 1 position in his eyes. I am no longer unique and special to him. He has lost respect for me."

Shared Dreams

Couples plan their future together. They make decisions about where to live, to have children or not, travel, what to buy, retirement, and all the experiences they want to share. They see a future with each other. Shared dreams often become a loss, because the future gets clouded for couples struggling with how to deal with any form of infidelity.

Alicia writes, "Cary and I worked hard for ten years to buy this second home in the beautiful Shenandoah Mountains. We both made sacrifices for this. It was eventually going to be a retirement home. We love to be outdoors. He says that we still can do it. I am not so sure. I think our dream has turned into a nightmare."

Health

It is common for the non-offending partner to experience physical symptoms, such as headaches, gastrointestinal disorders, muscle tension, sleep problems, and the loss or gain of considerable body weight.

When Jeanette came into the office, she looked haggard and thin. When asked about her weight, she said, "I lost twenty pounds—twenty pounds I couldn't afford to lose. My doctor referred me because she said I couldn't lose any more. I'm not sleeping. This other woman lives three thousand miles away. She probably feels hot and sexy, and I am miserable. Am I going crazy?"

The loss of emotional well-being is a major concern with cyber-infidelity. The losses that have been mentioned can lead to symptoms of anxiety and/or depression in Western culture. Depression is experienced as:

- ➲ Crying spells
- ➲ Sleep disturbances
- ➲ Difficulty concentrating
- ➲ Loss of memory

- Lowering of libido
- Slowing of physical movement or thinking
- Changes in eating habits
- Obsession with guilt or rage
- Difficulty starting the day
- Decrease of interest in previously pleasurable activities

Depression can cause changes in a person's ability to function at work, at home, and in other interpersonal relationships. For people in most cultures, if there is no improvement in these symptoms in two months, professional help should be sought. In various cultures, normal behavior is defined differently, and local professionals need to be consulted to determine whether someone is in need of professional assistance. In severe depression, people can become suicidal or homicidal. If there are thoughts of killing yourself or anyone else, professional help must be sought immediately.

Anxiety is experienced as:

- Worry
- A knot in the stomach
- A lump in the throat
- Hypervigilence
- Motor restlessness
- Sleep disturbance
- Fatigue
- Irritability
- Muscle tension
- Difficulty concentrating or your mind going blank
- Excessive sweating
- Racing pulse, heartbeat, or thoughts

Once again, cultural norms vary with respect to how much anxiety is to be expected within a population. In the Western world, anxiety disorders are diagnosed when a number of the above symptoms persist for more days than not over a period of more than six months. If, however, your distress is overwhelming and interferes with you day-to-day functioning, do not wait six months. Seek the aid of a psychotherapist to help you cope with your stress. These disorders cause clinically significant distress or impairment in social (which includes family life), work, or other important areas of functioning.

When Not to Reveal Cyber-Infidelity

As Rona Subotnik, M.A., MFT, and Gloria Harris, Ph.D., note in *Surviving Infidelity*, there are times when revealing an affair is dangerous. If you are in a relationship with a violent person, it is better to see a therapist than to risk being physically abused. They wrote, "Your priority is not the affair, but the problems of living with domestic violence."

Fragile partners, who may have attempted suicide or have a long history of depression or anxiety, may also be poor candidates for receiving the details of cyber-infidelity. In this case, it is better to work with a professional therapist to examine the reasons for your cyber-infidelity, and whether your relationship will be strengthened or seriously damaged by your complete honesty. Other people who might benefit from professional guidance include community and religious leaders who have a high public profile. These individuals may want to receive guidance on how to involve their partner in therapy to resolve the basic issues leading to the cyber-infidelity. Humiliation is typically acute when infidelity becomes public knowledge and becomes the subject of gossip and conjecture. It is difficult to resolve underlying relationship issues when the couple is in the public eye.

The impact of cyber-infidelity on couples and families can be significant. After the discovery of cyber-infidelity, a relationship can be permanently altered. To the surprise of many people, partnerships can improve as the result of dealing with the situations brought on by infidelity, and the committed relationship may even become stronger, if properly handled. The help of a professional is often required to assist with the transformation that is needed to make this happen.

Repercussions on Family and Friends

When someone breaks a sacred promise of fidelity, the effect is not limited to the couple and the third party, but is often profoundly felt by the couple's children, and to their frequent surprise, by their friends and parents. The couple can experience a deep sense of shame, a feeling stronger than embarrassment. Even very young children can sense the changes. They notice changes in voice and tension between parents, and intuitively know that something is wrong.

The entire world was witness to such a situation when the picture of the Clinton family was flashed across TV screens, as they walked to their helicopter to begin the process of healing at Martha's Vineyard after the president's affair with Monica Lewinsky. The pictures showed a downtrodden group, dealing with the wounds of infidelity on a family system.

Although the suffering of most families experiencing infidelity is not televised, the image of the presidential family is one to remember, because it shows how everyone is impacted. These wounds persist through time.

Children

In Chapter Four, we discussed cyber-sexual compulsivity and its effect on the family. Children can be harmed by parents' cyber-sexual activities in many ways. They often experience distress and embarrassment, and can easily be drawn into parental conflict.

Past studies have shown that children are adversely affected by arguments related to a parent's infidelity. We also know that children who learn of the infidelity experience anger toward parents, and they too can feel betrayed. Such uncomfortable feelings can make them think they are disloyal to their parents.

In therapy, children often express worries about the future of their family and wonder if they are to blame for the situation. They also lose faith in the parents' ability to take care of the family. It can be easily seen from research and clinical observation that infidelity can lead to often unspoken, yet painful insecurity in children of any age.

In today's world, children can learn of parental infidelity quite easily by locating hidden files on the hard drive, opening email that was intended for the parent, or finding records of a parent's exchanges with a virtual lover. Even if a parent thinks such files are adequately hidden, many children are more computer literate than their parents and have ample time to find and unlock supposedly hidden files. For some children and teens, it can become a challenging treasure hunt for unknown goodies, rather than an intentional search for anything specific. For others who have reason to suspect cyber-infidelity, it can become a painful obsession to find evidence by hacking into the family computer to get the facts.

When children or teens discover evidence of parental sexuality, either in the form of pornography or transcripts of a cyber-affair, reactions can vary. Their dilemma is one of wanting to help, but not knowing how to best intervene. They are burdened by needing to decide how to handle the evidence they find.

In the midst of this turmoil, the people who normally would be their source of comfort and direction are the source of pain. If they tell the faithful parent, they most likely will reveal a secret. If they tell the unfaithful parent, they might be punished. If they tell a grandparent or trusted friend, their parent may be confronted. The child or teen may fear that divorce will inevitably be the consequence, leading to the breakup of their family and home. Much like children who are victims of familial incest, these children and teens may choose to keep the secret to themselves, where it can fester and surface as depression, anxiety, acting out, or self-destructive behavior.

If a child has the strength to expose cyber-infidelity, one should respond honestly and simply, while avoiding details and overly emotional reactions. Parents have a right to privacy as they renegotiate their relationship in the light of infidelity. At the same time, children require an explanation—although a limited one.

Above all, children should not become the confidants of their parents. Confiding in children and teens changes the family structure and can cause undue anxiety. Parents must be family leaders and avoid the possibility of blurring the necessary boundary between parent and child. Parents how-ever, often find it difficult to discuss infidelity with their children. Such dis-cussions require care, sensitivity, and an awareness of the child or children's emotional development. A parent would speak differently to a child of ele-mentary school age than to a teenager.

The following shows how Gail and Jerry talked to their children about cyber-infidelity:

Gail told us, "My kids are nine and eleven, and I can see they are reacting to the anger I feel toward Jerry all the time. I decided they don't need to know Daddy has a girl-friend on the Internet. So Jerry and I talked it over and we decided on a plan, and spoke to the kids together. We told them that families sometimes have a problem and Daddy and I are having a problem now and we are working it out, and it may take some time. We are sorry about the arguing and we are working hard to change it."

Jerry added, "They wanted to know what the problem was, and I said that it was private. Sometimes we get sad, sometimes angry—just like you kids do—but we think things will be better soon."

"I am really sorry for what I did," Jerry said, "and I don't want my kids knowing about it. First, because I feel humiliated, but even more importantly, children nowa-days are really knowledgeable about the Internet. I want to protect them."

Gail and Jerry successfully handled their experience with their young children, but the task is more complicated when children are older. Today's worldly teenager may ask questions that are more difficult.

Alice and Jim had teenagers who were shocked by the discovery of their parent's infidelity:

Alice said, "When Stuart heard Jim and me screaming at each other about the Internet, he asked questions about it. Even though he is only fifteen, we saw he was pretty wise to cyberspace.

"So Jim really had to have a 'man-to-man' talk with him, not just about us, but about the dangers that a kid can get into online. As far as we were concerned, Jim told him that, just to pass the time, he started talking on the Internet and he became friends with a woman in a chat room, and that he spoke to her every night. It was a mistake—a big mistake, and he had hurt Mom. He told Stuart that he apol-ogized to me and will never talk with that woman, or any other, again.

"Jim apologized to our son, Stuart, as well. He told him that he understood his anger and that he had broken a sacred trust to him and his mother. And then Jim said, 'I promise to work hard to earn your trust again.'"

If your children ask about the tension they experience in the household, acknowledge that something is happening. If you do not validate their experience, children will get confused and start to doubt themselves. When left to draw their own conclusions from snippets of conversations, unspoken tension between parents, slammed doors, and other negative exchanges, children and teens tend to assume the worst. Much to their dismay, they typically draw erroneous and emotionally painful pictures of divorce and family dissolution.

These suggestions may be helpful in talking to your children. They probably need to know the following:

○ They are not responsible for your problems. The younger they are, the more naturally self-focused they will be. They may firmly believe the world revolves around them, and they are the cause of other people's behavior. For example, when something in a family goes awry, they often point to their most recent misbehavior as the cause, such as "Mommy and Daddy are getting divorced because I didn't eat my green beans last night." Older children may not give such simplistic explanations, but may ask themselves if they are too much of a burden, if they spend too much money, stay out too late, etc.

○ They cannot solve your relationship problems with your partner, but as adults, you and your partner can and will work to that end.

○ They only need to be aware that a problem exists, and that you are working on it.

Parents also need to:

○ Speak respectfully of the other parent to your children, regardless of how pained you are and how abused you feel. Speaking negatively of your partner draws children into adult issues and can produce split loyalties. Do not force your children to take sides. It can only hurt them over time.

○ Never ask children to carry messages. Deliver your own information to your partner, no matter how upset you are. If you are afraid you will get out of control, learn to calm yourself and take responsibility for delivering your own messages. If you think you will resolve the situation by withdrawing and refusing to communicate, think again. Your withdrawal is a punishment to everyone involved, including yourself and your children. Become proactive and resolve the situation as quickly as possible by initiating contact, clearing the air, and working toward solutions. The way in which you conduct yourself during this difficult time will serve as a model for them.

○ Keep up family routines as much as possible. If you go out for Sunday brunch or church, continue to do so.

○ Avoid discussing these problems during family time; keep the conversation on noninflammatory topics when you are with the family.

○ Have discussions with your partner when the children are in bed or out with their friends.

If your children seem anxious, depressed, or are misbehaving more than usual, and their worrisome behavior is not relieved after a few discussions with you, consider outside help. Books are available to help children sort through difficult emotional problems. Look for them through the Internet, your local bookstore, or the library. Spend time reading these books with your child, and carefully answer questions that may arise, using the principles we have previously outlined for you. If that doesn't help, take the extra step of caring for your child by seeking professional help for them individually. Many communities have low-cost or free clinics for children. Schools often have a school psychologist or counselor who may be available. Children worry and do not have the maturity or cognitive skills to sort through their feelings and concerns.

If you are considering divorce and have concerns about it negatively influencing your children, look into the research about the long-term effects of divorce for children of families struggling with infidelity. You might want to start by looking into research by Judith Wallerstein, Ph.D., at the University of California–Berkeley. She has been reporting on this phenomenon since the early seventies. In her book, *Unexpected Legacy of Divorce*, she interviews adults who came from divorced families. Some of her interviewees experienced the repercussions of their parents' divorce even thirty years later. As can be expected, most children experience the greatest difficulty in the immediate years following the breakup. Dr. Wallerstein has also found when children of divorced families grow into adulthood, a significant number marry late or not at all.

Try to find other sources of information about the effects of divorce upon children. Many Internet websites are devoted to this topic. Discuss the information you may have gathered with your partner. Consider divorce only as a last resort when you and your spouse have carefully weighed all the options.

Parents
Your parents may also sense the tension in your relationship, and it is best to follow the same general principles we have outlined for use with your children. That is, maintain a level of privacy about the details of what has occurred and be respectful to all parties. It is often best to inform parents of a problem in the relationship, and that you are working on it.

Parents or other close family members are usually in distress if they learn of infidelity. Many do not know what cyber-infidelity is. They may feel quite helpless, yet want to help you. They may be upset and add fuel to the fire rather than try to help ease the situation. They realize that their off-spring is hurting, and fear that the marriage may be in trouble. Long-held fears and resentments may surface toward either of the marriage partners. Many parents worry about the effect on their grandchildren. Reactions can vary from minimal to overly controlling. Some parents may minimize the affair because it was on the Internet and there was no intercourse. Other parents are alarmed because it sounds bizarre. Their pain can rebound, and cause yet another stress for you.

As Cathy told us, "My mother can't understand. 'He talks every night to someone with a phony name, and he has sex with someone that isn't there? It's weird.'"

"But," Cathy added, "my father says, 'It's nothing. There's no real person. I shouldn't worry about it, but he should see a doctor.'"

Joe's father, with whom he shared his problem, said, "I knew those damn computers were going to be nothing but trouble. You better stop this stuff. You are hurting her. There's no telling where it will end."

Lester said, "I am mortified. I don't know how I can face my in-laws after all of this. They've always been so nice to me. They are furious. Now I dread the holidays."

Lester's wife told us, "I am angry too, but I am embarrassed in front of my family. My father joked about it to my brother, and the news spread to everyone else. Now they are all laughing. I could just cry when I think about it. We've become the butt of family jokes about cyber-sex. The worst part is that my parent's fortieth wedding anniversary is next month, and the event is planned for my house because we have a great backyard. I want to cancel, but just can't."

Parents have feelings and reactions that must be addressed. If they are ignored, they will be angry and resentful. If they are given too many facts, they can become overly involved. In some families, parents stop speaking to the offending partner. If there are children, they can overhear intergenerational discussions or jokes and feel caught in the middle.

You can involve parents early in the process by suggesting ways in which they can be supportive. What you might ask of them depends largely on your relationship and their ability to help. Some of the ways our clients have asked for support is by requesting babysitting, telling parents not to ask questions, not spread gossip to other family members, stop any gossip they do hear, and to be compassionate rather than hurt by your mood swings. Express appreciation for their concern.

The offending spouse can ease the situation with an apology, a brief acknowledgment of the pain, and a promise to change. Doing so helps the family heal. We have seen many individuals who cringe at the prospect, but who meet the challenge. We will say more about apologies when we discuss recovery.

Friends

Friends react in much the same way as family members, but may feel the freedom to discuss sexual aspects, which parents typically avoid. Friends may have heard more private and personal information from you over time, and can often be helpful in giving their perspective.

As Lou told us, "My friend Ralph tells me I can't really trust Lorraine. She's always been a flirt and now she just found a new way to do it."

Karen responded, "I needed to talk to someone, but I felt so ashamed—almost like Larry was doing something sick."

Some friends see no harm. As Mel wrote, "Hey, man, it's cool. I never knew you could do this stuff!"

Reactions from friends will depend on their own history and their own views of infidelity. Some will try to tell you what to do. Not all friends know how to remain objective and let you make your own decisions. For example, when close friends learn about the affair, they sometimes take sides or show hostile behavior to the unfaithful partner. Other friends will simply listen and not know what to say.

Caution and common sense should be used in making your decisions. It might be best to start by telling friends who do not know your partner, and with whom your partner will not need to meet socially in the future. An online support group might be a good solution. Try the Cyber-Affairs Discussion Forum at <http://www.selfhelpmagazine.com/phorum/list.php3?num=22>. However, a support group or a therapist may be the better choice.

Although the problems caused by cyber-infidelity are serious, they can be resolved and couples can find that their relationship can be strengthened and grow, despite their initial pain and distrust. However, at this point in time, many people make a hasty decision to leave the relationship because the pain is so intense that they want to emotionally cutoff. Such action, despite intense pain, means that the individual is operating at a low level of differentiation. This is a time when staying emotionally connected, thinking through the issues, and being self-defined and self-validated is needed to make important decisions about the relationship. In the next chapter, we will discuss in detail what couples need to know to make decisions about whether to stay or to go.

7

Decisions:
To Stay or to Go?

A couple, Janet and Eric, in an apartment building in Brooklyn Heights, New York are facing a serious relationship dilemma.

"I am sorry you had to find out this way, Eric," Janet says quietly.

"Janet, it's not the way I found out," Eric replies. "It's the fact that you're having a relationship with another man on the Internet."

"I never meant to hurt you, but you know it's hard for me."

"I know, I know. I'm trying to lose the weight. In a couple more months I'll have it under control. I want to be able to make love to you just as much as you want."

"It's already been so long, though. We're young, and sex is important. I guess I needed something to satisfy my needs. The computer was just there."

"Do you still love me?" Eric asks.

"Of course I do."

"I still love you too. I want to make this work, Janet. If I go to the gym every day, can you stay away from the computer?"

"OK, we can do this together."

Another couple, Cheryl and Danny, are walking along the beach in Miami Beach, Florida.

"Please, for the hundredth time," Cheryl insists, "I want you to give up your virtual lover."

"I won't," Danny replies, looking away from her angrily.

"Why? It's hurting me. It's hurting both of us. I can't concentrate at work. My boss has noticed."

"It's not hurting me, and it's not hurting you. You have everything you want. A big home. Fancy cars. Vacations. How does it hurt you?"

"I want you."

"You've got me."

"The hell I have. What if I say I would leave you?"

Danny pauses. "You'd be making a big mistake. But I could handle it."

"Well, handle it. I'm going to stay with my parents, whether I'm ashamed or not."

Making a Decision

Eric and Cheryl find themselves in a situation many others have experienced when a partner has been unfaithful. They are trying to cope with many emotions, the shock of betrayal, the inability to concentrate at work, the doubts about staying in the marriage, and the reactions of family. They are making different choices. Why does Eric stay in his situation while Cheryl leaves?

This decision is commonly referred to as the "stay or go" decision. Such a decision is a life-altering one, so careful thought must be given to it. Most often, the unfaithful spouse is the one who makes the decision to stay or to go. That is not always the case. When cyber-infidelity occurs in a committed relationship, both partners need to be knowledgeable about the decision-making process. This requires stepping back and examining all relevant issues. It is best to wait for the initial reaction to pass and think with a clear head.

Reality Check

People often make decisions without understanding their own motivations. Powerful needs such as to be loved, to love, and to experience sexual gratification can easily cloud thinking about one's actions. The next section is offered to help you check your motivations when thinking about infidelity on the Internet.

Technology cannot be held responsible for human decisions. If people make poor decisions with any tool, they need to develop a greater awareness of how to use it, or choose not to use it at all. As we have seen with cyber-infidelity, the unscrupulous can now further confuse themselves and their partners with vague promises of fidelity. They can claim that having cyber-sex with someone from Panama City is not prohibited by their marriage vows, or that they were simply experimenting with a long-repressed part of their personality. Some say they were only "playing a game" with the newest pornographic software.

The techno-savvy philanderer can now defend any variety of illicit cyber-actions by saying he or she was home, did not touch anyone, and did not expose the partner to the possibility of sexually transmitted disease. We obviously need conversations and clarification that take into account the broad range of thoughts and behaviors now possible through technology. Are these reasons, or excuses?

Separating reasons from excuses for cyber-sex and cyber-affairs can be difficult. If you are wondering how you distinguish reasons from excuses, give yourself this reality check:

○ Are you denying that this is an affair? "*Hey, it's nothing. I just met this person.*"

- Are you minimizing the way your partner would feel if he or she found out? "*She will get over it. It didn't mean anything.*"
- Are you rationalizing your cyber-sexual behavior? "*It really is helping our relationship.*"
- Is your behavior deceitful to yourself and to your partner? "*This makes me a better lover. It's bound to be helpful to the relationship.*"
- Are you justifying your behavior by not taking personal responsibility? "*It's human nature. I'm not a bad person. Everybody does it.*"

If you answered "yes" to any of these questions, and you have promised sexual exclusivity to your partner, then it is possible you are making excuses. A frank discussion with your partner will probably be needed to remove any doubt of self-deception.

If, indeed, you realize that you have been deceiving yourself as well as your partner, it is time to look for the reasons behind your excuses. If you look deep enough, with the information we provide in this chapter, you will most likely be able to identify some reasons. However, if you are like most people, you have not discussed specific thoughts and actions related to fidelity with your partner. The vague definitions used to define fidelity in the past have been problematic for many generations.

Nonetheless, when promises of fidelity are broken, the issues that are important to understand are the emotional connection of your partner to the other person, the best interests of you and your family, and the reasons for the infidelity.

Emotional Connection to the Virtual Lover

The wounded partner must understand the degree of emotional connection the partner has to the virtual lover. This is indicated by whether or not the partner is willing to stop the cyber-affair. If he or she is not willing to end the affair, it is painfully clear that the lovers have developed closeness.

When people have an affair, they start telling the new lover many secrets while they are being deceitful with their partner. Naturally, they feel closer to the new lover. In his book, *Private Lies*, family therapist Frank Pittman, M.D., described this dynamic. "The sharing of facts and feelings can be relatively free and uncensored with the lover, while the opposite is true with the spouse. No matter what the potential for intimacy in a marriage, it is impossible to feel close to a person one is hiding from, confusing, throwing off track, or deceiving."

The following conversation between Heather and Ted shows how Ted is giving up his virtual lover and including Heather in the process. His willingness to do so is the indication to Heather that there was not a closer connection with his virtual lover than with her.

"Honey, I'm so sorry," Ted tells Heather. "It's over, I promise. I'm never going to talk to her again. We've been through this a hundred times. What can I do to make you feel better?"

"How can I trust you after all this? You broke our marriage vows. You were unfaithful to me."

"Please, honey, try!"

"Are you kidding? Get real! I trusted you before. Look what it got me!"

"How can I make it better?" Ted asks. "What if I email her and end it?"

"Only if we do it together. That way I can know for sure that it is done, and done completely."

"OK, whatever it takes."

They sit down together at the computer. Ted composes a message.

> *I am writing to say good-bye. Heather knows about us, and we are working on our relationship. I am putting all my energy into this because I love her very much. I have apologized to Heather for hurting her and lying to her. I also want to apologize to you for this relationship on the Internet. It wasn't fair to anyone. I am changing my email address. Don't try to track me down. If you do, I won't respond. I will no longer be in the chat room. I am determined to strengthen my marriage to Heather. I wish you all the best. Ted.*

Heather adds:

> *I'm sitting here with Ted. I am angry about what happened, but Ted promised me it's over between you two. That's it! Heather.*

They click the Send button together. "Do you feel better now?" Ted asks.

"Yes, but not as good as I want to feel."

"What can I do?"

"You can start by telling me why you did this."

By giving up his virtual relationship, Ted helped Heather make the decision to stay in their relationship and work things out. Repairing the damage caused by cyber-infidelity begins with ending the cyber-affair and the behavior associated with it, including visiting chat rooms and maintaining of personal or sexual relations online. From that point on, there can be no further contact with the third party, or any dating sexual chat room members. Sending a general notice about ceasing all chat room and personal contact is part of ending the triangle, and demonstrates good intentions to the primary partner. Ted is acting responsibly by emailing the virtual lover to terminate the cyber-affair and explaining that he is working on his marriage. He is building trust by showing Heather the email and changing his email address. Once the virtual lover is out of the picture, Ted and Heather can begin to work on identifying the underlying causes of Ted's self-defeating behavior without distraction.

If the unfaithful partner cannot give up the lover, then the question must focus on why that partner feels the need for a marital triangle. These situations are complicated, and emotions can flare. If this is the case, we strongly suggest enlisting the help of a couples therapist. Couples counselors can uncover and resolve the reason for the partner's inability to give up a cyber-affair.

After determining the emotional connection your partner has to the virtual lover, you will want to think carefully about your life and decide what is in your best interests. This, of course, includes acknowledging your feelings, but separating your emotions from your thinking. In doing so, you can come to a rational decision about what is best for you and your family.

Your Best Interests
Many people criticize others for staying in a relationship when infidelity is an issue. That decision is personal and can be based on age, fear, religious beliefs, health, family concerns, or a number of other factors central to the relationship.

Thoughtful decisions are usually based on a combination of acknowledging and understanding one's feelings, looking at all of the facts in a calm manner, and coming to a conclusion that is personally appropriate. All factors must be carefully challenged and considered. Let us take a brief look at what others have told us about their decision making.

"I am fifty-six years old, and I have no career," Sophie said, "so I am staying. I found out when I was looking for our passports and I came across some pictures of a woman in sexy underwear in very provocative poses. They came through email. I saw the addresses at the top. She calls herself 'Sugar Lamb.' He's been corresponding with her, I guess. Look, I've got varicose veins and high blood pressure. I'm pitiful next to Sugar Lamb. What's more, I thought he was impotent. I can't leave. I can't make it on my own."

Sophie decided to stay. Is that the right decision for her? Maybe, but other things are obvious. She does not feel good about herself, she does not envision a happy future, and communication with her husband is poor. Sophie would probably be helped by seeing a professional to clarify her situation before she makes her decision.

Lyza, on the other hand, writes, "Well, he's never been much of a husband and now our golden years are more like—well, never mind. Over the years we both expressed disdain for marital affairs. Now he has changed the rules. He won't talk or go for help, and he really doesn't care about me. People think of sixty-years-old as ready for the old-age home, but it's not true. I've got more living to do. I have friends. I'm going to travel and continue my volunteer work. So we are separating."

Lyza, at the same age as Sophie, is making a decision to leave her marriage. We see from her message that the relationship has been a disappointment for many years. Sophie is staying because she is frightened. Lyza is also frightened, but she is not immobilized.

Each person's circumstance differs. Some of these beliefs may be true, some not, and some may be based on the types of stressors we will describe in this chapter. They might also be based on beliefs developed in childhood. They must all be challenged to see if they are true. This means thinking clearly, gathering information, and speaking with others.

Reasons for Cyber-Infidelity

We will share stories with you that show the reasons that some people have cyber-affairs, and then give you an exercise that may help you pinpoint your stressors and other motivators. You will notice, as you read, that human behavior is complex, and many causes and underlying dynamics can motivate a single action. There are many reasons for cyber-infidelity.

Expected Transitions

Life involves many transitions. Whether planned or not, transitions create new expectations, roles, and stress. Nancy Schlossberg, Ed.D., adult and developmental psychologist, defines a transition as, "an event or non-event resulting in a change of assumptions about oneself and the world." Sometimes, the anxiety concerning transitions is so high that it can stress a family system to the point that an individual tries to cope by having an affair. Affairs often occur during periods of transition such as a move, engagement, birth of a child, retirement, illness, or death of a loved one. An accumulation of stressors can produce a high degree of anxiety from which people seek to escape.

Darlene was in tears as she told her story to her therapist. She shook her head in disbelief as she began, "For the past eight months, I have been walking on clouds, planning my dream wedding with my fiancé, Ron. We've known each other for a few years. It wasn't love at first sight. In fact, he really pursued me. That's why I find it so hard to understand his recent behavior. He has started going to chat rooms and flirting with other women. I found out from a mutual friend who thought I ought to know this before we go any further with our relationship. When I confronted him with this information, he didn't deny it. In fact, he cried and begged my forgiveness. He said that he couldn't explain his behavior even though he was uncomfortable with it."

Ron joined Darlene in one of her therapy sessions. Together, they examined his behavior and decided he was anxious about marriage in general, but had no doubts about his love for Darlene. He wanted to marry her, but was anxious and was unable to explain his anxiety. His courage led them to premarital counseling. The counseling helped them both understand their expectations and make agreements with regard to the Internet and to fidelity.

Many transitions in life cause anxiety and make people vulnerable to affairs. People often underestimate the anxiety caused by change, and the ways in which they can turn to a tool as powerful and easily accessible as the Internet to soothe themselves in times of stress. People are often surprised to discover that expected and desired transitions can lead to stress, such as graduation, the birth of a child, or an eagerly anticipated move to another city. Another example might be a highly desired job promotion. All these events can cause performance anxiety and worries about associated responsibilities.

Mid-life is another vulnerable time for individuals and for marriages. Lila and Guy experienced a transition at mid-life. Lila wrote us about the role that cyber-infidelity played in their marriage.

"I supported Guy while he developed his office furniture company. I created a home for him as he flew around the country and negotiated high-level deals for his new enterprise. After many long absences to keep the company viable, I began resenting Guy's time away. He was finding success as a businessman, and it seemed that the only success I had was in getting the ants to stay out of the kitchen, and that was on a good day!

"So I bought myself one of those fancy computers and decided I'd take classes. The other women in the class told me about the women's websites, and I heard about dating chat rooms. Before long, I found several of these rooms, and visited them when Guy was out of town."

Lila wrote that she did not feel the connection she once shared with her husband. When she tried to tell him how dissatisfied she was with their life, he dismissed her feelings. Lila confided in several people on the Internet, including two men. Within a month, she was having a cyber-affair.

Lila was at a mid-life transition point, trying to find fulfillment in the second part of her life. She was "out of sync" with her husband, who had devoted much energy to his business. Lila tried to solve her situation with her cyber-affair. A mid-life crisis is not an individual issue, but an event that affects the entire family. Therefore, appropriate family support and involvement is needed. These are times when people reach out to others, and are more vulnerable to affairs.

Daniel was a person who had difficulty with a new set of assumptions about himself after retiring from his medical practice.

"I never thought I would be writing something so personal, but I am stunned by what happened to me. I'm not a young, computer-savvy type guy. In fact, I'm fifty-seven-years-old and a retired physician. It was not long before I realized I was not happy in my retirement. I missed my work, the camaraderie with my fellow physicians, and the structure of my day. I have never developed any hobbies, so I felt a profound sense of loneliness.

"At my wife's suggestion, I bought a computer. This brought many new ways to occupy my free time. I became well known in several dating chat rooms and before long, I was having regular cyber-sex dates with a woman named 'RedhotMama.' I felt exhilarated and desirable."

Daniel's twenty-eight-year-old son found his folder of particularly erotic email exchanges. Daniel was so embarrassed by this discovery that he sought psychotherapy. He reluctantly broke off his relationship with RedhotMama. After a few months of self-examination, he began to see that the kind of love available through the Internet was not what he needed. He turned his attention to his wife.

Many seniors are turning to the Internet and discovering a wonderful world of support and information. But do not let age fool you. Promises of monogamy and fidelity can be broken after many years of faithfulness, regardless of one's age, education, or social class.

Unexpected Transitions

Dr. Schlossberg describes other transitions that produce stress. She calls them "non-events," such as when the realization hits that a marriage will never be realized, or a baby will never be conceived. These are transitions because a new set of assumptions requires a life adjustment.

Such a transition happened to Beth and Larry. They were married for seventeen years and were in their late forties. They had tried for many years to conceive a child. After undergoing expensive and painful medical procedures, Beth and Larry had abandoned their hopes of having a child.

When Beth went to see her therapist, she needed help in mourning the loss of this dream. She had always wanted to be a mother. "It hasn't been easy," she said. "We've decided to just get on with things. We've had some wonderful vacations and we renovated an old home in the city. But I can't get used to the fact that I will never have a child. Renovating the home was a distraction. While we were doing it, I met someone online who was an expert in fixing up older homes. He lived in our city, and his name was Louis.

"We met over lunch and I was very attracted to him. I started to chat with him by email without telling Larry. Our cyber-friendship has developed into a cyber-affair, with all of the secrecy and deceit that makes me feel very guilty. I am here because I am thinking of getting a divorce. I want to get away from Larry and all that disappointment."

Although it may seem that Beth and Larry were not experiencing a transition, their circumstance was indeed a transition. This couple needed to turn toward one another in their time of mourning over their inability to conceive. Transitions that occur at an unexpected time also can cause anxiety, such as the husband who suffers a terminal illness at age forty-three, or the daughter who leaves home at age fourteen.

Loneliness

Looking at the events before an individual engages in cyber-infidelity may reveal times of intense loneliness. When a client, Amber, was asked to look at her life events before being tempted by cyber-infidelity, she could not think of anything significant. Further questioning uncovered her true motivation.

"I would go to the computer in the evening," Amber said. "I never intended to find anything more than support. I have a disability. My husband's company moves us every couple of years, and we've now moved six times. I don't have friends. I thought I'd find some online. I found Benny. He also is disabled, and retired. Our conversations online led to a cyber-sexual relationship, and to the decision to meet. I guess I'm really lonely."

As we see, Amber has to deal with a variety of stressors, many of which can lead to infidelity. The Internet simply makes infidelity easier. Amber's most significant stressor is the daily struggle with a disability. Dr. Nancy Schlossberg coined the phrase "chronic hassle" to describe special conditions, such as long-term illness, which drain energy. They often prevent families from engaging in many normal activities. Chronic hassles not only cause daily stress, but often cause guilt and worry. Partners may blame themselves or each other. The repeated needs for adjustment and new resources are part of the chronic hassle.

Despite Amber's disability, her husband continues to work at a job that keeps him away from home. She bears much of this stress alone. Most likely, Amber, like many others, has gradually slipped into an uncomfortable, but seemingly permanent arrangement. She does not seek ways to create a positive change that would improve her life as well as her relationship. Not only is Amber overburdened, but she is also lonely because her husband is away so much. Her husband's work requires that they move frequently which, of course, makes it difficult for Amber to develop friendships and support. Amber is aware that she is at a point where she might do something she would regret. She catches herself fantasizing about Benny and having cybersex with him. She recognizes that she is in the process of establishing an intimate relationship with someone she has met online. Amber is on the slippery slope that Dr. Shirley Glass describes, when a friendship can easily turn into an emotional affair and then into a love affair.

Unavailability

People can also become involved with others when a partner is home, but emotionally or physically unavailable. Andy told us of his affair. "It was an accident. I just slipped into it. Janet was very busy with her oil painting.

She likes to be alone and spends much of the weekend in her studio. She's very content in there, and hates it when I interrupt. So I've learned to do things and not even bother asking her to join me. After I got my computer for Hanukkah one year, I spent the rest of the holiday setting it up. I tried interesting her in some graphics programs, but she preferred to be alone in her studio, without me. I wanted to talk, so I found someone to talk to. Within a few months, Cecile and I were having weekly cyber-sex. I look forward to time with her much more than any time with Janet. Janet still doesn't know. I'm not sure she would even care. I've been able to arrange a work assignment in Denver for the summer, and I'm planning to meet Cecile that week. Why not? I've never been happier."

It sounds as thought Andy is unhappy in his marriage, because he cannot get his wife's attention. That might be because either he lacks relationship skills, Janet is emotionally unavailable, or both. At this point, it is obvious that something is amiss in their relationship. Identifying the source of the problem is impossible to determine, given the limited information we have. Janet could have a problem relating to people, and find comfort by being alone in her studio. On the other hand, Andy could have a problem or behavior that disturbs Janet so much that she withdraws. The best solution would be for Andy to discuss his unhappiness with Janet and seek a resolution. To ward off any further complications, he would do well to tell her of his Internet activities before this planned meeting with Cecile. People imagine a virtual lover to be a source of relief, but often this does not prove to be the case.

Andy's wife is emotionally unavailable to him, but there are times when a partner is physically unavailable due to separations caused by military service, employment, educational pursuits, or other such conditions. In the past, these conditions would often be cited as a reason for infidelity. Paradoxically, now with the Internet, couples can continue to be close even though they may be thousands of miles apart, by communicating online and by using this technology as a tool to maintain their sexual relationship.

However, physical unavailability becomes an issue when a partner suffers from a debilitating illness such as a stroke, neurological disease, confinement for mental illness, or coma. Often, people have affairs when a spouse is unavailable in this manner. For some, it is clear that "for better or worse" is the agreement, and for others the situation is the reverse, and still others are not sure. Usually, young people in the throes of love do not imagine such conditions, but such situations do occur and even to the young. Once again, a forthright discussion and understanding of expectations regarding infidelity is needed, so that future decisions can be made without breaking vows or promises.

Jerome, a thirty-three-year old gay man who was grieving the loss of his companion of eight years, told the following:

"When Bill and I decided to move in together, we talked about AIDS and what we would do if one of us became HIV positive. We decided to be monogamous even if one of us became ill. Shortly after that, Bill became HIV positive and he died a year after developing AIDS because he was not able to tolerate the medication. That I kept my promise of monogamy because during that time has given me some peace today. It is fortunate that we had the foresight to talk it over."

Communication

Poor communication skills often contribute to infidelity. Good communication provides a way for people to hear one another and to bring needs, misunderstandings, and problems to the surface so that they can be addressed. Individuals differ in their ability to communicate and resolve issues for many reasons. A primary reason is that many have never seen an effective model of communication in their family of origin, and so they continue to follow the pattern they learned from observing their parents' interactions. Some of these responses are anger, rage, violence, silence, or acceptance with resentment. These are indications of poor differentiation and may be correctable by learning communication skills. This legacy of ineffective communication inevitably creates conflict or emotional cut-off.

A second reason for ineffective communication may be due to gender differences. Women, in general, are more expressive and want to talk about their feelings. Of course, this may not be true if their expressions are met with anger or violence. Men, in general, prefer to discuss the content of a topic rather than the feeling, and move toward problem-solving. Women often need to have their feelings understood before moving toward a solution.

A third reason for ineffective communication may be due to issues at a deeper level. Effective communication may not be possible for poorly differentiated people, people with difficult personalities, or people with serious psychological problems. Good communication requires the use of "I" statements, honesty, self-validation, concern for the other person, and a willingness to work toward a solution. If a couple cannot find a way to solve their problems through communication, their relationship becomes or continues to be unstable. One way that people try to cope is by forming a "triangle," which diverts attention from, and temporarily stabilizes, the situation at hand. The third point of the triangle can be any number of behaviors, such as workaholism, use of drugs, excessive spending—or another lover.

Many people are not able to state their emotional needs effectively, and many partners are not able to demonstrate that they can listen and understand. Sadly, some partners simply do not care enough to listen or understand. "I've told him," Megan said, "that I am last on his priority list. He's there for everyone else, but he doesn't hear me. I guess I gave up trying to make him understand. So I found someone on the Internet who listens to me."

A partner cannot always meet the other's needs, and in fact, it is not always a partner's responsibility to do so. Some needs are reasonably met by the relationship itself, but others must be met by the individual. Howard explained, "When I think carefully about my relationship with James, I can trace some of the reasons for his dissatisfaction. I put him in a difficult situation, insisting that he take an active role in all of my interests. He later told me that I asked too much, demanding that he attend all my tennis matches and that he learn to play poker. I realized that my need to share every moment was unrealistic. Now James joins me when he wants, and I've learned to be OK with him having his own interests."

Boredom

Boredom can be complicated by other situations. The reasons that lead to cyber-infidelity often are not simple, but can be a combination of things— boredom, no excitement in life, problems at home, or dissatisfaction with the relationship.

Babs told us, "My teenage kids are busy with their activities. I am really bored. So I started playing around on the computer when I had some free time. It was a distraction. No one knew. It's fun, and I need fun. I am not serious. I pretend to be someone I'm not. There's no harm. If Anthony hadn't found out, I'd still be doing it."

In addition to having to cope with family situations, Babs is in need of "getting a life." Her therapy was centered on her own personal development. She began to explore activities that exhilarated her and brought interest into her life.

"I understand now," she later explained, "that my 'pretend games' on the Internet did hurt. My husband told me he felt inadequate, but since he began to realize how difficult things were for me and started helping me, we have actually grown closer."

Expectations

Clifford Sager, M.D., noted for his work on the *Marriage Contract and Couples Therapy*, said that when people form a relationship, certain expectations are present. Some are verbalized, others are unstated but understood, and still others are beyond consciousness.

Karen explained her cyber-infidelity. "At first, Beth took charge of our finances and it was a relief for me, because I made a mess of my own finances before we met. Over the years, I've noticed that she totally took charge of everything. I work too, but she plans our vacations and decides what we buy and what we do.

"I felt really awful, and so I got on a chat room for some advice. I hit it off with one woman who is a good listener. We ended up having cyber-sex. I loved the control it gave me. The more assertive I was, the more she got turned on. I found that whenever Karen planned our activities, I longed to be on the computer."

Karen had expected support with her poor financial abilities, and Beth delivered on that, but her planning abilities went too far and she became "controlling." Karen expected Beth to only organize some areas of her life that needed help. She didn't specify where Beth was to stop. People need to fully express their expectations before assuming their partner is uninterested or unwilling to comply.

Chronic Cheaters

Some have many online or offline affairs over a long period of time. They make little emotional connection with any of their many partners. They cannot appreciate how others are feeling. They are narcissistic and it may very well be that they have had a history of self-centeredness, which one may only notice after discovery of the affair. The problem lies within individuals who are unable to honor the vows they have made. However, people involved with chronic cheaters need to ask themselves why they become involved with someone who treats them so badly. Margo's story about her husband will illustrate this pattern of behavior.

I remember it well. It was midnight, about a year ago, when Terry came quietly into the house. I was waiting for him in the family room.

"Where have you been?" I asked.

"I told you. I have been working on an important project at the office." Terry replied.

"I called the office and you weren't there."

"Come on, Margo. There's no one on the switchboard at night."

"I called Security at 10:30. The guard said your door was locked. He opened it. The office was dark, and you were not there. He checked the entire floor. You just weren't there. You were out with some woman again, weren't you? When is this going to stop? Every year, it's a different one."

"I was at Hank's house," Terry answered, "working on the computer."

"We have a computer," I said. "You could work at home. For this you missed your son's honors award at school? You're up to your old tricks. You and Hank have been picking up women."

"No we weren't. We were working on an important computer project."

"More important than your son?"

"Come on, he'll get over it."

"Look, Terry, none of us will get over the damage your cheating causes."

"I don't owe you any explanation. But call Annie and she will tell you I was there with Hank."

So I called Annie, and she told me they were on the computer all night. Then the rest of the story made more sense. 'Margo,' Annie said, 'the guys were just fooling around on the computer. They visited a chat room. I know it sounds sick, but it's not like it used to be in the past. They don't actually meet anybody.'

Well, Annie was wrong. Terry got involved with Hank. He finally told me they've been having an affair for the past six months. He won't go to counseling. He says he's bisexual and wants to stay married to me. It's so confusing, I don't know what to do.

Margo has not been able to face some of the facts about Terry. She has endured his affairs for years, and naïvely agrees to stay with him despite this latest news. Terry is a chronic cheater because he has had a series of affairs and refuses to stop. It is important to note that bisexual people are not necessarily sexually compulsive. In fact, most bisexual people are not sexually compulsive, and are monogamous.

But in this case, Terry seems to be both. He shows no awareness or compassion for the impact of his behavior on his wife or son. His lack of remorse is indicative of a personality disorder, and he has little chance of changing if left to his own devices. Given Terry's sexual compulsivity, unwillingness to seek treatment, and lack of remorse for breaking his promise of fidelity, he is a poor choice for a marriage partner. Most importantly, Margo is personally at risk for sexually transmitted disease, whether Terry is having sex with men or women.

The future of relationships with chronic cheaters depends largely upon the reason the partner is unfaithful. From our observations, the prospects are poor with narcissistic or psychopathic individuals who show no remorse or feeling for the effect of infidelity on the partner. The prospects are better for sexually compulsive individuals if they can find help. There are times when such behavior may stop, usually because of public humiliation, a change in health, or altered financial or social status. Many must hit rock bottom to want to change.

A variation of the chronic cheater is the philanderer. Philanderers are individuals who take advantage of sexual opportunities when they arise. Such people usually are on the lookout for sexual opportunities. They were identified in Chapter One as the Seducers.

Regarding her husband seducing women in cyberspace, one reader, Cheri, angrily asks, "Why does he do it? Because he can. If the opportunity is there, he's a willing participant. He has decided he isn't hurting me, no one has to know, and he is just having the kind of fun I can't or won't give him. I'm furious."

Sexuality
There are people whose sex life is so disappointing that they reach out to others for sexual pleasure. Although limited to the virtual world, Internet sex can give some level of sexual satisfaction.

One client, Jerome, told us the following, "It was just easier to have cyber-sex with 'Karma Sutra' than with Rosie. KS would say—I mean, type—the whole little sex game I liked. She typed in things like—sexy laugh, with bedroom eyes, deep-breathing—to let me know how much fun she was having. She would do anything I asked, and with gusto! Rosie is suspicious now that I am not approaching her for sex anymore—she's asking more and more questions."

Some clients tell us that cyber-sex is improving their relationship. Actually, what may be happening is that one partner's interest is revitalized by the virtual lover. This is reflected in the attitude and behavior of unfaithful partner. The partner may be responding to renewed vigor and interest, but not aware of the source. However, the damage to the relationship may soon become apparent.

The same revitalization can come with a refocus on each other, accompanied by honesty and open mindedness. Sometimes, the mediation provided by a marriage counselor is needed, but often, these discussions can occur without a therapist. Long-lasting and satisfying results come from regular time spent on nurturing the relationship.

The Exit Affair

Some individuals plan to leave their marriage and search for someone to support them emotionally, and sometimes financially, during the exit phase. These are the people we describe as Dumpers in Chapter One. The Internet is a fertile meeting place for those looking to exit a marriage. While they may be experts at seduction, these people may not have the skills to maintain relationships over time. They most likely will be emotionally unavailable for the next partner, since he or she is probably a mechanism or excuse for exiting the primary relationship.

Some people break their promise of fidelity to exit a relationship, then bring their partner to therapy and leave it to the therapist to take care of their hurt and angry spouse. They may not see their promise of fidelity as applicable anymore, because they have already made the decision to leave their primary relationship.

Others use an affair to leave a relationship by provoking their partner into a predictable rage response. If a partner tends to be hostile when angry, it is then easier to justify leaving, to get away from the hostility. This is a particularly harmful way to leave a relationship because it is a setup for the faithful spouse to feel responsible. Provoking someone is a way to blur the lines of responsibility and hide the guilt of having broken the promise of fidelity.

Revenge

There are times when individuals have affairs for revenge. Usually, it is retaliation for the pain and humiliation of their partner's infidelity. The fact that the partner had an affair is an indication of a problem that needs to be addressed. Seeking an affair does not address the original hurt, and those that do so usually do not get the satisfaction that they expected.

Bill, a thirty-four-year-old accountant told us, "I found out she was having an affair on the Internet while I'm struggling to build a business for the two of us. I cannot explain the rage I felt at what she had done. I decided 'an eye for an eye' was a good payback. So I got into a chat room, cybered, and told Ellen about it. She was furious and somehow I didn't feel very good about it."

Cyber-Sexually Compulsive At-Risk Individuals

Another reason someone might become involved in an online affair is that they are "at-risk" to be cyber-sexually compulsive. To understand how this group of people can unexpectedly become involved in cyber-infidelity, let us look in on Carmen and Mac in their first session with their therapist as they try to explain their problem.

"It's hard for me to believe this has happened to us," Carmen begins. "I don't know where to begin. As I remember, it started when the dishwasher broke and I was looking for the warranty in our file cabinet. I hate to say this, but I came across a box of dirty pictures with dates printed on them over a two-year period."

"Dirty pictures?" the therapist asked.

"Well, that's what they looked like to me—computer photos of many women in provocative poses, only partially dressed.

"After finding this, I decided to look more carefully into our computer files. It seems that Mac left a trail of email messages that showed he had many sexual contacts on the Internet. These emails were full of sex talk and bringing each other to orgasm. I can't go on...Mac, you tell the rest."

"It's true," Mac confessed. "The pictures were sent to me on the computer from women I've been emailing. It's been horrible in our house since Carmen found out and I promised to stop, and I did for about a week. And then I kept thinking about it. I thought I would just go on to a chat room and be friendly, and not get involved. Yet before I knew it I was going private with women and doing the same thing as before. Every time I got off the computer, I felt like an old pervert. I tried to stop again. I knew it was wrong, but I couldn't stop. I can't believe that I got involved in this."

"Neither can I," Carmen said. "Mac is the last guy on Earth you would think this would happen to. He had always been a model father and husband. He does community work. But, I think he's developing a serious problem."

The behavior Mac and Carmen disclosed was completely out of character for Mac. As identified in the research led by Dr. Cooper, Mac is typical of a newly emerging "at-risk" group who are indulging in sexual behavior on the Internet. If not given the opportunity by the Internet, he probably would never have acted on his impulses.

Criminality

As mentioned in Chapter One, some people enter into affairs because they are criminals who prey on others for their own needs. They, of course, are not seeking an emotional connection, but they may be skillful at appearing compassionate and concerned, which is part of their deceitfulness.

Matilda, an eighteen-year-old student, said, "I am not usually a suspicious person, but my curiosity peaked about a man I had met online. I found him to be very charming and intelligent. He seemed very interested in me, and fascinated by my name, which is an old family name. He also was intrigued by the fact that I lived in Las Vegas. He is a gambler.

"I was worried about whether he was a compulsive gambler, yet he seemed very worldly and compassionate. When he wanted to meet me and wanted several photos of me, I decided to hire a private investigator who specialized in computers. I found out that he was married and had six kids. He had been arrested on child pornography charges, and served time in prison. He is still in the pornography business, only this time it's on the Internet. I feel sick at how close I came to being involved with such a person."

The pseudo-intimacy that developed quickly online can easily trick someone into believing the sincerity of the person with whom they have shared so much.

Considering the reason for cyber-infidelity in decision making gives some indication of the probability of success in recovery. Based on clinical observation, there is a good chance of successfully resolving infidelity when the reasons stem from transitions, communication difficulties, boredom, the unavailable partner, unfulfilled expectations, and sexuality issues. The exit affair usually has a poor outcome, because the exiting partner has already made a decision to leave. Those falling somewhere in the middle in terms of ability to reach resolution—the revenge, mid-life transition, and sexually compulsive affairs—can respond successfully if there is therapeutic intervention. The most difficult affairs to resolve involve the chronic cheater and the criminal.

In conclusion, uncovering the reasons for cyber-infidelity is usually a painful process for a couple. However, this process is best done when couples work together because both must understand the reasons for the affair. Assessing the reasons will often clarify whether the underlying relationship problems can be resolved. If this assessment is not completed and the partners make a decision to stay, they could continue to harbor feelings of anger or cyber-infidelity could reoccur.

If the decision is to go, both partners will be helped by gaining an understanding of the reasons for their conclusion. They will be able to use this information for their respective personal growth and to avoid repeating the same mistakes in future relationships.

Whether the decision is to stay or go, assessing the reasons for cyber-infidelity requires self-control, patience, understanding, and persistent effort. The next section will help with this assessment by outlining the common underlying dynamics that occur with couples experiencing cyber-infidelity.

Underlying Dynamics

Now that we have identified the three factors needed to make a stay-or-go decision about cyber-infidelity—the emotional connection to the virtual lover, your best interests, and the reasons for the affair—you may want to examine more closely the underlying dynamics of your relationship. When a couple deals with infidelity, there are two underlying areas to explore: current stressors and unconscious or conscious messages from the family of origin driving the behavior of one or both partners.

Current Stressors as an Underlying Dynamic

A good way to start the process of understanding the dynamics of cyber-infidelity is to review the life events and stressors of the year preceding the affair. In your review, you and your partner must carefully examine what happened personally to you as individuals and as a couple before the cyber-affair. Look for potential stressors in all spheres of your life—health, family, work, finances, and future:

- ❍ Have you or a loved one experienced a dramatic change in health, such as the onset of an illness or the need for a surgery?
- ❍ Has there been a death in the family?
- ❍ Have you been coping with a chronic hassle or a severe problem on a day-to-day basis?
- ❍ Have you had a baby? Have you given up on trying to have a baby?
- ❍ Were you experiencing unusual problems with children, parents, or other extended family members for whom you are a caregiver?
- ❍ Have you been coping with a serious illness in a child or parent?
- ❍ Have you been worrying about how to finance a big purchase, such as a new home, a child's education, or a new car?
- ❍ Have you experienced a serious financial setback, job changes (promotion or demotion), a move, or a perceived loss of status in business, religious, or community organizations?
- ❍ Are you suddenly facing a forced retirement or caring for elderly parents?
- ❍ Are you planning for a significant change in the near future?

Considering the stressors in your life is an important first part of looking at the breadth of factors that can lead to infidelity. Many couples are not aware of how stressful life had become. By carefully looking at these events and your reaction to them, you may understand part of your problem.

Looking over a span of years, ask yourself:

- Do you feel your spouse is emotionally or physically unavailable?
- Are you lonely in your relationship?
- Are you feeling badly about yourself?
- Are you hooked on cyber-sex?
- Have you repeatedly had affairs online and offline?
- Do you want out of your marriage?
- Are you bored with your relationship partner?
- Do you feel your partner expects too much of you?
- Are you willing to change?

When together, honestly answer these questions about your relationship:

- Do you believe your communication is effective?
- Do you feel a power struggle as a couple?
- Do you believe your lives are boring?
- Do you believe you are overworked?
- Over the years, have you felt satisfied in your sexual relationship?
- Do you communicate effectively when making love?
- Do you communicate effectively about making love?
- Do you make love, do you just have sex, or are you capable of both?
- Do believe you are capable of being intimate?

When alone, ask yourself these questions about your partner:

- Does my partner have emotional problems that complicate my life?
- Does my partner have poor self-esteem?
- Is my partner willing to change?

These questions are designed to help you find answers to the most often asked question by couples:

- Why did you do it?
- Why did I do it?
- How do I know this won't happen again?

If you take the time to answer these questions with the intent to understand rather than blame, you may find that solutions logically present themselves. For example, if you are bored with your partner, the first step to sharing this information constructively is to describe the actual behavior (something that can be seen or heard) that you would prefer.

Your request must be positive in nature, and avoid detailing the behavior you do not want. For example, your request could be, "I'd like more variety, more surprise, more initiative on your part."

Notice how easier this last statement is to hear than a statement such as, "I am bored with you. You always do the same thing, never surprise me, and always leave it up to me to introduce a new idea." The first request is rooted in dissatisfaction (boredom) but stated in terms of desired behavior change. It is more likely to get a positive response, accompanied by actual behavior change. The second request is also rooted in dissatisfaction, but is stated in terms of blame and criticism. It is likely to get an angry and defensive response, and is unlikely to prompt positive behavior change.

If your communication style is the latter rather than the former, you may need to take a class in communication skills building for couples. If you can read a book and follow instructions as a couple, there are several good self-help books available on this subject. If your attempts to be positive and make requests to alleviate the stressors contributing to cyber-infidelity go unheeded by your partner, or if cyber-infidelity has occurred multiple times, you may need the help of a good couples counselor or psychotherapist. Seeking to remedy your sources of relationship stress may also lead to an appreciation for the next step as well, that of understanding the influence your family of origin has had upon your current relationship skills.

Family of Origin Patterns as an Underlying Dynamic

The second part of your work as a couple is to look at your family of origin to understand the attitudes and values that have influenced you both positively and negatively. Many people would like to believe that their childhoods have nothing to do with their current life choices. Unfortunately, much research has proven this untrue. While there is variance with how early life experiences can influence adult choices, in most cases the effect of parental modeling as well as child-rearing practices is profound.

Most people are greatly influenced by childhood experiences. For better or for worse, they carry those influences into their adult relationships. Just as we speak English because we learned English from our environment, we relate to other human beings in the ways we observed and experienced relationships as children. Just as with language, we may be more sophisticated about our relationship as adults, but the basic patterns of relationships are learned in childhood and adolescence.

When partners take the time to examine the influence of their families of origin, they often find it explains their behavior and the choices they made. This process helps partners understand the other as well as themselves. People often are both surprised and relieved to see how many of their actions are rooted in attitudes, decisions, and behaviors that determined family interactions.

Reviewing the current stressors and the messages from family of origin is a way to gather information that you need to understand some of the reasons for the cyber-infidelity. The following examples are of two couples in which cyber-infidelity is causing a partner to make a stay-or-go decision. Let us look at the underlying dynamics of this process for each couple.

Stay-or-Go Couple No.1: Brandi and Tyrone

Tyrone and Brandi were asked about the stressors in their lives prior to the cyber-infidelity:

Brandi said, "I didn't cheat."

"But you were hardly home. I was alone so much," Tyrone replied.

"So the affair is my fault? I'm working late hours to get the down payment for our house."

"No, of course not. It's not your fault. I wish you didn't have to work. My job doesn't demand as many hours as yours, but it is stressful for me to watch how hard you need to work, and how many hours you need to put in."

"Well, we need the money. I want to have the house so we can start a family."

The therapist intervened. "It looks like the two of you feel badly about this situation. Brandi, you are working hard, and it's not what you really want to do. And, Tyrone, you are lonely and uncomfortable that Brandi is not available. And you are struggling financially as well. You both agree that this cyber-affair is regrettable and should not have happened. It looks like you need to focus on your goals, your finances, your schedules, and past influences on your life."

Brandi said, "When we looked at our backgrounds, I began to understand how we tick. Tyrone's father was a big flirt, but Tyrone was sure he never had an affair. He always lectured Tyrone about marriage vows and his religious beliefs. Tyrone's mother always looked the other way when he flirted and laughed it off. So it was never taken seriously.

"I was pretty involved with my work. I am very ambitious. I always knew I could count on Tyrone. Like his father, I knew how he felt about the sanctity of marriage. Well, after I discovered the Internet thing with Tyrone and his 'pen pal,' Tyrone told me that she was not a real woman, there was no real sex, and he never broke his vows. Just like his father, he followed the 'letter of the law' but not the 'spirit.' So the message he got from his family was that it was OK to flirt. He convinced himself that he was just flirting on the Internet, although he was spending lots of time with his pen pal, having cyber-sex with her, and keeping it all a secret from me. My message was to put blinders on and work really hard, just like my mother did.

"We now know what to do and that is to communicate with each other. Until we started doing that, neither of us was aware of how resentful we were of the little time we had together."

Tyrone agreed. "Brandi secretly blamed me for how hard she worked, and I blamed her for my loneliness."

"I don't think we will slip into this situation again," Brandi said.

Their therapist told them, "You have developed an understanding of one another, and in the process, more effective interpersonal skills."

Tyrone and Brandi now see how their current situations and past family messages are related. The late psychiatrist Alfred Adler coined the phrase "private logic" to describe the seemingly logical conclusions people come to based on their own private or personal experience. However, such logic dooms people to replicating the past and adopting self-defeating solutions to their problems. Infidelity is one such solution.

Stay-or-Go Couple No. 2: Marge and Kurt

In our second story, Marge is trying to make her stay-or-go decision on her own. She is having lunch with her friend, Claire. They are friends from high school, and Marge has been confiding in her about her agonizing over her decision to leave her husband, Kurt.

"I can't make up my mind about leaving Kurt," Marge tells Claire. "This is the third cyber-affair in four years."
"Well, it wouldn't take me long to figure out what to do," Claire replied.
"It's not a decision you make lightly," Marge answered.
"Neither is the one to cyber with someone for months. Three different women."
"I know, but..."
"But what?"
"He didn't have real sex. So maybe I'm overreacting."
"Is he stopping?"
"He promised before, but he broke his promise. I think he really likes this woman. He won't stop. I am afraid he is planning to meet her, because he is going to an annual conference he never attended before."
"Does he love her?"
"He won't say, but he tells me that he won't give her up."
"So what's going on?"
"I don't know."
"Do you fight?" Claire asked.
"No, he is very quiet. We don't argue, but then he just doesn't say much."
"Is he hooked on sex? What's the story?"
"I don't know. He won't go to counseling. He says if I don't like it, I can leave because it's not really sex."
"So, why don't you leave?"
"It's hard. The twins are starting high school. Maybe I should wait until they go to college. It would be better for them and me. I don't know what to think about all this."

Claire is helping Marge think through her decision. Marge cannot understand the reasons for Kurt's cyber-infidelity, but she is searching for possible reasons. Claire suspects Kurt may be sexually compulsive. We can see that Marge and Kurt have a problem with intimacy because he is having many cyber-affairs, and he shares very little with Marge. Kurt may be narcissistic, because he seems to disregard Marge's feeling. Marge does not know if he is engaging in cyber-infidelity as an exit strategy from their marriage, or if there are other reasons for his behavior. He presents her with a "take it or leave it" choice.

We see that Marge knows only a little about Kurt's closeness to his virtual lover. On one hand, he will not give her up, which we know is critical to resolving the affair. Kurt has had other cyber-affairs. Most likely, he cannot develop closeness or intimacy with anyone. He may be attracted to affairs on the Internet because they create a false sense of closeness, which is less threatening than true intimacy.

Since he is not willing to disclose his feelings about this person to Marge and refuses to go for counseling, Marge has little information about his closeness directly from him, only from her observations of him.

Marge is beginning to think that it is in her best interest to leave, because she sees that without Kurt's cooperation, they will not resolve the issues that led to cyber-infidelity. However, she realizes that the timing is not right for her or their children. Essentially, Marge has made her decision. She will leave, but on her own terms.

Looking at the three factors in making decisions about cyber-infidelity—what is in your best interests, the reason for the affair, and the connection to the virtual lover—will provide important information. From many of the stories, you were able to see how people made their stay-or-go decisions. Because this is such a crucial decision, it must be made according to individual circumstances. To help make a decision that is best for you, we suggest that after you gather the information you need, make a list that shows the case for staying and the case for going. This may help you clarify your thinking.

If You Have Strayed

If you have been the unfaithful partner, there are many different paths to help you proceed and recover. We will outline some of your options in the following sections. If you are undecided about whether to terminate your offline or online relationship, perhaps the following sections will provide an appreciation of the work involved in either choice. The tools previously described for your partner can also be helpful to you. You are likely to experience emotional reactivity and need to learn to calm yourself and proceed thoughtfully and rationally.

Returning to Your Committed Relationship

For some people, the decision to return to the committed relationship is a relief from deception and betrayal, but for others, it may be tainted with the feeling of loss of the virtual lover and the dreams that have begun to develop with that person. This feeling is normal, and while these feelings may not be reasonable to discuss in detail with an angry partner, you can acknowledge them for yourself and share them with a trusted person. If you are experiencing sadness over your decision to leave the virtual lover you were emotionally connected to and stay in your committed relationship, you must also be tolerant of the pain that your partner is feeling as he or she sees the depth of your feelings for the lover and he pain you feel at the loss.

Be cautious about relying on yourself to successfully navigate these waters alone. Many people prefer to simply forget the past and move on. It is more appropriate to understand the causes of cyber-infidelity–more specifically, the dynamics between you and your partner at the time of your infidelity. Reread the sections in this chapter related to the reasons for cyber-infidelity. In addition to struggling with issues of newfound passion, intimacy, past and current stressors, or perhaps even sexual compulsivity, you probably had not been communicating well with your primary partner. If you have not yet ended your relationship with your virtual lover, you are most likely comforting yourself in the fantasy life you have built with him or her, rather than getting the emotional satisfaction you need from your primary relationship.

Our best suggestion for you is to realize that cyber-infidelity is a symptom of a larger problem. Take the time to understand your contributions to your failed relationship before you head toward a fantasy you have built on the Internet. Returning to your committed relationship takes courage and emotional strength.

Find someone who can help guide you—a friend, a religious leader, a support group, or a therapist. If you cannot do so face-to-face, join an online support group for cyber-affairs. Closely examining a failed relationship can take from six to twelve months or more of regular psychotherapy. If you do it without professional help, it can take even longer.

As you can see, decision making involves information gathering and introspection. Decision making precedes recovery. Recovery is both an individual issue and a couple's issue. If the decision is to go, both individuals still need to recover from cyber-infidelity so that they can continue future relationships with inner strength and increased interpersonal skills.

Conclusion

Regardless of your decision, understanding the process of recovery is helpful to building a satisfying relationship in the future. The next two chapters about recovery will be helpful at this crossroad in your life.

Path to
Recovery

8

Beginning Steps to Recovery

In an upstairs bedroom in a gated community in Potomac, Maryland, seventeen-year-old twins Cindy and Andrew are on their father's computer, looking for the files of their college applications. They come across a file called "StudOne."

"What the hell is this?" Cindy asks Andrew.

"It's not mine. It must be Dad's. It's his computer."

"I'm opening it," Cindy says.

"Wait!"

"Too late. Ewwww, what is this?!"

"Oh, my God!" Andrew says. "This stuff is dirty!" They both start reading, and then look at each other in astonishment.

"I can't believe this,'" Cindy says with disgust. "I really hope Mom is GalaxyQueen, because if not, Dad's in big trouble." They read further and find that GalaxyQueen lives in another state.

"How could Dad write this stuff?" Andrew asks. "I bet he was whacking off with this woman when he wrote this!"

"This is really sickening. I'm turning the computer off. Sooo...what should we do?" Cindy asks.

"Well, I guess Dad doesn't love Mom anymore, but I'm not telling her."

"Fine, then I will—she needs to know, Andrew."

"Screw that, Cindy! Do you want Mom and Dad to get a divorce?"

"We've got to do something."

"Maybe we should call Aunt Maggie."

"Good idea. She'll know what to do."

After learning of the cyber-affair from the children, Aunt Maggie tells Steve and Nadja what she knows. Later, Steve and Nadja are talking in bed.

"I've been sick ever since we met with Maggie," Nadja tells Steve. "Your messing around is bad enough, but now the children are involved. I feel so alone, like I'm sinking into a black hole. I lie here at night beside you, but its like I don't even know you, and don't want to know you. You carried a secret that kept us apart. I'm really upset. You've put 'GalaxyQueen' between us."

"I've been a damned fool." Steve admits. "I can't believe what I've done. I am sorry. It didn't go on for long. She and I never even met."

"So what?! That's supposed to make it OK?! You were sexual with her, and told her about our problems. The two of you got really close. I saw your Instant Messages. I can't stop thinking of them. I feel like I'm going crazy."

"I'm very, very sorry."

"You may be," Nadja says, "but she still took something away from us. She took our intimacy and the special way we felt about each other. Maybe I was fooling myself all along. I don't even know what to think anymore.

"At the time, it didn't seem so serious," Steve tells her. "Now I know. I'm so sorry. What you and I had was wonderful. We can have it again. Please trust me again?"

"NO!"

"I love you—passionately. I know it's hard for you to believe that right now. You're the one who turns me on. I have been such a fool, honey. I've caused you so much pain, I wish I could turn back the clock and make it all right again. I'll never do it again."

"How do I know that?"

"I'll tell you everything I do. I promise."

"Everything you do?! I don't want you to do anything except with me. That's the point—that's what we promised each other when we got married. Now, you cheated on my with some bimbo called GalaxyQueen. GEEEEEZ! What a dirt bag. Now your promises are worthless."

"I deserve that. But you are the one I want to be with."

"I'm afraid of you now. I'll just get hurt again. I don't know who you are anymore. Sometimes I think I want a divorce."

"Oh c'mon. I'll make it up to you, and to the kids. Just tell me what you want me to do."

"Oh, like I'm supposed to know how to fix this? All I know is that I can't sleep. I haven't slept well since Maggie spoke to us. I'm worried about the kids."

"Honey, look, we've been married twenty-two years. We've been through a lot together. We'll get through this together.

"I don't want to be in bed with you."

Nadja gets up and goes into the guest bedroom. Steve turns over and stares at the ceiling.

Nadja's remarks to Steve give us a good picture of her emotional reactivity. When she says that she feels as though she is sinking into a black hole, she is essentially describing her depression. Such a description speaks of hopelessness, despair, and powerlessness. She also talks about feeling as though she is going "crazy" because she cannot stop thinking about her husband's cyber-infidelity. She is referring to the intrusion of thoughts that normally follow a trauma. When she talks of the distance between them, she describes the feelings of separateness she feels from Steve. Her concerns include fears of not being able to trust or regain intimacy, and she worries about the effect of their marital struggles on their children. Nadja speaks of her anger and her desire at times to leave him. This means she is considering an emotional cut-off and, in fact, acts out those feelings when she leaves their bed to sleep in the guest bedroom.

The path to recovery has four basic steps. Although these steps are presented in logical order, people and their relationships are complex. Couples often find themselves quickly moving from one step to another, and back again. Overall, you can regard any involvement with these steps as movement that takes you from cyber-infidelity to recovery:

1. **Coping with Emotions.** The first step in the process is learning to cope with the emotional aftermath of the cyber-affair, by strategies that will help you deal with emotions such as depression, anger, and anxiety.
2. **Searching for Understanding.** Couples cannot get to this most critical step until they are able to reduce their emotional reactivity and thus think more clearly. The second step involves improving communication skills, finding the reasons for the affair, looking at stresses and family history, and reaching an understanding about the infidelity.
3. **Reconstructing the Relationship.** At this step, the couple can build the type of relationship they need. The emphasis is on correcting the cause or causes of infidelity, looking at history, identifying individual needs, renewing their promise of fidelity, finding caring ways to relate to each other, and learning skills that bring them closer together and allow them ways to trust again.
4. **Finding Closure.** The last step puts closure on the cyber-affair through an apology, symbols that signify the end, and an agreement for the future of the relationship.

Infidelity is a challenge to overcome because of the strong response to betrayal, and the length of time it takes to reach full recovery. When dealing with infidelity, it is most helpful to work with a therapist who is impartial and who views the relationship as the "client." Because many couples, for whatever reason, are not able to see a therapist, we have developed the next two chapters to demonstrate the complete process of recovery as experienced by two different couples. The chapters are provided to help you find validation for your reactions to infidelity on the Internet. They are also designed to help you understand the strategies that can most often lead you to recovery from infidelity, whether on the Internet or in real life.

While both chapters will take you through the complete recovery process, Chapter Eight will emphasize the first two steps: Coping with Emotions and Searching for Understanding. Chapter Nine will emphasize the last two steps: Reconstructing the Relationship and Finding Closure.

Coping with Emotions

Many of the skills we have discussed earlier in this book will be needed at this point. As Dr. David Schnarch suggests, learning to tolerate your own anxiety, avoiding your partner's anxiety, and remaining connected to one another is the path back to true intimacy and love.

As Nadja's anxiety decreases, she will be able to think more clearly and logically about why she and Steve are dealing with infidelity after years of a stable and satisfying marriage. It is important to understand that through this process, she undoubtedly will continue to feel hurt, betrayed, sad, and concerned about trust and intimacy. This does not mean that she is not making progress. It will take time for Nadja to manage her own anxiety, but when she does, she will be able to look more objectively at the situation so that she can understand the reasons for Steve's infidelity and work on the recovery.

For relationships to recover from infidelity, both partners must recognize their own family history and current stressors that contribute to the difficulties in the relationship. They must find a way to stay emotionally connected to each other. As each partner manages his or her own anxiety and reduces emotional reactivity, the wall that was built by secrecy, deceit, and betrayal will slowly disappear. Effective communication will remove the wall so that information can be shared and intimacy restored. Obviously, this can require months and often years of consistent effort.

Let us begin looking at this process of recovery with Nadja and Steve in more detail. Two weeks after Nadja and Steve had their bedtime talk, they began psychotherapy, having been referred by Maggie. With this appointment, Steve and Nadja are taking the first step toward recovery. Steve has given up his cyber-lover and is recommitting to his relationship with Nadja.

However, Nadja suspects that Steve has developed a strong emotional closeness with his cyber-lover. She has pulled away to protect herself from that pain, and has expressed confusion about the issues, their future, and whether she wants to stay. In her first session, Nadja talks about a "wall" that has come between them.

Making Sense of Reactivity

Psychologists Shirley Glass, Ph.D., and Tom Wright, Ph.D., compare an affair to a wall that separates relationship partners from one another. On one side of the wall is the faithful spouse; on the other side are the partner and the cyber-lover. This wall prevents the primary couple from sharing intimacies; which are instead shared between the unfaithful partner and the new lover.

Steve has not only created a wall between himself and his wife, but also between himself and his children, Cindy and Andrew. In fact, they are also aware of the wall that Steve has created between himself and their mother, and are reluctant to speak to their mother about their discovery. Instead, they chose to speak to their Aunt Maggie.

As we have discussed throughout this book, cyber-lovers are free from the intrusions of everyday life, so they see each other through rose-colored glasses. Facing challenges such as an overflowing toilet, sick children, and late mortgage payment are not part of their romance. Instead, they experience each other with promise and excitement. Each time the cyber-lovers connect deeply, the wall between the faithful and unfaithful partners grows.

Infidelity on the Internet can foster feelings of distance from one's partner, as feelings of pseudo-intimacy are intensified toward the new lover. It is easy to fool oneself into believing that the problem is with the committed relationship, and happiness can be found with the more understanding, caring, and exciting virtual lover.

People also erroneously convince themselves that an affair is a sign that they have fallen out of love with their partner. When this happens, the twin concept of trust and intimacy for the committed couple is lost, and must be recovered. At this point, Nadja is reacting to the loss of intimacy and trust. As she lowers her anxiety, she will be able to focus less on these questions and move toward an understanding of the cyber-affair.

The first step toward the goal of recovery is to reduce emotional reactivity. At times, Nadia wants to leave Steve because of the intense pain she is experiencing. This would be an emotional cutoff, and would not free her from her pain. When Steve gives up the cyber-lover, maintains honesty with his wife, and shares intimacies with her, Nadja will no longer feel walled off. Nadja is experiencing many losses and accompanying anxiety. She is also depressed, just as others have whose lives have been touched by infidelity.

Harriet Lerner, Ph.D., marriage and family therapist, writes in *The Dance of Deception*, "After the secret is revealed, relationship issues may still be obscured because so much emotional focus is on the breach of trust that it is difficult for each partner to examine her or his part in the marital distance that predated the affair."

As we can see, Nadja is exhibiting the emotions typically felt by one whose partner has betrayed them by breaking vows of fidelity. Nadja and Steve's first step to recovery must begin with helping Nadja manage her obsessive thinking.

Coping with the Obsessive Review

As Nadja described, it, she cannot stop thinking about the file found by her teenagers. She feels as if these thoughts are driving her "crazy." Most faithful partners have the experience of repeatedly thinking about the facts revealed by discovering infidelity. Betrayal of a sacred promise predictably leads to constant thinking about events that might have been red flags, peak times of harmony, and times of distress and anxiety. Events related to the infidelity are repeatedly examined and compared with memories of surrounding events. After discovery of any affair, it is normal to have thoughts about sexuality, the meaning of the affair, and the future of the relationship. Faithful partners often become obsessed with how they might have missed any clues, and whether the affair is continuing.

In his book, *Marital Separation,* psychiatrist Robert Weiss, M.D., calls such a process an "obsessive review." These types of thoughts, as they relate to cyber-infidelity, often include:

- Why did this happen?
- Is that what (s)he was doing the night I was out with my friends?
- Does he/she still love me?
- Does he/she love this other person?
- What does this mean for our relationship?
- The holidays are coming, what will we do?
- This is the worst thing that could ever happen.
- Our marriage is ending.
- I'll never be able to trust him/her again.
- I don't know if I should stay or go.

These repetitive thoughts are the mind's natural way to try to manage a sudden increase in anxiety. Thoughts become automatic and incessant in an effort to gain an understanding. Obsessive review occurs at times of trauma or great distress. It occurs not only with cases of infidelity, but with other traumatic events as well. To illustrate, think back to the tragic and untimely death of Princess Diana, or even further back to the assassination of President John F. Kennedy. You may remember how many people obsessively reviewed the same media coverage. With such events, people often collect newspaper clippings and compare stories for details they might have missed. Therapists are aware of this repetitive need by some clients to review the events of the infidelity.

While obsessing to control anxiety may seem normal to psychotherapists, it is highly distressing to faithful partners who have been subject to deceit and betrayal. They not only must deal with feelings of surprise and anxiety, but they are also frightened that they cannot control their thinking.

Emily Brown, L.C.S.W., author of *Patterns of Infidelity and Their Treatment,* considers the obsession to be a difficult aspect of resolving the infidelity because it interferes with understanding the reason for the affair, and prevents the couple from working on underlying issues. She has identified some common obsessive themes, such as rage, jealousy, abandonment, victimization, rejection, and powerlessness. Unfaithful partners can also experience obsessive review, but it is more often seen in faithful partners.

Early in her psychotherapy sessions, Nadja reported, "On the more difficult days, I feel like I am going crazy. All I do is go over and over what I know about this affair. I picture him on that keyboard in our bedroom, and me not knowing anything about it, working on our checkbook in the other room. Every time I think of him telling her how hard his erection is, I get furious. Sometimes, I just can't stop thinking about it. Then, when he comes home, I just want to scratch his eyes out!"

In therapy sessions, Nadja was assured that she was not "going crazy," and that the review is how we eventually come to terms with distressing events. Gradually the review diminishes in intensity and frequency. "I am relieved to know that," Nadja replied.

Nadja was told to accept the review as part of recovery, and to practice obsession-management and anxiety-management techniques.

How to Stop Obsessing

The relaxation skills described in Chapter Six can be very helpful to lower overall levels of anxiety. For maximum benefit, slow, rhythmical breathing can be practiced four times a day for four minutes to the count of four.

Another technique to manage obsessive thinking is to schedule a review time every day. The goal is to confine your review to a specific period so it will not be intruding upon your thoughts throughout the day. The technique is not for everyone, especially not for people who are suffering from a mental illness. However, if this is not an issue, the following steps will help you gain some control over the review:

- ◉ Pick a time that you will not be disturbed. For example, you may decide that 7:00 P.M. will be your time to obsess.
- ◉ Sit alone and let your mind explore all the details. Look at all the angles and consider all the possibilities. Let yourself cry, be angry, or have any other feeling that accompanies your obsessing. This is your time to devote to thinking and reexperiencing your side of the cyber-infidelity.
- ◉ Once your scheduled review time is complete, you may be tired or feel emotionally drained. Call a friend, send an email to someone you love, or read a soothing book. Whatever your activity, make sure that it will engage your mind and not let it wander back to the obsession. If you find yourself thinking about it again, remind yourself that you have done all your obsessing about the affair for that day.
- ◉ Stick to the schedule. Keeping yourself on schedule will minimize the tendency to be plagued by intruding thoughts throughout the remainder of your day. Some people find it helpful to say something such as this to themselves when the obsession returns at unscheduled times: "Stop! I won't let myself dwell on the affair when I need to be doing other things. I've scheduled an appointment for 7:00 P.M., and that's when I'll deal with this."
- ◉ Limit review time to an hour or less per day.

Decrease the schedule as your need to review lessens. You can do this by shortening the time each day and by skipping sessions. Nadja reported back the following in one of her therapy sessions, "It was not so easy to do this review when I first started thinking about all of this, but I stuck with it and eventually it started working. It is helping, because I think less of it during off times."

Unrelenting thoughts about a partner's cyber-infidelity will diminish in their frequency and duration as time goes by. Eventually, people come to terms with such a transforming event, make it part of their personal history, and the obsession stops. People report that as they move toward understanding why the cyber-infidelity occurred, they do not need the review time as they did before.

There are other creative ways to consciously take control of your thoughts. Wear a rubber band on your wrist and snap it when you feel yourself reviewing. The pinch of the rubber band will serve as a signal to stop. A second thought-stopping skill is picturing a big, red stop sign in your mind when your thoughts are veering in that direction. Nadja told us of another way she handled it, "Every time I start to think of Steve at the computer, I just pop a mint into my mouth and tell myself to chill out. Sometimes I say, 'Get out of my mind.'"

Like Nadja, you may be able to think of a creative thought-stopping skill that can help you.

Writing the Love Letter

The obsessive review is not only disturbing to the faithful partner, but causes a great deal of concern to the straying partner who feels very remorseful. One of the strategies that clients have found helpful is that of the love letter.

Steve was asked to write a thoughtful letter that expresses his feelings of love for Nadja, how important she is to him, and all the things he cherished about her. Nadja was asked to read, then put away his letter. When her obsessive review seemed out of control, she was to take it out and read it carefully, to help bring back his loving thoughts. Nadja and Steve shared their experience with the love letter.

Steve said, "I'm really not the kind of guy to write a love letter, but I found that once I got into it, I was on a roll. Some very important stuff came to the surface and I poured out my love for Nadja. I was even moved by the depth of my own feelings!"

Nadja said, "One day things just weren't working right, and the obsession came back, stronger than ever. I began thinking about that computer and what he had done, and how it upset the kids, and my feelings got all twisted again—and then, I suddenly remembered the letter. I took it out and read it, and it calmed me down."

Steve added, "It helped me with my feelings of guilt and it made me feel more able to help Nadja. You know, I work in Washington, D.C., a power city, and yet at home I feel so powerless to help Nadja. Writing this love letter gave me a way to help her get rid of those thoughts that keep plaguing her. I think it is important that we both focus on what is happening between us in reality, not what happened in that fake Internet world.

"I now understand that where I went wrong was hiding my need for comfort from my family, finding it with some other woman online, and lying about it in the real world. That shook my whole family's trust in me, and how I fooled myself into thinking it was nothing, that my actions had no repercussions. I got a bit long-winded about it, but I really wanted to make sure to mention some of that in my love letter, just in case she thinks I don't know what I did wrong. If there's one thing I learned in therapy, it is that when she feels like I understand what I put her through, she can relax a bit."

Other clients have put their creativity to work in variations of the love letter. One woman, rather than write a love letter, wrote her husband a Personal Bill of Rights after her cyber-infidelity affair. Another man, who was an artist, designed and painted a valentine for his wife, which he called "Valentine's Day Is Every Day," and on this, he wrote his feelings of love for her.

Essentially, the love letter is tangible evidence of love and understanding that can be referred to at any time of stress. It is an excellent self-soothing technique for both the faithful and unfaithful parties.

Challenging Distorted Thinking

Self-talk is the thinking that occurs to you as you go about your daily activities. When things are calm, you might be thinking, "I need to bring Jenny to school, then stop and buy those notebooks for the office today." When you are a bit more anxious about infidelity, it might sound more like, "I feel and look terrible today. I wonder if Steve will think about GalaxyQueen when he sees me." Such thoughts can give rise to an entire sequence of other thoughts that are not based on fact. Drawing premature conclusions and making early decisions can be self-defeating and alarming, and will most likely raise your level of anxiety.

Once these negative thoughts enter your mind, you will need strategies for extinguishing rather than fueling them. Once again, the slow, rhythmical breathing techniques are always a good place to start. Nadja was taught a few other helpful techniques.

In one of her therapy sessions, Nadja said, "I began to feel better when I stopped telling myself that I needed to divorce Steve. Sure, I was furious for a few weeks, not talking to him and being cold, sleeping apart and slamming doors. But I realized I was frightening myself with my own thinking. The fact is that Steve was staying in the house, with me. In his own way, he was insisting that he wanted to work things out—with me. GalaxyQueen was thousands of miles away. Those were the facts, and I forced myself to stick with them, rather than letting my mind run amuck.

"When I finally got a grip, I began to wonder if he was trying to tell me something is wrong, but was too frightened to say it directly. Suppose he told me, 'Yes, I want to end the marriage.' But then I reminded myself he was staying in the marriage, that maybe something was wrong and he couldn't say it.

"The more I reasoned things out, the better I began to feel. The facts told me that he wasn't rejecting me—he was running away from himself. I decided I'm not going to scare myself anymore. We're going to talk about this like two adults. He owes it to me, and I owe it to myself."

Nadja had to *work* at stopping her self-defeating thoughts. She forced herself to think of other possibilities, despite her anxiety. Some of the new thoughts she told herself were:

- "Steve is here with me, in the house. That other woman is thousands of miles away."
- "Maybe this is Steve's way of calling for help."
- "I'm not going to scare myself anymore. We're going to talk about this like two adults. He owes it to me, and I owe it to myself."

Other self-reassuring and calming thoughts could be:

- "Even though I am hurting, I need to remain calm."
- "More important than the details of the affair, I need to know why it happened."
- "This is not the end of the world."

Nadja realized that focusing her thoughts and preventing her emotions from ruling her behavior would be more helpful than losing her temper with Steve. She remained in control of herself and the situation. She said, "I practiced a few breathing and relaxation exercises for a few minutes before I approached him, but we had our talk and I was able to remain calm. I felt very proud of myself after that. Understanding how our thinking influences our behavior has been very helpful to me. I was rational and reasonable."

It is important not to go to the opposite extreme. Some people choose not to say anything. This is an emotional cutoff, and is damaging to relationships. That approach is not constructive. It is best to find a way to talk about it, but retain your composure.

David Burns, M.D., in his book, *Feeling Good*, says that self-defeating beliefs and thoughts fall into predictable categories. Some of them are all-or-nothing thinking, overgeneralizing, labeling, catastrophizing, mind reading, fortune telling, minimizing, personalizing, and negative filter. Another common type of negative thinking is called emotional reasoning. This means that you draw conclusions from the way you feel rather than from the facts. These self-defeating beliefs are called "cognitive distortions." When used excessively, they lead to anxiety and depression. To help relieve anxiety and depression, these beliefs can be challenged and replaced with truths. Here are some examples of distorted beliefs that could have fostered Nadja's obsessive thinking, and how she stopped them with factual thinking:

1. *"Now that Steve has cheated, our marriage will always be in danger."* This is generalization. Using absolute words such as "always" and "never" are tip-offs, and often indicators of overgeneralization. A better approach would be: *"He has made a big mistake in using the Internet in this way. It jeopardized our marriage, but it does not mean that we can't learn from this and move on."*

2. *"Steve's a womanizer. I guess I can never trust him."* This is labeling and fortune telling. A better approach would be: *"I am labeling him. We will have to talk about the behavior that disturbs me. I am fortune telling when I say 'never' trust him. I trust him in lots of ways, and I am sure I can trust him again if he gives me reason to do so."*

3. *"If I can't trust Steve with a computer, then I can't trust him anywhere."* This statement is an all-or-nothing statement. A better approach would be: *"For twenty-two years of marriage, Steve has been faithful to me. We will have to talk about how I can learn to trust him with computers again."*

4. *"It must be me. I'm just too boring."* This statement labels and personalizes. A better approach would be: *"I'm a good person, and I am not boring. If Steve wants something new and different, he can learn to ask me for what he wants. If I am making it difficult for him to ask, then I want to learn how I'm doing that so that I can stop."*

5. *"I feel responsible for Steve's cyber-affair."* This is an example of accepting responsibility for a behavior that is not one's own. It is called emotional reasoning because it is based on the way your feel, not on the facts. A better approach would be: *"I'm not responsible for his actions. I am only responsible for my behavior. Steve made the choice."*

6. *"Steve thinks that I'm ridiculous for carrying on about this. His mother hasn't visited lately. I guess she must know."* This is mind reading. You cannot be sure of another person's thoughts unless they tell you. A better approach would be: *"I really don't know what his mother is thinking, but I am justified in feeling upset about this cyber-infidelity. We took our wedding vows and Steve promised he would be faithful to me. My feelings are appropriate to what has happened."*

Challenging dysfunctional beliefs and replacing them with facts can help you control obsessive thinking, tolerate anxiety, and thus reduce emotional reactivity. You will see a reduction in the strong reactions, such as anger, depression, shame, diminished self-esteem, and guilt, that accompany the discovery of cyber-infidelity. Keeping track of your strong emotions and what you are thinking at that time can help you change your distorted thinking.

Nadja and Steve were both asked to keep a log for when they felt a negative emotion, and at that moment jot down what they were thinking. When they had time to review it carefully, they were asked to see if they were using any type of distorted thinking. If so, they were asked to challenge that distortion.

Steve said, "We were in the video store, looking at what we wanted to rent, and I picked up *Fatal Attraction*. Suddenly, I felt bad. I thought of the pain I caused Nadja and I said that I was a real S.O.B. and deserved whatever I got.

"Then I challenged my thinking, like you told me, and realized that I was labeling myself. I changed my thinking, and said 'I made a big mistake, but I deserve another chance to make it up to Nadja and the kids.' This helped me a lot."

Nadja said, "I also saw that video and my heart sank. I thought he's just like Michael Douglas in that movie and I'll never be able to trust him. But I challenged that thought and said 'No, I'm overgeneralizing.'"

When your thinking is not distorted by faulty beliefs, and distortions are replaced with facts, recovery is near. Separating emotions from thinking reduces anxiety and depression. When Steve and Nadja learned to recognize their distorted thinking, their communication improved.

Relieving Anger

Anger is much like fuel, in that sometimes it can be burned. Anger is a form of energy, and physical activity temporarily relieves the edge. As much as possible, engage in vigorous physical activity on a regular basis—run, swim, walk, or bike.

Nadja reacted to this suggestion with great enthusiasm. "Of course, I love to swim and I stopped doing it a few years ago. The weather is so bad here it just seems easier not to bundle up and go to the pool. But we do belong to an indoor swim club and I could go there." Nadja reported that she found swimming to be invigorating, and she would continue.

When Steve was asked about exercise, he said that his work kept him so busy that he did not know when he could exercise. As part of his therapy, he was asked to find a solution to his unmet need for exercise. Steve now has an exercise bike to use before dinner, which Nadja also uses when she does not want to go to the pool.

Other people find relief by punching a pillow until they are exhausted. Some boxing buffs dig out their punching bags. Sometimes these techniques backfire, and emotional reactivity only increases. Gauge yourself, and as with any of these suggestions, if they do not help put them aside and try something else.

Journaling

Some people find journal writing to be a safe way to find words to express their feelings. Once on paper, obsessive thoughts often can be viewed more objectively, and their grip can be thereby loosened. Writing is a way to let go. Journal entries also give needed evidence of progress over time.

Reactions to this technique also differ, however. Some people report that writing increases their emotional reactivity. Try it and see if you benefit. If journaling intensifies rather than dissipates your negative emotions, put it aside and try something else.

Writing an *unmailed* letter is a technique similar to journal writing. You write a letter to the person with whom you are angry. Since this letter will be for your eyes only, you need not worry about style, grammar, or spelling. Although you might be tempted to mail such a letter, do not mail it. Burn or trash it. Both writing and destroying such expressions of negative emotion often brings added relief.

Nurturing Yourself

It is important to maintain self-nurturing behavior throughout life, not just at times of crisis. Taking care of yourself means making time for you, your pleasures, and your preferences. It also means eating well, exercising, treating yourself to something special every day, and keeping contact with people who know and love you. The experience of recovery from cyber-infidelity is a bumpy road. There will be bad days and good days, but every day should have something positive in it for you, whether it is a pleasant walk, a lunch with friends, watching a movie, or reading a book. The choice is an individual one, but you must plan and create your own pleasurable activity.

When asked about her progress on this, Nadja replied, "One of the things that made me feel better was to actually schedule in my calendar specific times to walk, go to a movie alone, and visit the bookstore that has big, comfy chairs and a coffee bar."

Finding the time for solitary relaxation or meditation is also useful for managing negative feelings. The deep-breathing and progressive muscle relaxation previously discussed to reduce emotional reactivity can be continued every day in a modified way. Take a few minutes to relax, and replace the mental rehearsal with an image of yourself in peaceful surroundings, such as a garden, beach, floating in a pool, or whatever scene brings you serenity.

Active Solitude, Social Action, and Distraction Revisited
Other ways of helping yourself include distracting yourself with a change in activities, such as renting a video, looking at a magazine, or following a weekly TV show. Try reading a book or working on a new project. Freshen an old bookcase with a new coat of stain, plant new seeds in your garden, or begin taking piano lessons. Participating in sports, calling friends, writing a letter, or visiting a loved one can help. Despite the immediate feeling of relief, the following acts do not help:

- Drinking
- Using drugs
- Overeating
- Overspending
- Gambling
- Compulsively seeking sex
- Driving in a rage
- Engaging in acts of revenge

You may recognize some of the above as the negative reactions to loneliness. They are called sad passivity. In Chapter Two, we outlined some of the work of psychologists Carin Rubenstein and Philip Shaver on loneliness. Their suggestions for combating loneliness are relevant at this juncture. Infidelity causes the faithful partner to feel a deep sense of emotional loneliness. Therefore, the suggestions in Chapter Two are presented once again at this point. They fall under the categories of active solitude, social action, and distraction. Rereading the section on loneliness at this time may be helpful.

Remembering Your Resourcefulness
At times of stress, it helps to look back at other difficult times in your life and remember the activities that brought you serenity. Go to a ball game, sail, or write letters. Contact old friends. Prayer and meditation help many people. Support and therapy groups are often an enormous aid. Plan a future activity to give yourself something positive to anticipate.

Steve joined a support group for people who had cyber-affairs. He reported, "I started going to this group, and it was really weird. I mean, all these people had been having affairs on the Internet, and here we were, sitting in a real room, with a real therapist. It made me realize that I was living in a fantasy world, but it had real-life repercussions."

Nadja also extended her activities. She decided to go to church, and reported, "It's remarkable, but I feel a great sense of peace from just being in that building. The people are great, too. I also started going back to something I did twenty years ago—yoga. I can't believe I stayed away from it so long—it's really helping me."

Although many of these self-help measures provide only temporary relief, they will have beneficial results and begin the process of empowerment. Taking control, even in small ways, will bring relief for the anger and the obsessive thoughts. To the degree you work at helping yourself, you will begin to alter your feelings of powerlessness. If these techniques are not effective, and your thoughts run wild in spite of your best efforts, medication is available to help reduce the amount of energy you spend obsessing.

Searching for Understanding
As Nadja, Steve, and the children learned to cope with their emotional reactivity, they shifted into the second stage of recovery. They were now ready to understand why Steve had an affair online. Nadja had questions about why this happened, and about Steve's cyber-relationship.

Learning to Talk and Listen
Although the recovery period is a time to talk, it is also a time to listen. That, of course, does not mean only listening for the opportunity to begin speaking. It means listening with a goal of understanding one another, and coming to a resolution about issues. One approach to learning to talk and listen involves the fishbowl technique. The fishbowl technique may help you more than you can imagine.

Using the Fishbowl Technique
Psychologists Shirley Glass, Ph.D., and Tom Wright, Ph.D., have written and spoken extensively about their "fishbowl technique." This coping strategy has become very popular for helping with difficult conversations and finding a way to look at the issues with a tolerable comfort level. They suggest that as questions come to you during the week, write them down on a slip of paper and place them in a fishbowl or any handy container. The questions are answered at a scheduled time, which we call "Talk Time." Drs. Glass and Wright recommend discussing the most difficult questions only when closeness and trust have been rebuilt.

Developing Talk Time
Scheduling time together is a common exercise given as homework by therapists. We have called this Talk Time, and found it to be a crucial strategy for couples to work through the contributors to cyber-infidelity. Couples are asked to set aside time to connect with one another or discuss relationship issues. This technique is also used to manage anger. We suggest that you combine the fishbowl technique with Talk Time. The fishbowl allows you to collect your questions for Talk Time, and prevent you from hassling each other during the week with accusations. If the question is potentially too explosive, return it to the bowl to be answered later.

The following guidelines will help you make the most of this time:

◐ Set thirty to forty-five minutes, three or four times a week, to talk about the cyber-infidelity. Agree to bring up the infidelity only during these times, and at no other times.
◐ Ignore distractions. Do not answer beepers, telephones, or doorbells. The world can wait.
◐ Do not schedule Talk Time for when you have something else that needs attending. Do not talk in the few minutes before leaving the house, while others are waiting, or just before going to bed.
◐ Be sure to have complete privacy.
◐ Begin and end on time. Do not go over the agreed-upon schedule. You will not get all the issues addressed in a brief period. Resolution takes weeks and months. Talk Time regulates the time for expressing yourself and helps assure that things will not get out of control. If you don't talk about everything you want to at one meeting, you may agree to extend the time by another ten minutes, but no longer. Extended time is not usually productive.
◐ Take turns talking, and make one or two points at a time.
◐ When your partner makes a statement, repeat it so that you can be sure you understand. If you cannot repeat it accurately, ask it to be stated once again. Listen carefully and reflect back to be sure you understand what is being said. Once you have understood the other person, you are free to respond from your own point of view. Then your comment can be repeated back to you, so that you can be certain that you are understood. Proceed in this way until Talk Time is finished.
◐ You cannot expect to gain closure on every issue you discuss. Your goal is to understand each other and to have your questions answered. In time, as your relationship improves, you may be able to make specific requests, such as moving the computer to the living room, or about time spent on the computer. Avoid vague requests, such as, "I would like you to spend less time on the computer," because it is not specific and therefore compliance will be much more difficult to determine. A more specific request would be, "I would like you to limit the time you spend on the computer to one hour each evening."
◐ As your relationship improves, you will be able to reduce the number of Talk Time sessions. The number is determined by your needs. In the beginning, you will need more time. As your questions are answered and you begin to understand more, you will need less time.

Remember that recovery is a bumpy road, and there are times when you may find you need to increase the number of sessions after they have already been reduced. Do not let this concern you. It is not an indication that you are not making progress. Just be prepared for the bumps in the road. However, we strongly advise that you continue to set aside a regular time throughout your relationship to talk. It can become a time of closeness and sharing.

There are many benefits to be derived from Talk Time. If you wait until Talk Time, you will both be more likely to be ready for discussing difficult topics. Another benefit is that you will have agreed to a limited amount of time for "heavy duty" discussions. Being willing to set aside time for difficult conversations is also a sign that you value the relationship and your partner.

Steve told us, "My hat's off to Talk Time. I don't have to walk on eggshells at home and around the children."

Nadja said, "To my surprise, this process is bringing us closer."

Steve added, "I'm more willing to answer the questions because I know when they are coming. I can rest assured that we won't have one of those horrible all-nighters where we both are sick and exhausted from hashing it out."

Even Cindy and Andrew were thrilled with the results. Cindy said, "We know that Mom and Dad have their 'Talk Time' and we just leave the house or stay in our rooms. They usually are nicer to us after those times, so yeah, they're great!"

Most importantly, Talk Time is an effective anger-management technique. It reduces the free-floating anger that can create setback on the road to recovery. Without regularly scheduled periods to talk to each other, your home can become a battleground. Fearfulness and tension are likely to predominate if unpredictable anger is likely to erupt. Knowing that a time is set aside for the difficult discussions can channel those emotions more effectively, allow people to better manage their anxiety, and reduce overall emotional reactivity at home.

Although talking about relationship issues is a part of effective communication, another essential benefit of Talk Time is developing and demonstrating compassion for the other person's point of view. This is called empathy, and it requires putting your reactions aside to understand the other person. You will move toward empathy by repeating your partner's message until you are both in agreement regarding content. Angry exchanges often decrease when one partner recognizes the other's experience. Denying that experience results in anger.

If Talk Time does not work for you, consider seeing a psychotherapist. The presence of a neutral third party can help you lower your emotional reactivity. The therapist becomes part of a triangle with the couple. This is known as the therapeutic triangle. By talking through the therapist, couples learn to hear each other and discover that he or she will be heard. This has a calming effect and helps to reduce emotional reactivity. As the emotional reactivity decreases, the couple will begin to think more clearly and the individuals will start to speak to each other. With the help of the therapist, they will begin to become more differentiated. These professional approaches will move you toward gaining an understanding of the under-lying as well as current problems pertaining to the cyber-infidelity.

Discussing Details of the Affair

The need to talk about the specific details of an affair varies from one per-son to the next. Typically, the unfaithful partner does not want to discuss details. Some wounded partners want to know all the details, while others want to know nothing. Therapists differ with respect to this decision as well. Emily Brown, author of *Patterns of Infidelity and Their Treatment,* feels that the obsession can keep the couple from dealing with the underlying causes. Other therapists believe that all the details must be discussed to demystify the affair.

Our view is that uncontrolled discussion promotes obsession and becomes a distraction from dealing with the underlying causes of the affair. Time and energy are better spent focusing on stressors in the relationship before the cyber-infidelity and underlying dynamics in the relationship. Nonetheless, some discussion may be necessary to satisfy questions from the wounded partner. The faithful partner has experienced a painful gap in the couple's shared history. The amount of information needed to fill that gap is deter-mined by the need of the wounded partner, aided by the judgment of a skilled psychotherapist, if one is involved.

One important factor must be understood if the decision is made to discuss the painful details of the affair. The unfaithful partner will most likely have difficulty revealing the details realistically, even if he or she tries. Describing infidelity is similar to the process of describing a painting. The overall sense of the picture can be captured and verbalized, but many people will have dif-ficulty conveying the emotions experienced and the artistic details repre-sented. The verbal skills of the reporting party are also an important factor. Art historians will be more adept at using precise language to describe the emotional overtones and artistic approaches to the painting. Similarly, some-one with a good vocabulary for describing emotions and interpersonal dynamics will be more able to relay the details of a cyber-affair.

For better or for worse, technology can reproduce the details of sexual-ized contact through the Internet in ways that are more accurate than ever before. Couples can now be privy to the details of an affair in unprece-dented ways. Instant Messages, emails, and photos are often saved as spe-cial files to which the unfaithful partner can return for immediate gratification and a continuation of the fantasy about the cyber-lover, even in the absence of any further interaction. These records can often be accessed, even if the unfaithful partner has tried to remove them from a computer hard drive. Faithful partners may or may not want to see that level of detail.

The immediate emotional response to reviewing such records is likely to be profound pain. The memories of such review will most likely be difficult to forget over time. Our opinion is that sharing such records will most likely increase painful obsession. Such sharing should be done cautiously, if at all.

Looking at Family of Origin

Much information can be gained by having each couple review and discuss their families of origin. If you come from a family in which affairs have taken place, it is crucial to discuss not only this history, but also your views of fidelity with your partner and how they were formed. Infidelity in one's family of origin does not mean that one will automatically engage in affairs. However, a full discussion of the boundaries of acceptable behavior within your relationship will help both you and your partner understand what has happened in the past, and most likely prevent the heartbreak of betrayal in the future.

Therapists often see a very strong reaction to current infidelity in a partner who experienced parental infidelity. In these circumstances, an affair by the spouse can be experienced as a reawakening and deepening of the pain of parental infidelity. Therefore, rather than ignoring generational infidelity, couples need to discuss and make clear agreements related to infidelity, and in the case of cyber-infidelity, the use of technology.

During the course of therapy, Nadja and Steve also completed a genogram. This therapeutic technique is much like drawing a family tree, but has information that can be helpful in assessing the roots of relationship issues. Genograms are used to graphically depict family relationships, including important dates, significant patterns, messages, anxieties, illnesses, and family tensions.

Steve's genogram showed him to be an only child. His extended family lived close by, and he saw only a few concerns. The most important connection he made was that his father was a hardworking lawyer who died at age forty-seven of a heart attack.

Steve explained, "I know my Dad died when he was only forty-seven, really a young man. And rather young to have a heart attack. I'm almost that age, and I'm afraid I might go before my time, too. Sometimes these things run in families. My doctor feels I'm in excellent health, but he keeps trying to get me to change my lifestyle."

"What do you mean?" Nadja asked.

"Well, he thinks my work is too stressful."

"Is it?" the therapist asked.

"Yes, it is very stressful."

"Then you need to stop," Nadja quickly added. "We have all the money and things we need. You've worked so hard to get where we are. What good is it if you aren't around to enjoy it?"

"I know," Steve said. "We own this house. The kids' college money is there. We have investments. I could slow down."

"But?" the therapist prompted.

"I can't seem to do it."

After further discussion, Steve realized that he carried a childhood message from his father to work hard and to be a success.

"Can you visualize your life without work?" the therapist asked.

"Not really," Steve replied. "Yet, I don't know what I would do otherwise. I've never learned to have fun."

"What about that Internet woman?" Nadja asked. "How does she fit in this whole thing?"

Steve answered, "Well, I'm just beginning to realize that my father's father had an affair. I didn't connect it to my own behavior. I guess it was always there, in my family history."

Nadja asked, "Why didn't you ever tell me about this?"

"It's just not something anyone talked about," Steve said slowly.

Nadja was very curious at this point, and pressed with yet another question, "Why did your grandfather have an affair?"

"I don't know," Steve replied. "In my family, nobody ever talked much about anything but work and the weather. I actually found out about it by overhearing my mother and my aunt whispering when they thought I was out of earshot."

Nadja seemed to understand, "So you did what your grandfather did. You were feeling anxious and went looking for comfort, but this time with a computer."

"Well," Steve said, "No, it wasn't like that. I've just been worried about the heart problem, and I thought I'd see what the Internet had on heart conditions. I was looking up heart disease on the Internet and decided to go to a related chat room. I had a lot of fun just talking. I couldn't believe how fast the time went. You were at some meeting. When you got back, I realized I had been online for three hours."

Nadja said, "So you continued."

Steve dropped his head, too embarrassed to look at his wife. "Yes, I did. I'm very sorry, Nadja. It was just a friendship in the beginning. She was someone to talk to. I became so relaxed that I realized this heart disease problem and the pressures of work were really getting to me."

"You became *relaxed*?!" Nadja screamed. "You masturbated at your computer because you got relaxed with a 'friend'?! Right! Why didn't you tell me?"

Steve defended himself from his wife's emotional attack with, "I didn't want to worry you. I thought you would never know. I lied to myself, and to you, and to the kids. It was really wrong."

Nadja was encouraged by the therapist to calm herself with slow breathing, and to apologize for her outburst. She began seeing the effect her reactions had on him. She recognized that the thought of Steve's death sent her into a panic, and she lashed out at him when he was making himself vulnerable to her. When he did, she would use it as an opportunity to strike out at him.

Steve had a secret world. He secretly feared his own sudden death. He was unable to share his worries because he came from a family that did not discuss such things. He threw himself into his work, which only added more stress to his life. He was living in a "pressure cooker," and he secretly was letting off steam with GalaxyQueen at every available opportunity. Nadja wasn't extremely interested in the details, but Steve did confess that he had met with GalaxyQueen over twenty times after that first meeting, and every time they had cyber-sex.

Much to Nadja's surprise, Steve also confessed that he had a history of seeking pornography when he felt stressed, "When things got too rough at the office and I just couldn't stand it anymore, I'd drop a message to GalaxyQueen and ask her to meet me. Then I'd come home early from work and have cyber-sex with her. I'd also pick up a few little bottles of Jack Daniels on the way home, and completely forget my stress. I guess I don't know of many good ways to relax. I need help."

Upon closer questioning, the therapist determined that Steve did not have a problematic history of alcohol use, but he had used pornography extensively before his marriage. Nadja confirmed her husband's lack of a drinking history, but sat in shock as he revealed his sexual history, "I'm here to get help, so I might as well tell you everything. I had a reputation for 'anything goes' in college. Then I caught a venereal disease and needed to be treated with antibiotics for gonorrhea. But even that didn't stop me. I...now Nadja, just know this was a long time ago...slept with a few men, and decided it just wasn't for me. But I'm glad I tried it. By the time I got to law school, I'd pretty well burned out on a lot of wild sex, and just stuck to pornography, and now this cyber-sex."

Nadja immediately wanted to know, "This GalaxyQueen, is that a guy?

Steve understood her motivation for the question, and calmly answered, "Honey, I'm not gay, and if I were, you'd be the first to know, believe me. No, she's a woman. But I've also been around enough to know that being gay or having gay sex isn't the end of the world. My problem is that I can't relax without cyber-sex, not that I had a few gay encounters in college."

Nadja was anxious about the new information, but took comfort in the fact that Steve agreed to undergo an individual evaluation and psychotherapy for his compulsive use of sexuality under times of stress. Steve's recent cyber-sexual behavior would place him in the "at-risk" category of people who have been described in Chapter Four. Until recently, he did not use sexuality as a coping mechanism, but now, with the added convenience of the Internet, he found himself out of control. He uses cyber-sex to calm himself in times of stress. Nadja was uncomfortable with the whole topic, but decided, "I think I can live with it if he gets help."

They also continued their couple's work. Nadja and Steve were given short-term exercises to practice various types of relaxation together. They were also given a long-term assignment—to plan a new lifestyle around Steve's possible retirement. They were to discuss it during Talk Time and to investigate all possibilities. They were only to gather information; they did not have to make a decision.

Nadja's genogram revealed a family with the traditional values, that a woman's place is in the home and the man's role was to be a provider. "I felt out of step with a lot of my woman friends, but I could not see myself in any career. So I kept a lovely house and raised our kids."

"Except," Steve said, "Nadja did develop a small part-time business for herself through her class in photography. She takes portraits of children in natural settings—a lot of them in our own backyard which is wooded and very beautiful."

Learning To Communicate

Understanding is basic to finding solutions and requires good communication skills. The basic components of face-to-face effective communication are:

○ listening—hearing the content of what is being said, without interruption;
○ attending to all parts of the message, such as tone of voice and body language;
○ repeating back your understanding of the message, and receiving confirmation from the sender;
○ communicating to each other respectfully;
○ using "I" statements to explain and to define oneself; and
○ appreciating the other's point of view, even though you may not be in agreement with it.

Good communication is fundamental to successful relationships. It is normal to have changing goals, needs, and beliefs over time. Couples need the skills to be able to adapt to these changes as they move through various life steps together.

It is also important to include children and teens at this point in therapy. Nadja and Steve were asked if they thought it would be helpful to include their twins in a few psychotherapy sessions.

They agreed that it would probably be helpful because of their involvement in the discovery of Steve's relationship with GalaxyQueen. Nadja and Steve both agreed, and the twins came in the following week. They were not invited earlier because Nadja needed to learn to cope with her emotions before the children were exposed to the process. At this point, Nadja had also made considerable progress in managing her anxiety. The teens had been doing well in school, so there was no need for immediate intervention.

Coping with Children's Reactions

In the first psychotherapy session with the teens, Cindy and Andrew were asked how they felt about having found their father's file. The teens seemed ready, because they responded after only a few minutes of prompting. Cindy answered, "Well, I'm pissed." She had already written an unmailed letter to her father, after Nadja had suggested it to her the previous month.

Cindy reported, "I took that letter down to Great Falls Park in my neighborhood. It was Sunday afternoon. Andrew came with me. I didn't even share the letter with him. I sat on one of the rocks and read the letter several times. When I was done, I tore the letter into tiny pieces and flung them into the water. I watched them swirl away. I imagined my anger going down with them. On the way home, we stopped at the Village, where I decided to buy myself a necklace—to symbolize my freedom from those angry words. Now, whenever I wear it, I am reminded that I am past those feelings."

Cindy reduced some of her anger with that note, and nurtured herself with a symbol of strength. During this psychotherapy session, she asked her Dad about the cyber-affair, and if it was over. Steve was shocked, but also proud that his daughter had the courage to approach him,

"Yes, Cindy and Andrew, it's over. I should never have done it. I love your mother very much. I realize I hurt her, and both of you. I made a very big mistake, and can only hope that you will forgive me. I am working things out with your Mom, and this won't ever happen again. I know it must not be easy for you."

Cindy asked, "Why did you do it?"

Steve sadly replied, "It seems to be a combination of things. But it has nothing to do with not loving you kids or your mother. I love all of you. I'm here to stay."

Cindy found a way to free herself from anger, not only by freely writing her feelings, but also by using her energy to tear the letter apart and let the water wash away her emotions. She also found a nurturing way of reminding herself that she is in control of herself. She then was able to approach her father with her questions in the safety of the psychotherapy session. Luckily, he was caring and sophisticated in his response. She felt much better after hearing his apology and reassurance that it would not happen again.

When Andrew was asked about how he was coping with his feelings, it became obvious that that he distanced himself from his father. He stated flatly, "I stayed away from the house for a while, and played a lot of basketball. I couldn't tell any of the guys, it was just too weird. I think Dad noticed I was away a lot. I ran into him in the garage one day. It was really uncomfortable. We didn't say anything to each other. Dad, you're a hot shot lawyer. Talk is your trade, but you didn't say anything to me that day."

Steve replied to his son, "At work, talking is easy. Talking with my family is different. But I know what you mean. My father was just like me, and I felt just like you. My father could talk to everyone but me. If you only knew how much I wanted to hear my father say 'I love you.'"

There was silence in the room. Andrew said, "I know, Dad."

Steve said, "Oh, my God." He got up, walked over to his son, hugged him and said, "I love you."

A dam of repressed emotion broke at that moment, and flooded the room as everyone heard and responded to each other's pain. This is the power of psychotherapy. A simple discussion of how to distract oneself can unexpectedly lead to a healing exchange that will be remembered for decades.

Finding the Miscommunication

Nadja and Steve had a relatively smooth marriage up to that point. In many ways, they have shown that they can use the basic skills of communication previously described. Even in their opening dialogue, Nadja used "I" statements, even though she was emotionally reactive. Steve, on the other hand, was empathic as he recognized her pain. Yet, their communication was missing something. It was not the secret of the cyber-infidelity, because it had now been revealed and discussed. We soon learned that Steve carried much anxiety about his work and his fear of dying.

According to Dr. Alfred Adler's concept of private logic, individuals form conclusions that develops from childhood experience. Steve developed a logic based on his family history. The message for Steve, based on his childhood, was that he needed to work hard, make a name for himself, and support his family well by his own efforts.

Along with that message was another, "You don't share your thoughts or feelings." He had not considered, and therefore never shared, these concerns with Nadja until his therapy. When Nadja understood, she showed empathy for his feelings, but did not condone his unfaithful behavior. Steve's silence was apparent in his relationship with his children as well. Cindy was worried about the future of the family. Andrew needed Steve to give him an open expression of love.

Now that Steve was able to understand that the cyber-affair was the result of a combination of many factors, including his work stress, his anxiety about his health, his inability to communicate his feelings to his family, and the history of an affair in his family of origin, he was able to ask for family support. He and Nadja were able to move forward in their relationship—to the third step of reconstructing their marriage.

Reconstructing the Relationship

At this point, Steve and Nadja were able to make an agreement regarding their concept of fidelity and the use of the computer. They both agreed that they wanted their relationship to be monogamous, and that friendships on the computer were not allowed for them. They agreed that while the computer is a valuable tool for knowledge, information, and amusement, they would restrict their use because of the effects it had on their relationship.

Nadja and Steve had already been given an assignment: to talk about the lifestyle changes they could afford. They needed to make a drastic change in daily living, but they were stuck. Their stage-of-life problem had been compounded by their inability to communicate about Steve's inner fear of dying, and the role modeling he obtained in his early life from his grandfather. When faced with overwhelming stress, he used sexuality, secrecy, and deceit to cope. With those issues revealed and addressed, Steve and Nadja were able to get their relationship back on track and make the lifestyle changes that were needed for a continued life together.

Couples often face lifestyle changes when confronted with anxiety in the family. If they do not understand their motives, such as intergenerational infidelity, they can easily overreact. If, during this process, they take the time to reflect, they can make significant lifestyle changes instead.

In the year that followed, Steve resigned from his position with his law firm to practice only three days a week with an advocacy program. Steve and Nadja spent the time taking continuing education classes, exploring hobbies, and searching for new ways to enjoy each other. They made plans to have family time with Cindy and Andrew each week. Although typically, family time is not on teenagers' top ten list of things to do, Cindy and Andrew cherished the opportunity. For them, it was an indication of reconciliation between their parents.

Finding Closure
A significant element of finding closure after cyber-infidelity is making an appropriate apology. Although Steve had repeatedly given apologies, it was necessary to bring closure with an apology that included an understanding of Nadja's pain, remorse for what had happened, and the promise to never let it occur again. Such a promise must be made with sincerity and contrition.

The Apology
Steve apologized to Nadja for the pain he caused her and the children, and apologized to Cindy and Andrew as well. Steve had spent time finding a book for each family member that would send a message that he felt was important. He took them to dinner and presented his gifts to them.

Follow-Up
The follow-up came in the form of another psychotherapy appointment. Nadja and Steve wanted to say goodbye, to discuss their plans, and to, as Steve put it, "Get a twenty thousand mile check-up."

Nadja and Steve bought a smaller home in Annapolis, Maryland. Steve became a part-time consultant. When Steve worked, Nadja developed her photography business. In their spare time, they explored the charming parts of Old Annapolis and the beauty of Maryland's Eastern Shore. They had become interested in antiques and collectibles, and took drives to estate sales throughout this beautiful area. They met new people and reestablished old friendships. They continued Talk Time once a week to resolve issues and make new plans. Steve is also focusing on healthier eating and regular exercising. Cindy and Andrew are in college, one in Connecticut and the other in North Carolina.

Steve concluded by saying, "I put my family through the wringer on this, and I will regret it always. Yet, I am relieved to have not just changed our lives, but maybe break a generational pattern for the kids."

In this case, infidelity was the result of sexualized contact through the Internet. Its discovery led to a family crisis and its successful resolution. Unfortunately, not all couples have the strength to see infidelity through to such a successful transformation. If you are facing infidelity through the Internet or in real life, it is our hope that you will see how couples can weather such difficult storms and build a new relationship together, one that is often deeper and more rewarding.

In the next chapter, we will illustrate the way a therapist helps a younger couple with different issues work through cyber-infidelity that led to an affair in real life. The emphasis of this second recovery chapter will be on reconstructing the relationship and gaining closure.

9

Concluding Steps
to Recovery

Katie and Chuck were both twenty-seven years old, and had been married for three years. They first met each other at an international pharmaceutical company where they both held management positions. Chuck called for a psychotherapy appointment after his wife Katie returned from a trip to Peru. He wanted a couple's session. During their first psychotherapy session, it was obvious that Katie was very upset. Chuck sat and listened, with his fists clenched. Katie explained that she had an affair that started on the Internet, and that it later developed into a real-life romance.

"It started innocently. I had just received what appeared at first glance to be a message for 'Petra,' on my email. I soon realized that it was sent to me by accident, but I just kept reading because the letter was really steamy. I guess I was titillated and because it was written by Miguel, our company's largest client.

"I don't know what possessed me, except that I was having a fight with Chuck that evening. I decided to answer Miguel and flirt a little. I let him know that his letter to Petra had been delivered to me by mistake, and that he was 'looking for love in all the wrong places.' He answered immediately, saying that he was 'open to suggestions.' I had some time, so I invited him to chat with me.

"It got to be a routine. Chuck and I were fighting all the time, so I just didn't care. In fact, I almost hoped he'd come into the den to see me having cyber-sex with Miguel.

"One night when Chuck and I had a fight, I retreated to my office to work on a project. The project soon became Miguel. It helped me forget these ugly fights. Chuck never came to me at bedtime, not even to say good night. I was angry that he didn't ask me to join him. It had gotten so that if we fought or weren't connecting, I had to always be the one to go to him. Chuck hurt me so much, I had stopped trying to calm him down, or trying to fix things, or anything."

When Katie gave details of their arguments, she was embarrassed. She knew she had been tolerating verbal abuse, but did not know how to change it.

"A few months after I started my affair on the Internet with Miguel, he urged me to come to Peru. He arranged for my company to send me there on assignment. After one of my fights with Chuck, I accepted Miguel's offer. Trying to be honest, I asked Chuck for a divorce and I told him the whole story. He was furious. I packed my bags and left the next morning."

Chuck, who was sitting quietly in the therapy session, tried to appear stoic, but he was fighting the tears as he listened to Katie. Finally, he said, "I told her that if she preferred Miguel over me, to go ahead. She left the next morning."

The Full Process of Recovery

In this chapter, we will review how Katie and Chuck learned to cope with their emotions and reach an understanding through communication. Then, we will more fully illustrate the last two steps to recovery, which are Reconstructing the Relationship and Finding Closure.

Coping with Emotions

Katie was anxious about her inability to connect with Chuck. She was comforted by Miguel's reassurances, and when he invited her to join him in Peru, she thought she had found the answer to her problems. After her fight with Chuck, she accepted Miguel's offer. It was an impulsive attempt to deal with their problems by an emotional cutoff; that is, to distance herself rather than stay connected to Chuck, manage her own anxiety, and work toward solving their problems.

When Katie informed Chuck of her cyber-infidelity and her decision to leave him and go to Peru, he was stunned, deeply wounded, and very angry. Later, in one of his therapy sessions, Chuck said that he had felt a wall between himself and Katie for months, but hadn't considered its seriousness.

"Well, when I got to Peru," Katie said, "things were not what I thought. Miguel hadn't mentioned that he was the father of three little girls, and the husband of a very generous wife. The project was a disaster, as was the whole affair. He wanted to keep me as his mistress, and had rented an apartment for me on the other side of town. I felt deceived and degraded, but didn't know where to turn."

She went on, "One evening, in the middle of a minor disagreement, Miguel left me stranded on a dark street corner as he drove off in his shiny black Mercedes. I couldn't believe it. My first thought was of Chuck and I knew he would never dream of doing a thing like that to me, even now, after all I had done to hurt him."

Katie said she had wept for hours after she managed to return to her hotel room. Finally, she sheepishly called Chuck to ask if he would take her back. She was expecting silence, not the blast she received.

In the wake of her abrupt departure, Chuck retrieved the love letters exchanged between Katie and Miguel from her hard drive. Katie had tried to erase them before she left, but Chuck knew they might still be traceable, so he took the computer to his local repair shop. They found the files within minutes. When she called to come home, he was still fuming and he let her know it.

Nonetheless, he loved Katie and eventually accepted her pleas to come home. He had remained emotionally open and connected to her, despite his best efforts to stop caring about her. He told the psychotherapist, "I was outraged, first at Katie for leaving me, and then at Miguel because he treated Katie like dirt. 'Come home,' I said, 'We'll work this out.'"

He decided that if she were to come home, they would take a serious look at what had happened, but only with the help of a psychotherapist. He expected the process to be painful because he knew that having an affair was a sign of serious problems. Chuck was very concerned about the fact that the cyber-infidelity proceeded to an even more involved level, because Katie and Miguel had continued their cyber-affair in the physical world. Chuck suspected he had contributed to this problem and was willing to face that reality to get his wife back.

Katie was conflicted and uncertain about her ability to be honest. She knew she was wrong, and dreaded psychotherapy because she not only hated herself for her infidelity, but also for begging to come home. Her old feelings of resentment toward Chuck returned quickly. As she later said, "When I heard myself begging to come back, I knew I had reached a new low." When Katie said this, she was expressing her feelings, but her thinking was distorted.

Identifying Distorted Thinking

In Chapter Eight, we discussed how most people fall into anxiety traps with distorted thinking. Katie was prone to all-or-nothing thinking, name calling, catastrophizing, and fortune telling. During her therapy, she learned how to cope with her emotions by correcting her distorted thinking.

In a private psychotherapy sessions, she said, "I can't imagine why Chuck would take me back. I did the lowest thing anyone could do. This may sound terrible, but I have no respect for him. I think he is a worm for taking me back. And I'm a worm for coming back. I also don't see how psychotherapy can help fix any of that!"

Despite her protests, Katie was capable of learning and changing. She learned that her negative thinking only got in her way, and was not based on fact. Katie was instructed to list the ways in which she admired Chuck for his willingness to work toward reviving their relationship. She also admitted that she would not be coming to psychotherapy sessions if she did not hope it would be successful. She began to understand that she had been responding with her emotions rather than her intellect.

As therapy continued, Katie was able to realize that her cyber-infidelity was a reaction to stress in her life. She understood that she was putting up a strong, defensive front because she was scared and anxious that she would need to face the roots of her pain. She worked on many of the techniques previously identified to help her cope with her emotions.

Searching for Understanding

Katie and Chuck soon came to understand that effective communication skills help couples live comfortably with differences. Couples need not agree, but they must resolve their differences. To help them learn effective communication techniques, they were asked to describe their arguments. They each spoke from their own viewpoint. While one spoke, the other listened carefully. This reduced their arguing, which was replaced by more appropriate listening and responding. By doing this, they each became aware of the accusations, feelings of pain, and the past hurts that emerged.

In looking at their respective families of origin, Katie exclaimed, "I feel stupid talking about my family because Chuck says I should stop bellyaching about it. He says I'm a crybaby and need to grow up."

Chuck jumped in with, "You are a crybaby. Every time something gets tough, you go on and on about how your father treated you. I don't care how your father treated you! I'm the one that needs to deal with your constant excuses, and I'm sick of it—and of you!"

The therapist started to intervene when Chuck said, "OK, OK! I did it again. I see what I'm doing." Chuck had previously had an individual psychotherapy session to look at his name calling and dismissal of Katie's reality. He was embarrassed to have such an immediate demonstration of his outbursts.

Like many people, Katie and Chuck had a history of being thoughtless during fights. They had often focused on the goal of winning, not of learning about one another. They had a tendency to let their emotions run wild with name calling, ridiculing, and other hurtful behaviors. These communication styles are typically learned in childhood, and are a sign that people lack skills for making themselves understood. In other words, Katie and Chuck needed to learn new communication skills. Their unmanaged anxiety was at the root of all these behaviors.

Practicing "I" Statements

Chuck was first asked to directly apologize for his name calling, rather than just assume Katie would forgive him because he acknowledged it. Such precision is often needed to correct the pain that results from angry outbursts. He was also asked to make his position clear with "I" statements. This would force him to take more responsibility for his statements, and more accurately define himself as a person. It would also help Katie to accept his comments.

He rose to the occasion, and said, "Katie, I want to apologize for the way I spoke to you. There's no need for me to say those things to you now. We are here trying to fix things, and if I call you names and get mean, it won't help. I'm sorry, I need to learn to control myself. I do care about what happened to you as a child."

Chuck was encouraged to dig deeper, and find the reason for his insensitive statement about not caring. He sat quietly, then admitted, "I get frustrated because she keeps bringing up her father, and I can't do anything about her past. I love her, and want her to know that she doesn't live with her father anymore."

Katie responded, "But when you do that, you sound just like him. So it's like I never left home."

With further discussion, it became clear that Chuck felt frustrated when listening to Katie's history because it made him feel helpless. When he felt helpless, he experienced anxiety. To stop his own anxiety, he used name calling and belittling to quiet her.

Setting Boundaries

The other side of this dynamic was that Katie had a history of pulling back from these exchanges with Chuck because she did not know how to set respectful boundaries. When attacked, Katie did not know how to set limits on the things that she said, or the things he said to her. In the therapy office, she practiced setting boundaries by making "I" statements. Sitting up straight, she spoke to Chuck, and said, "Chuck, I want you to respect me. That means listening to me and not calling me names even when you are frustrated or anxious. Are you willing to do that?"

Once again, Chuck was asked to not be judgmental. It takes a while to break old habits; change does not come quickly. Gentle reminders and patience are required by each person. Chuck mumbled, "Yeah, of course."

The therapist asked Chuck if he would respond to the chairman of the board with that attitude. He mumbled, "No." The therapist asked Chuck to speak in complete sentences, look Katie in the eye, and say it more convincingly.

"OK, Katie, I will control my anger and speak to you with respect when we fight, and I won't call you names anymore." Chuck added, "I guess I need to learn to calm myself down when you need to talk about yourself. When I try to stop you, I only make it worse."

They were learning! They began to see that respectful communication is the brush with which we paint our relationships.

Understanding Family of Origin

As couples cope with their emotions, make "I" statements, set boundaries, and establish Talk Time, they develop an understanding of their behavior. This is further enhanced by looking at their families of origin. Couples find this to be an interesting part of their therapy, and most participate enthusiastically, even though they may have had a problematic family background.

Katie and Chuck were guided by their therapist to describe their family tree, and a genogram was developed. As explained in the previous chapter, this graphic depiction of an extended family usually clarifies patterns of behavior and emotion that have roots in previous generations. Katie and Chuck, like most couples, found this to be a fascinating exercise.

Katie and Chuck both realized that they had learned their destructive conflict resolution skills from their families of origin and had never learned how to improve those skills along the way. Katie's father was an alcoholic who regularly berated his mother. Katie never saw her mother stand up to her father and win, so she learned to suppress her hurt and anger. Chuck was not an alcoholic like his father. In fact, he was very reluctant to drink at all. He was a successful manager, supervising many people every day. When the therapist asked if he would talk to his employees as he does with his wife, he admitted that such behavior would not be tolerated at work. Chuck had been raised in a home where his parents "didn't argue." When upset with each other, they kept it behind closed doors. Yet, upset with their children, they used name calling, sniping, ridiculing, and screaming as primary modes of discipline.

Now, Katie and Chuck as a couple were recreating the unsuccessful conflict resolution patterns they learned in their homes as children. Chuck said that he just learned that, "Relationships are just chilly after a fight and eventually warm up if you wait long enough."

In their arguments, Katie typically was the one to break the ice, to apologize for their disagreement, and try to move the relationship forward. Katie resented Chuck's refusal to approach her when they fought. This was similar to the models of conflict resolution they each learned in their families of origin. When Chuck was anxious, he would distance himself from Katie. Neither partner saw himself or herself as having a communication skill or conflict management deficit until Katie "fell in love" with Miguel.

Although Katie and Chuck saw the patterns of their behavior, they were not aware of their origins. Once the puzzle that motivated her to seek romance outside her relationship with Chuck was unlocked, they would better understand how to make changes. The answer lay deep within her. After several more sessions, and with the use of the genograms, she revealed that she had spent many childhood years watching her parents fight over her father's alcoholism and extramarital affairs.

"He was a mean drunk, and when he came home smelling of another woman's perfume, my mother couldn't contain herself. She'd say a few things, and before we knew it, milk cartons and eggs were flying around the kitchen. He'd rip at her, often tearing her clothes, and she'd be crying in the corner of the kitchen. Then, he'd have the gall to stand over her, screaming at her to pick it all up. I swore I'd never let anyone do that to me, that I'd leave before it ever got that way."

Katie's mother did not know how to set limits with her husband, who blamed her for his misbehavior. Lacking self-esteem, she was unable to teach Katie how to value herself. Katie's low level of differentiation showed

in her feelings of inadequacy, her inability to set small limits before reacting with all-or-nothing behavior during a disagreement, and impulsive
behavior such as declaring that she was going to Peru to be with another
man. She experienced Chuck's anger in the same way she did her father's
when he went into a drunken rage. Given the role modeling she received
as a child, she was blocked from changing an undesirable situation in her
marriage.

Similarly, Chuck learned to be domineering and berating in his family of
origin. When faced with stresses in his marriage, he either pulled back, as
his parents did with each other, or used name calling, ridiculing, and
screaming to control unwanted behavior from his wife.

Katie learned to tolerate her anxiety about setting limits with "I" statements when she felt disrespected. When Chuck saw her strength grow, he
respected her more and trusted her to provide support when he felt the need
to discuss his own doubts and pain. They learned skills to resolve their con-
flicts respectfully when they realized the role that empathy plays in building relationships. Now that they had achieved a degree of mastery over their
emotions, they were ready for the third step on the path to recovery, that of
reconstructing their relationship.

Reconstructing the Relationship

Katie and Chuck had progressed through the first two steps to recovery from
infidelity. They had learned ways to better manage anxiety and reach an
understanding of their patterns of behavior. They were fascinated with how
they were replicating long-standing family patterns. Through the genogram,
they could see how extended family members and even grandparents had
similar situations in their relationships.

They were not only surprised to see how their patterns of dealing with
stress were handed down from previous generations, but also wondered
how far back these patterns had been present in their families. What was
more interesting is how each managed to find a marriage partner whose
family patterns complemented the other. They were well suited to com-
pleting the "dance" needed to replicate intergenerational patterns in their
own marriage. Once couples begin to understand the origins of their
behavior, they can begin reconstructing their relationship to change the
dance.

A Second Look at Family-of-Origin Issues

Family-of-origin issues typically continue to emerge throughout psychotherapy. Therapists and clients refer back to family history when new
information comes up in sessions. New insights or connections become
apparent. With this, the trail from the past to the present brings understanding. This information also provides the material needed to reconstruct

the relationship. Katie had reached this point in her therapy, but the hardest part was yet to come.

Katie did not appreciate her own strength. She unconsciously withheld herself from being honest in many other ways, fearing that Chuck would treat her as her father had treated her mother. With his name calling, belittling, and other careless actions, Chuck had stepped right into the role Katie feared the most, but nonetheless, had cast for him.

Katie was overwhelmed with paralyzing anxiety when Chuck mistreated her. She reacted emotionally, with the helplessness of the little girl she used to be. When this pattern seemed insurmountable in her marriage, she escaped into the virtual arms of another man, a stranger who spoke the words she wanted to hear.

She had a secretive affair, just as her father did when she was a child. When she realized that her dream with Miguel was not real, she called Chuck and fully expected him to take her back, as her mother had taken back her father when he had betrayed her. She was not prepared to have her husband break the silence and insist on psychotherapy to force a change in their relationship.

Part of reconstructing a relationship involves learning to be sensitive to one another and showing empathy at the appropriate times. Before moving into deeper levels of their painful histories, this couple needed to learn these skills. As we mentioned in Chapter Eight, the steps to recovery are not always linear, and movement is sometimes unpredictable.

Expressing Empathy

Understanding how others feel is the essence of empathy. Katie also needed to demonstrate an understanding of the effect her behavior had on Chuck. In the next week's psychotherapy session, heatedly describing his experience, Chuck gave her that opportunity.

"You didn't even give me a chance. All of a sudden in the middle of fight, you announced you'd been having a ridiculous 'cyber-affair' with Miguel, and that you were leaving the next morning to be with him in Peru! All I could think of was what a slut you were!" Chuck had tears in his eyes, and looked away.

In his pain, Chuck resorted to less-effective communication. He did not use the "I" statements he had been taught, but instead, used accusatory and inflammatory language that would surely bring an emotional reaction from Katie. Katie was quick to try to defend herself, but the therapist stopped her. If she could not demonstrate her understanding of the pain she caused him, her probability of healing this wound would be very low.

She was asked to take a few slow breaths, as she had been taught in previous sessions to control her emotions. She allowed herself to be coached into avoiding defensiveness, regardless of Chuck's emotional outburst. This is a difficult process, but defensiveness must be put aside for recovery.

Katie replied, "Chuck, you felt hurt and betrayed by my leaving you and flying off to Peru. I'm beginning to see how your frustration hides your pain and anxiety. I'm sorry for what I did to upset you."

Chuck responded, "Thank you. I appreciate your apology. I guess I'm just not over it yet. When my head clears a bit and I'm not so angry, I can see that I push you away when I get mean like that, like your father probably did to your mother when he wanted her to be quiet. I know it sometimes doesn't show, but I'm really trying to change and not call you names. I'm sorry."

In the next psychotherapy session, the therapist took Katie back to some of the specific events of her childhood related to her father's infidelity. As the details emerged, tears welled in Chuck's eyes. He quietly listened to his wife talk about being four years old and hiding in the closet with her older brother, Tim. Tim would gently rock her and put his fingers in her ears so she could not hear their parents fighting about their father's infidelity.

Chuck said that he wanted to know more details of both affairs, so they would have no more secrets. Over the next few months, she told him about both affairs, hers and her father's.

Katie and Chuck were instructed to use the fishbowl technique previously described, and to answer the questions Chuck put in the bowl during their regular Talk Time. Their relationship grew stronger as they became more open. Katie was healing from the wounds of long-held secrets. Chuck realized he could control his temper by understanding that it flared as his anxiety increased, and that hearing his voice rise was a cue to apply the skills he learned to relax and change his thinking. It was more work than he liked, but he practiced relaxing and thinking through the facts, rather than blowing things up in his mind.

Chuck explained, "I can feel the hair on the back of my neck begin to bristle and my voice getting louder. I need to realize that those are cues for me to relax and control myself. I am getting better at focusing on the facts and not letting my mind run wild with how she is ticking me off. I'm the one who is ticking me off. She might be doing something I don't like, but I'm the one who's getting enraged and either calling her names or walking off."

Accepting Responsibility

Cyber-infidelity is a choice, regardless of the reasoning. Katie admitted that regardless of how she felt with Chuck, no one forced her to be unfaithful. She accepted responsibility for her behavior and her deceit. In one session, she declared, "I need to learn to control myself, too. I can see that I felt humiliated and belittled, and how I played a part in it by not standing up for myself. I just reacted by secretly blaming you for everything and pulling away. It drove you to a frenzy, and didn't solve anything. I was doing to you what my mother did to my dad."

Although Katie had difficulty at first in assuming responsibility for her part of their fights, when she was able to do so, her defensive wall began to disappear. This was the first step in helping her soften her heart in psychotherapy. She came to the next therapy session with this insight, "I can't believe what happened the other day. We were dressing for the Valentine's Ball, and Chuck told me how sexy I looked in my new black dress. I felt guilty, and didn't respond.

"I put the dog into the kitchen and was turning off the lights, but as I checked all the rooms before leaving, I was telling myself a lot of really cruel things, like how I was really a liar and a cheat and didn't deserve to be going anywhere with him that night, and how our friends would all be talking about me behind my back. By the time we got to the car, I was in a really foul mood.

"Within five minutes, I had picked a fight with Chuck. I accused him of saying cruel things to me. When he reminded me that all he said was how sexy I looked, a light bulb went off in my head! I had said all those mean things, and was blaming him!

"It made me wonder how many times he had said something nice to me, and I had twisted it into the kind of thing my dad would say to my mom. Maybe I'm creating a lot of this in my own head!"

This is an example of how anxiety increases when thinking is distorted. Clearly, Katie was not separating her thinking from her feelings, and became emotionally reactive. In her thinking, Katie was jumping to conclusions and labeling. When her defensiveness had been decreased through psychotherapy, she could see these patterns. In sharing this information with her husband and their therapist, she was accepting responsibility in a deeper and more constructive way.

This was a turning point in Katie's therapy. She felt the freedom and power of admitting her truth. These historical revelations and ensuing insights helped them move toward one another in newer, deeper ways. They began to look at one another with understanding.

Reestablishing Trust

Building trust is one of the most difficult aspects of reconstructing the relationship after a cyber-affair. Trust must be built up over time. It is a slow process, and it involves many different behaviors. In her book, *After the Affair*, Janis Abrahms Spring, Ph.D., states, "When I speak of trust, I'm referring, of course, to your belief that your partner will remain faithful to you. But there's another kind of trust that matters too—the trust, essential to both of you, that if you venture back into the relationship, your partner will address your grievances and not leave you regretting your decision to recommit."

Chuck spoke in a very solemn way about an issue that had been secretly worrying him. He began, "It boils down to trust. I want to trust Katie but I still have worries." The therapist told Chuck that trust builds up slowly over time. With good communication and honesty, the foundation is laid for trust. Chuck was still holding back and he was asked to talk about his obvious concern.

"Well," he said, "I know we're working on all this, but it seems as if it's an awfully long and drawn-out effort. We're young and without children. Sometimes I think we could walk away from this without much complication. I don't know what to think. I love Katie and I want it to work. I guess I wonder if it is right to have kids in a troubled relationship."

Recovery from infidelity takes more time than most people would like to believe, because they must not only reconstruct their relationship with their partners, but each partner must work to achieve personal growth. As individuals move toward greater mastery of their own feelings and understanding of their own motivations, they can easily get overwhelmed with the tasks they see in reconstructing the relationship.

Having gotten better at controlling her reactivity, Katie calmly showed empathy and offered a reasonable solution, "Chuck, you are right. This is a lot of work, and it's too soon to have kids. We need to learn more about ourselves and take the time to make it right between us again. We're getting there. Please give me time to earn your trust again."

Chuck replied, "I'm planning on doing that, but the therapist asked about my doubts, so I thought it would be good to tell the truth. I don't know what it is, but I need something more." Chuck continued talking and revealed that Katie's continued use of the computer and the attention she gave other men still bothered him.

With this added information, Katie was able to accommodate his need. She offered to move the home computer to the living room and share her online activities with Chuck to earn his trust. They made agreements that she would bring up the topic of how often and in what ways she used the computer, rather than wait for him to ask.

The therapist also encouraged her to keep a log of when she wanted to flirt with other men and the circumstances surrounding her at those times. After keeping the log, Katie was surprised to learn that she wanted to flirt when she felt emotionally disconnected from Chuck. She laughed at herself when she explained, "It probably seems obvious, but it never occurred to me that I was flirting to get attention from a man when I was feeling disconnected from Chuck. It was usually when he was busy with a work project, or had friends visiting from out of town. Once it was when he decided to spend the weekend cleaning the garage. I went to the grocery store and found myself seriously making eyes at this good-looking guy in the checkout line.

"It seems kind of silly, but after writing down what I was thinking when I wanted to flirt, there was no denying the pattern. So I learned that those are the times I've got to go home and tell Chuck how I am feeling, and maybe flirt with *Chuck*. The good thing is that he is always responsive and when I ask him directly, I get exactly the kind of attention I need—probably because he really loves me."

Through treatment, they learned to make themselves trustworthy. They learned to trust each other emotionally and then sexually.

Igniting the Sexual Spark

When the therapist explored their sexual connection, it became obvious that their double standard of "hold me close while I mistreat you" was still apparent in their bedroom.

During their psychotherapy, they avoided sexual contact until this point. As their hearts softened, the old spark returned, but they were anxious about how to resume their sexual relationship.

Upon further discussion, it became apparent that even when they thought their sex life was acceptable, they were avoiding intimacy. As previously discussed, true love is an expression of passion, intimacy, and commitment. While they may have felt passion, they were not aware of how to experience full intimacy, and therefore, their commitment wavered.

The therapist asked them if they looked at each other during lovemaking. Chuck answered first, "Well, I sort of look at her. I mean I see her, and I like what I see."

Chuck was trying to answer light-heartedly and his embarrassment was obvious. Katie was slower in responding, but when she spoke up, she demonstrated that she had learned how to be more direct. "Well, we look at each other a bit, then we both close our eyes and go off someplace. It isn't very satisfying."

Chuck was visibly upset again. "Other women have found me to be a great lover. I don't understand what our problem is."

Many Americans have not learned to deepen their intimacy through eye contact. Chuck and Katie visually closed each other out, would retreat into fantasy and expect the other to bring them wild, passionate sex. They both excused themselves from making love to one another, and focused intently upon their own fantasies. They tried to stimulate themselves mentally while insisting that their lover stimulate them physically. While Chuck thought he knew how to make love to a woman, he did not know how to make love to his wife. She did not know how to love him, either, because she couldn't keep contact with him, to guide him through what she wanted. Their sexual trust for one another changed when they practiced making love with their eyes open and communicating more fully about their respective desires.

Chuck later reported energetically, "I am beginning to have sexual daydreams about Katie again! It's the strangest thing, but I am having sexual fantasies about coming home to her. This eye contact thing is really working!"

As Katie and Chuck continued to experiment with making contact and keeping agreements, they rebuilt their relationship and reestablished trust.

Making Internet Agreements
Because the anonymity, accessibility, and affordability of the Internet make it easier to commit infidelity, couples recovering from cyber-infidelity need to be in agreement regarding their respective uses of the Internet. People whose marriages have been harmed by improper use of the Internet need to attend to the role of the computer in the reconstruction of their marriage. When they move further along the path of recovery, they may think about using the computer together for fun and education. The Internet offers many mutual areas of interest to explore, not just sexual playgrounds. If you are able to do this, your computer can be returned to its rightful place as a tool, rather than a messenger of pain.

Reducing Codependency
In the classic definition of codependency, partners of individuals dependent on a substance are seen as participating in the problem. Their participation is due to their lack of skill in asserting their own needs. In exchange for being accepted, codependent individuals seek and find others for whom they can care.

In Chuck's case, he worked long hours to improve his sales management position with the pharmaceutical company. His efforts were not being rewarded at work or at home. Codependent people often experience themselves as victims who are powerless to change the situation. Compounding Chuck's feeling of helplessness at work was the realization that he pushed Katie away with his own behavior, by badgering, humiliating, and belittling her.

In effect, before the affair and the resulting psychotherapy, they were locked in a dance that indicated a low level of differentiation. Chuck worked harder to maintain his job, but was cruel to Katie. In turn, Katie was hurt and refused to give him the devotion he wanted. Katie distanced herself from Chuck. Rather than connecting with them to work out their problem, she was cutting off emotionally. It was clear that they were functioning at a low level. They did not know how to self-define and self-validate and reacted emotionally rather than rationally.

Making Peace with Separateness
Katie and Chuck were a young couple, and the rupture in their relationship occurred before they could experience the normal individuation that occurs

in long-term relationships. To complicate matters further, they were still operating with the weak self-management and communication skills they had learned in their families of origin. Once they had learned new means of coping with their emotions and communicating, they needed to learn to accept each other's separate desires without feeling threatened. At this point in the relationship, Katie and Chuck were ready to learn how to tolerate their separateness.

They needed to learn to not only take responsibility for their actions, but also to give each other the space to make their own decisions and live through the consequences of those decisions. Chuck wanted to have a private meeting with Miguel that next week, when he flew in for a meeting at their office. Katie was horrified at the idea, fearing that Miguel would try to get Chuck fired. Worse yet, they both could be fired. Chuck was adamant that he needed to settle this matter for himself.

Chuck ranted, "This has nothing to do with you. It is man to man. He won't fire me because he knows I can expose him and all his little dirty secrets. He invaded my life, and he's going to hear about it. Besides, I want to look into his eyes and see what you found so attractive about him." Katie remained silent at the prompting of the therapist. Much of the focus of the therapy had been on Katie and her needs, and Chuck deserved some understanding as well. He was finally voicing some of his needs, although they initially surfaced indirectly.

Chuck continued, "Who the hell does he think he is anyway? He just left you on that street corner, at night, in Peru. What a jerk. I'd like to punch his lights out."

Feeling the need to assess his threat, the therapist responded at this point, "Really?"

Chuck lowered his voice a bit, and said, "No, not really. Well, yeah, I'd like to, but I wouldn't. I'm bigger than him, and I might just hurt him." He smiled. "But I would like to face him and tell him what a low-life I think he is."

Katie had been noticing how the therapist allowed them both to speak their minds, then come to their own decisions with occasional prompting. She did the same, "OK, say you meet with him, then what will happen?"

"Well, I'd tell him he's a low-life, and then I'd walk out."

"OK, then what would happen?" Katie asked.

"Well, I'd go to my office and shut the door." Chuck began laughing. "Then I'd probably be worried about how he'd sneak around and do something really slimy, like tell my boss that I'm messing up his account, or call you in to tell you what I jerk I am, or God knows what. I'd probably be a wreck all day. I hate him. I still wish I could punch his lights out."

Much to her credit, Katie stepped right in, with empathy and a good interpretation of his emotion. "Yeah, I don't blame you. But I'll bet you're more upset with me for falling for him. We've both known what a slime he is from the beginning. Do you think maybe you need something else from me, like for me to tell you how much I love you, or to tell you how much I'm devoted to you?"

"Yeah, I probably need a lot more of that," Chuck said. "But there's more. Since we've been married, I'm just not the same guy. I think I need to just get some time to myself. I think I might need to go away for a couple days after the vacation we have planned before your promotion. Maybe I'll go spend a couple days with my brother in Phoenix. It's warm there, and I could just relax. And I know you will be faithful while I'm gone."

Katie wasn't expecting that answer. She thought she was being generous, but now he wanted to visit his brother without her. She did not like the idea, but understood. At the prompting of the therapist, she said, "Well, if you think that will help you, I support you doing it. I don't like us being apart, but Jerry is good to you, so sure, go ahead. I promise I'll be here when you get back. And both before and after, I'll tell you how much I love and am devoted to you, OK?"

Katie and Chuck were learning not only to communicate with their intellect, but also to make the type of difficult decisions that would allow them to separate and come back to one another. Chuck needed to assert his manliness with his expression of hostility toward Miguel, and when he was given the time to do so, Katie was able to move in and connect with him emotionally. She did not expect that he would take that as an opportunity to take yet another step away from her by announcing his need for a few days with his brother. She did not fuss, but rather expressed her support of his taking the time he wanted for himself.

Katie and Chuck were coming to peace with their ability to be two separate people. When couples learn to allow for differences, they can reconnect in new and more energized ways, including a new type of courtship.

Courtship

Courtship is a crucial part of reconstructing a relationship. When a couple is willing to soften toward one another and resume the courtship activities that initially drew them together, recovery is significantly advanced. Katie and Chuck planned time together and made it a priority. During those times, they were instructed not to bring up anything related to the infidelity. They were working on reestablishing the feeling of 'specialness' to each other that had been lost.

Therapists working to reconcile infidelity routinely ask about weekend plans, trips, and ways in which messages of caring are sent to each other. Couples must get in a habit of planning time to spend together. Psychologist Bonnie Eaker Weil, Ph.D., writing in her book, *Adultery: The Forgivable Sin,* says that couples need to learn how to enjoy each other and have fun together. She suggests that having fun becomes a top priority for a couple.

It is serious business and couples who are revitalizing their relationship need to have enjoyable events every week, whether they are dancing lessons, picnics, roller skating, or surprise dates.

At one session, Katie reported, "Now that our Talk Time is less emotional, we have started to use it to plan our activities for the week and the weekend together. And it is really great. I no longer wait for things to happen, Chuck and I make them happen, and so there is less resentment between us."

Affection

The affection couples may have shown each other in the past naturally disappears on hearing about cyber-infidelity. However, it must be gently coaxed back as part of the process of reconstructing the relationship. Katie and Chuck initially had difficulty resuming the kiss on the cheek, the hand on the waist, the long hugs, and the frequent smiles they once shared. Research has shown that these little signs of affection are often the "glue" that helps cement a broken relationship and maintain a good one. The wound to the heart brought through cyber-infidelity requires tenderness, delivered by word and deed. As Chuck said, "At first it was awkward because it felt like a homework assignment. We kept at it, and the awkwardness eventually passed. Now I look forward to seeing Katie's smile and getting a hug when one of us walks through the door."

Finding Closure

As we have seen, recovery from cyber-infidelity occurs in steps. In the beginning, the most important tasks are identifying, expressing, and coping with a roller coaster of emotions. The next step involves the search for understanding. Then, couples must reconstruct the relationship by working through individual and couple issues that led to the affair. The final step includes the apology and closure. This concluding step makes cyber-infidelity part of the couple's history. They have learned and grown from it, but it is no longer the focus of their relationship. Katie and Chuck were ready for a sincere and believable apology.

Making the Apology

Katie accepted her responsibility for her role in the cyber-infidelity and gave Chuck the apology he needed. Her apology shows the growth and understanding she has achieved:

"Chuck, I know I hurt you. Honey, I understand the anger you feel because I started a relationship with Miguel on the Internet and flew down to Peru to be with him. I was wrong to do that. I thought I was falling in love with him and out of love with you. That was silly. I didn't even know him. Meanwhile, I broke my promise of fidelity to you. I lied and cheated on you. You have the right to feel betrayed not only for my infidelity, but also because I've held you responsible for my happiness in this marriage. I see these things now, and am grateful that you are willing to be with me. I am willing to do whatever it takes to restore our relationship."

The apology must have all these ingredients: sincerity, contrition, remorse, empathy, and a pledge never to let it happen again. An apology must be sincerely felt and given. It took Chuck time to accept Katie's apology, until he felt her true remorse and understanding of the suffering and pain she had caused both of them. Sincere apologies include an admission of responsibility for incorrect behavior. They also indicate an understanding of the suffering caused by deceit, and the impact of betrayal on the emotions of one's partner. Remorse must be apparent. Apologies will be accepted more easily over time, after evidence of day-to-day effort to sincerely rebuild a relationship.

Early and profuse apologies are often rejected by the faithful partner who needs time to overcome the shock, cope with the pain, and express these emotions before being capable of accepting an apology. Katie apologized in her telephone call to Chuck from Peru, when she asked if she could come home. She and Chuck were in the midst of an emotional storm, and that apology was not of the same depth as the one she gave in therapy. Chuck's shock and anger prevented him from hearing Katie's early apology. Her first apology was necessary, but could not be the kind that is offered after coming to an in-depth understanding of their issues. Initial apologies are important, but are akin to dowsing a house fire with a bucket of water. Her initial apology was laced with fear of being belittled, and resentment toward herself for what she saw as crawling back to him. It did not heal their wounds, but did allow her to regain entry to their relationship.

Renegotiating the Promise of Fidelity
A sincere apology also includes a promise not to engage in any further infidelities. A promise of fidelity should also include a pledge to continue the work of mending the underlying problem that led to the affair. This includes an agreement to communicate any future discomfort, problem, or worry as it arises. The pledge also works toward building trust that future problems and dissatisfactions will be discussed and worked out rather than acted upon without the knowledge of the other partner.

As time passed, Katie renegotiated her promise of fidelity with Chuck by writing the following to him:

Dearest Chuck,
I know I've caused both of us a lot of pain. I promise to be faithful to you, and to be sexual only with you. If problems arise in keeping my promise, I will speak with you about it. I will not betray your trust. I will always be honest with you.

Chuck found this note on his birthday, folded neatly in his birthday card. He was very touched. In our next therapy session, though, he took out the written promise and admitted he wanted Katie to add that she would never use the Internet or any other technology to be sexual with another person. He also requested that she apologize to his parents, because they were both aware of Katie's cyber-infidelity. Katie respectfully added the sentence to the bottom of the note, and then asked him to give her a similar written promise about his behavior toward her. They had successfully renegotiated their fidelity agreement!

Apologizing to Loved Ones

Katie's work continued with her apologies to Chuck's parents. It is often most difficult for an unfaithful partner to apologize to an in-law. When Katie apologized to Chuck's parents, she said, "I cannot tell you how sorry I am for the pain I have caused to both of you and to Chuck. I am responsible for and ashamed of what I have done, and I will never do this again. I love your son and will do everything to regain his trust, and yours as well."

The apology to Chuck's parents helped them support Chuck in his reunion with his wife, put an end to their questioning of their son, and helped Katie and Chuck heal the wound of her infidelity.

Katie also wanted to apologize to a coworker who was privy to the affair and had become overinvolved. Katie told her coworker, "Faith, I'm sorry for the pain I caused you in sharing too many of my problems about my affair. It was unfair of me to tell you so much. Chuck and I are now in therapy and working things out. We are OK now."

After Chuck received Katie's apology, he said in one of the therapy sessions, "I appreciate your apology for the hurt that you've caused me. I also want to apologize for my verbal abuse."

Making Amends

It is also important to make amends through words and deeds. Making amends is also helpful to the unfaithful partner, because it helps to alleviate feelings of guilt.

Dr. Janis Abrahms Spring writes in her book, *After the Affair,* "Trust is not a gift. It must be earned, and not with verbal reassurances alone, but with specific changes in behavior. You, the unfaithful partner, need to demonstrate to your partner through bold, concrete actions that 'I'm committed to you. You're safe with me.'"

Breaking off the affair with your virtual lover, making specific agreements about your future use of the computer, and keeping your partner informed of your Internet activities are steps in the right direction. Initiating conversations about your commitment to the relationship is also a way of reassuring your partner that you are committed to working on the relationship. Making Talk Time a regular part of your life provides a structure for discussion of problems and plans, and for building structure for your work together as a team.

Talk Time can continue to be an established way of working together even after the cyber-infidelity is resolved. Asking your partner for specific behaviors you can accomplish daily or weekly to reassure him or her of your intention can also be very helpful in making amends and rebuilding trust.

As partners feel they are well along the path of recovery, we have seen many ask something special of the other. The request usually comes in the form of a gift—a "makeup gift." Chuck said, "Yeah, I want something. I want her to quit her job at the company. I know she is upset with Miguel, but he worked his charms on her in the past, and I still am not comfortable with her seeing him when he comes to our office. I know it's a big building and she only sees him when other people are around, but whenever it happens I go insane. I have tried to control myself and not say anything, but I live in constant dread of their meeting. This is very self-serving, but I want her to take the time she needs to find a reasonable job elsewhere and leave. And as soon as I can leave, I'll do it too. Given what's happened there, working there is tainted for both of us." Later he added, with a chuckle, "And oh, an occasional breakfast in bed would be great."

Katie responded appropriately, "Oh no! I was afraid it would come to this. I'm in line for a promotion to regional manager with a huge budget next month, and this has been my dream for years. The product I'll be promoting is really hot, and likely to be a market first. It would involve lots of traveling and being away, but it also has lots of perks that would be good for both of us.

"But to be honest, I'm not sure if I'm getting the job because Miguel influenced it somehow, or if I earned this on my own. Breaks come in interesting ways in such a large company, so it's hard to tell, and I certainly didn't ask any questions when my boss announced the news to me last month."

A willingness to leave her promising future with this pharmaceutical company was a symbol to Chuck of his wife choosing him. It was an acknowledgement that she had tainted the company for both of them with her decision to have an affair with an important client.

Chuck visibly relaxed when he heard his wife express the fear he had not been willing to voice. He too, suspected the promotion. He had not wanted to upset Katie, so he had kept quiet. He now said, "Wow, I never thought I'd hear you say that. You really are trying to be honest with me, aren't you? Look, I'll make a deal with you. What if you accept the promotion and plan to leave the company once that new product is launched, like in six months or so? That way, everyone will benefit, but I know there will be an end to my worries."

Katie's heart softened, and she once again rose to the occasion, "OK, that will be our plan. Chuck, I promise you that I will act in a completely professional way in any meeting or correspondence I have with Miguel. I will not engage in any small talk or banter. It will be strictly business. I will also tell you of any contact that I have with Miguel in person, by phone, or by email.

"Meanwhile, I'll let you know whenever I've got a meeting with Miguel, regardless of how many other people are there. I don't want you to worry about any of that. You are my husband, and I don't want anyone else—especially after all the work we've been through to find each other again!"

Many people who have endured tragedy or trauma in their lives have the need to symbolize its end with a ritual or a demonstration of love and caring that shows the importance of the relationship. In expressing his concerns about Katie's forthcoming promotion, Chuck was able to give Katie the opportunity to demonstrate her love for him. By taking the risk to voice the suspicion they both had in their hearts, she was able to demonstrate her commitment to him in yet another way. Her willingness to leave her prestigious job was a symbol of her devotion to him and gave him reason to trust her yet again. They had negotiated a compromise that worked for everyone.

Finding Meaning

It is important for couples that have been coping with cyber-infidelity to know that suffering eventually deceases. However, it is important to find meaning from suffering. If not, it can leave bitterness and lingering resentment. As Katie said, "It was a horrible experience, but I am finding strength and making sense of it all. I suffered, and I made Chuck suffer. But I know from this suffering, a happy life is ahead of us. If we had not continued on our path to recovery, we would not have learned the lessons we needed to learn to grow up and be mature adults. We would not have learned how to communicate properly, and we would probably have taught our future children to react in ways that are similar to the ways we were taught to react. Well, the generation 'buck' stops right here. We paid a high price, but we have reversed the training of our families and will teach our children to understand themselves and be more respectful of the ones they love."

Tolerating Setbacks

If you are like most couples, you will experience both good and bad days. The ratio of good to bad days will increase, and the number of good days will eventually predominate. Bad days might occur at anniversaries, holidays, and other significant dates. You might not be aware of any particular reason for sadness. These dates can include the date the infidelity began, was discovered, was admitted, and the date it was revealed to family and friends, or any other related occurrence. During the course of psychotherapy, couples often take steps forward, only to slip backward for any number of reasons, such as the emergence of new information, personal and family events unrelated to cyber-infidelity, or because of miscommunication. Final closure on the wounds of cyber-infidelity is difficult to predict. Closure occurs over time, and at whatever pace is needed by each member of the couple.

"Christmas sucks this year," Chuck told us. "I was looking for decorations in the attic and found a folder of her email to Miguel! I can't believe she kept them. I threw them away, but it slipped me right back to where I was a year ago. And I was beginning to forget that intense kind of pain. Will these feelings ever go away?"

Recognizing Loss

Setbacks can also be the result of a specific loss. As we discussed in Chapter Six, couples experience a variety of losses when infidelity is discovered. These losses often include the loss of innocence, commitment, specialness, confidence, shared dreams, and health.

At times during the course of therapy, both Katie and Chuck showed signs of sadness. They were encouraged to use their newly-learned communication skills to express these feelings. Once, early in therapy, Katie replied, "I feel like I really blew it and messed things up. It's like I killed something in our marriage. I feel so terrible that I have a knot in my stomach. I can't eat, and I can barely sleep."

Chuck added, "I'm worried about her. She's lost fifteen pounds."

Katie replied, "I've lost more than that. I've lost Chuck's trust, and I can't look at myself in the mirror. I can't stand who I see."

Chuck was asked what he thought of what Katie said, and he answered, "Well, we've lost a lot. It hurts. But we haven't lost our love for each other, our passion, and although Katie's commitment wavered—she's back. We still have our shared dreams for the future. We haven't lost that. So we have some important things left. And I haven't lost my love for her. "

When cyber-infidelity touches a relationship, it feels like a death, and many of the steps in death and dying are similar to what Katie and Chuck were feeling. Often, there is denying or minimizing the significance of what happened. When those defenses are no longer operating, anger, bargaining, and depression follow. The sadness is depression over their losses.

The final stage of loss is acceptance, and with that, depression is likely to lift. Working together on the path of recovery, Katie and Chuck eventually accepted what happened and were able to continue to build a good life together.

Closure is gradual, as couples realize they have become safer with one another. They feel each other's comfortable presence and find that infidelity is no longer paramount in their thinking. A ritual of closure or a celebration of renewal can mark this meaningful period. It is beneficial and appropriate to decide upon such a closing event together.

Thinking of smashing the computer is not closure. Thinking of a romantic getaway to a place you both yearn to visit is a sign of being on the right track. A book of love poems, new music, or any special symbol can bring closure to this difficult time.

Conclusion

When we assess Katie and Chuck's situation, we can see that they were willing to stay emotionally connected to each other; even with the high levels of anxiety they felt. However, they had not learned to communicate their needs in many areas. They each lived a secret life of despair. As with many couples healing from infidelity, it took time to uncover their individual contributions to the situation, and then mend the hurt of the affair. There were many interruptions along their path toward recovery. This is to be expected with all couples. It is important for you to understand this so that your anxiety will not rise when having a bad day. Remember to look on such days as minor setbacks, only to be inevitably followed by forward movement.

They started with reducing anxiety and increasing communication skills. Katie and Chuck learned that intimacy meant sharing their inner thoughts and inner lives. Neither Katie nor Chuck were aware of inner thoughts, and did not know themselves well enough to recognize and communicate these thoughts as they occurred. When they were able to communicate with each other, improvements took place in other areas of their life. When they appreciated each other's history, they developed more understanding and compassion for one another, and were able to renew their commitment to fidelity.

Follow-Up

Six months after the end of therapy, Katie sent an update.

"We are doing great! We are not arguing as much, but when we do, Chuck is holding up his end of the bargain, that is, working on being sweet to me after a fight. He approaches me at least 50 percent of the time after we argue, so it isn't only my job to make up again. The best part of it all is that we are hardly fighting. And I'm learning to forgive myself for the error I made with seeking false comfort in a cyber-affair. Now, I'm putting all that energy into learning new ways to work things out with Chuck. Not only is our sex life improving, but also we plan to have our first baby soon."

Had Chuck and Katie left their marriage, they could have taken the time to learn to control their emotions, understand their motivations, and develop better relationship skills—but that is unlikely. Most people find someone new, get swept into new passion, and "fall in love," only to discover that they have, in essence, picked a partner with similar dynamics and with whom they construct a familiar pattern of interaction.

Couples have much invested in one another—time, dreams, memories, and often children. Before closing the door on all that is shared and all that is hoped for, make a solid attempt to rebuild on the foundation of your current relationship.

Infidelity on the Internet

New technology expands and assimilates past technologies. The quill pen was sequentially replaced by the ink pen, the manual typewriter, the electric typewriter, the word processor, and now email. Marconi's early radio has evolved into technologies that send invisible signals to televisions and wireless telephones. The World Wide Web integrates them all, and promises to deliver a host of new features to serve our basic communication and entertainment needs.

Unlike our recent ancestors of one hundred years ago, people float in and out of face-to-face contact, extend the conversation via car phone on the way to work, zoom down the freeway encased in metal and fiberglass vehicles, and without giving their shifting reality a second thought, resume conversations started a day or a week prior with coworkers. They do not experience these shifts in time and space as anything unusual, but rather, the conveniences are seen as luxuries, as time-savers. These conveniences expose human weakness as well as strength, however.

With ever-increasing Internet power, we will have the opportunity to learn more about how individuals and groups use such powerful tools to break their promises of fidelity, or to strengthen them. We will discover how closely technology can replace or enhance human relationships, and how often, if ever, we need to intersperse email, chat, or video contacts with face-to-face meetings to keep them reliable, flexible, and alive.

Technology blurs reality in subtle and yet powerful ways. For example, people sometimes exchange a series of voice mail messages, and fail to remember if they actually spoke with each other, or if the information received was only from voicemail. It seems reasonable to assume that people will use technology to have new experiences, define themselves differently, and grow from their learning.

Similar yet more fundamental questions arise when considering the impact of telecommunication technologies upon our committed relationships. With estimates of Internet sexuality skyrocketing in the future, it is likely that we will see an increasing number of people integrate their experience of heightened emotional and sexual arousal through technology. For whom will these experiences become integrated into their committed relationships? For whom will they develop into private worlds where infidelity can flourish in evermore secretive ways? It is obvious that we are increasing our potential for infidelity through computers, pagers, and cell phones. The impact upon different people in different circumstances is yet unknown.

Given the increasing development of these potentially clandestine technologies, it is likely that some individuals will not invest the time and energy to improving their committed relationships, but rather relieve their tensions and frustrations by grabbing a "quickie" from a stranger, anywhere, anytime on the Internet. Some of these escapades will be experienced by their committed partners as betrayal and deceit. For other couples, openness about such activities may become commonplace, and the full range of associated behaviors will be accepted. For them, such behavior may simply be considered a high-tech form of innocent masturbation. Current indicators show these reactions vary according to gender. It is likely that future research into cyber-sex will show that reactions of primary partners will also vary according to age, religious training, culture, and other important variables.

Just as we can see diversity within definitions of Internet-based sexuality, it is likely that society will struggle to understand individuals in relationships made more complex through technology. Such concepts challenge the imagination and raise more questions regarding human values and definitions of relationships. Deb Levine, health education consultant from San Francisco, writing about Internet attraction in the article "Virtual Attraction: What Rocks Your Boat," discusses the potential of online relationships. "For some people, online attraction in relationships will become a valid substitute for more traditional relationships. Those who are housebound or rurally isolated, and those who are ostracized from society for any number of different reasons, may turn to online relationships as their sole source of companionship." For these people, living through technology will be better than real life. It is yet to be seen how many people will be able to integrate this technology into developing more gratifying primary relationships.

For others, technology will rob the human experience of the soulful, essential qualities of real life. Dr. Schnarch, in the June 1997 *Journal of Sex Education and Therapy*, writes, "...a cyberrelationship may approximate a real relationship—but then, so does sex with an inflatable doll. Neither one is likely to help people develop substantial capacity for an intimate relationship when they are subtly capitalizing on ways either one differs from the real thing." For those who fight impulses toward infidelity, the temptations of the Internet may lead to the demise of their current relationships.

The central issue is that we have developed the technologies to extend our freedoms, but we do not yet have the systems to control abuse of those freedoms. Our existing value systems are profoundly challenged by the previously unattainable, and the previously unimaginable. As a group, in terms of computerized and global networking, humanity is like a precocious child, where social and intellectual development are out of step with one another. Many people are not emotionally equipped to handle the range of free choice we have developed for our desktops. But they will learn. The ever-accelerating Internet will force this learning. Definitions of human behavior will become more precise, values will be learned, and social mores will be created to protect people from each other and themselves. We will inevitably mature through this time of transition into a global community. Meanwhile, as a global population integrating telecommunication technologies, we will learn to communicate more effectively, and suffer the required growing pains inherent to such a process. Through the lessons we bring to ourselves and our children, our values will undoubtedly be stronger. Our sense of personal responsibility and freedom to choose will eventually be tempered with more wisdom.

The Internet enigma is that we have developed tools that give us more choices than ever, improving our functioning on one hand and harming ourselves on the other. Yet, the solution to the complex problems posed by the Internet is simple. It is to be found in the present moment and is comprised of individual behavior and responsibility. The key to the future is in how we handle this moment, this frustration, this loneliness, this stress, this breath, this flirtation, and this sexual impulse. It is in how we accept the repercussions of our behavior upon ourselves, our loved ones, and those with whom we interact on the Internet.

As previously described, cyber-infidelity occurs when a partner in a committed relationship uses the computer or the Internet to violate promises, vows, or agreements concerning sexual exclusivity. Our choices will begin with how we respect the promises we have made to ourselves and our loved ones, moment to moment.

Our choices will be reflected in how we communicate our fidelity agreements, and how we include or exclude agreements about behavior made possible by telecommunications technologies. They will also determine how we mend the relationships we have broken through misuse of the Internet. Those decisions will serve as examples for our children, and will shape their development through this age of technology. We have the opportunity to make new decisions, reach new people, and determine our fate more than ever before. The choices are ours to make. The task is great and the stakes are high.

Let us begin with ourselves and our families. Let us look at how to communicate our core values about fidelity with our partners, negotiate our differences, and teach these values to our children. It is the challenge of this new century to aim for improvement through technology, for us as human beings and for our world.

We live in a technological world: it calls for brave definitions and clear communications.

Appendix A: Understanding the Internet

The following appendix provides an introduction to the Internet for anyone unfamiliar with its structure, usage, and common terms.

Navigating the Internet

Welcome to the virtual world. We are going to explain the technology of cyberspace, how to get there, and how to find your way around it. Your knowledge of how to navigate the Internet will be needed to help you understand cyber-infidelity. Let us start with the basics of where people meet and how technology helps them to connect.

Components

The basic components are a computer, a connection (modem, cable, or high-speed telephone line), and a service provider. Service providers can be small, local operations, telephone companies, or large, international groups such as America Online or Prodigy.

Types of Communication

There are two fundamental types of communication online: synchronous and asynchronous communication. Synchronous connection is also known as "real time." With synchronous communication, people connect and can respond to each other immediately, thought-by-thought, such as talking through a walkie-talkie. With asynchronous connection, messages are sent to people and they are free to be retrieved at the recipient's convenience.

Channels for Meeting in Cyberspace

There are several communication channels where people can meet large numbers of potential dating partners on the Internet. To help you understand how people function on the Internet, here's a description of the various lanes of the information superhighway, and how people generally navigate each one.

Websites

If the Internet were indeed a superhighway, the World Wide Web would be the access lane, the lane where you could get on and off and could maneuver to reach almost any other lane. In essence, the Web is being increasingly developed to allow access to many specialized services, as detailed below. Websites are by far the most visually appealing, with special features that make participation fun, easy, and often quite stimulating. Viewing websites requires software called a Web browser, which transports users to other Internet computers anywhere in the world.

Ads

Many different sorts of websites offer a wide variety of types of information and opportunity to their users. Some websites also offer readers the opportunity to post a personal ad. The ads have the same function as those in newspapers and magazines, that is, to search for someone, to sell, to buy, or to notify, and they can be and usually are explicit.

Profiles

In larger websites, people typically create a profile of themselves using an alias as their name or identifier. They might include a photo and history, which can be either fabricated or real. These profiles are frequently used by those who notice someone's writing and want to know more about them before making an approach.

Website Features

A website can display fancy fonts, layouts, pictures, or can send music, voices, moans, groans, and heavy breathing noises, as well as any other sounds heard through your computer speakers. Pornography is widespread on the Internet, and with all the features available, is just short of actual physical contact. Of course, often there is a fee paid with a credit card. But people looking for love and relationships tend to avoid the pornographic websites and communicate through places such as dating websites.

WAV files can be listened to by anyone with speakers attached to their system. They are files that record sound. With improved technology, video clips and even live images can also be stored and displayed at websites. These environments often hold information or entertainment, and usually are free or very low-cost to any individual user. There are also many consumer-oriented sites, where goods and specialized services can be purchased.

Newsgroups and Bulletin Board Systems (BBS)

These are electronic versions of the bulletin boards, like those found at most large grocery stores. They do not include pictures–they are text-only environments and are cataloged by general topic. You can read what other people have posted, or can post your own message. You can write down someone's information and contact him or her privately when you have time.

A newsgroup name usually gives an indication about its theme. Postings on a newsgroup can range from a few messages per day to a few hundred. An example is <alt.singles>, which contains thousands of messages every day. Newsgroups are asynchronous, in that messages are waiting to be retrieved by the user. This is similar to email, in that it also can be viewed when convenient.

Email
Electronic mail (email) operates much like having a post office box in your home. People send you mail which you can retrieve at your leisure. Email is similar to old-fashioned letter writing. It is correspondence on a page, but in its electronic form you see it printed on your computer screen. One of the primary features of email is that it is asynchronous, and thereby able to be retrieved at any time of day or night by the recipient. This benefit provides flexibility and convenience unknown to those of us who grew up with telephones that often demand attention, even when screening calls through an answering machine. Email also offers the ability to send a message to a small group, or to thousands of people at once.

Attachments
Pictures and graphics can be added to an email as a special feature, called an "attachment." Newer technologies have made pictures available directly in email.

Other Features
Newer technology for videomail is available and gaining popularity. It is possible to send email as a file containing a video clip of you delivering your message in your own voice, whenever your intended recipient is ready for you.

Email addresses look like the following: seekingluv@hostname. All email addresses have the @ sign in them. Many email-related problems still need to be corrected, such as privacy, copyright, sales, taxation, and the confidential safekeeping of financial and healthcare information. Accounts can be obtained without a fee, purchased from small companies in your local area, or from large national and even international organizations. Examples of some of the larger service providers are America Online, Prodigy, Juno, and Compuserve.

Anonymous Servers
These services take incoming email, automatically change the email address to a fixed identification number or an "alias" name, and forward the mail

to its intended recipient after a random time delay. The email can then be successfully delivered to the appropriate party, but it is almost impossible to trace the identity of the source of the original message. Individuals seeking cyber-infidelity and cyber-romance are frequent users of these services. A few popular services of this type include Hotmail (email), Dejanews (news reading and posting service), iName (email), and Mailmasher (email). People use combinations of anonymous servers and identifiable servers for different purposes.

Other Text-Based Environments
A number of other text-based environments exist on the Internet. They include chat rooms, Internet Relay Chat, MUDs (Multi-user Dungeons), and MOOs (Multi-User Object Oriented Sites).

Internet Relay Chat (IRC)
These are live, or synchronous, areas of the Internet, but they do not use the World Wide Web. Rather, users are required to download a program to dial into available servers. This software also allows people to set up chat rooms (called channels), set up different aspects of the chat room, and choose their "handles." Handles are essentially aliases, whereby people can participate without fear of being discovered. IRC was the basis for chat rooms as described above, but has continued to thrive in its own right, separate from chat rooms accessible through the Web.

Chat Rooms
Chat rooms usually exist in websites, although they originated from Internet Relay Chat rooms. However you access them, they are similar to party lines for text conversations. A large number of people can "talk" (type) to each other simultaneously. When people communicate with each other and receive responses within seconds, the interaction is said to occur in "real time." In chat rooms, messages are sent immediately in response to messages on a screen. They typically are brief. Answers, comments, and questions appear on the screen within seconds of being typed–all at the same time, as received by the mediating computer, wherever it is located in the world. This makes for a fast-paced and exciting world, where new thoughts bombard the user from nowhere and anywhere. Despite its apparent complexity, ongoing discussions successfully continue simultaneously.

Chat rooms are an example of synchronous connection, in that people type a sentence, send it, and the other person sees and responds within seconds. By approximating real-time conversation, some people can communicate for hours. Others get frustrated with the slowness of the medium, and prefer to simply pick up the telephone and speak their thoughts more quickly.

Purpose
When people return to a chat room or any other text-based environment with regularity, others come to know their handle, and over time make them feel as though they belong to the community. Newcomers are welcomed and regulars settle into roles with each other. People are people, doing what they do. They can hang out with the larger group, flirt, gossip, and exchange information. In fact, many interactions in even the romantic chat rooms have nothing to do with romance.

Wherever people connect, they are people, and inevitably bring to the situation their own dynamics. It is surprising to many that chat rooms can offer some of the same types of exchanges that can be experienced in the real world. In chat rooms designed for romance, special features make the environment particularly conducive to flirting and dating. Couples can easily meet in a large area, converse, and agree to meet privately in another room. Anyone can set up a private room and invite someone else to enter. In essence, they can lock the door, prohibiting others from viewing their exchanges.

Instant Messages
Such invitations are sent via public messages to the large group room, but most often they are sent by private email messages to the personal email address or name required of all who enter the room. Some larger services have become creative and developed their own terms and programs to send such messages. For example, America Online (AOL) has developed the term Instant Message for such private exchanges or invitations.

To provide a measure of safety, some chat rooms allow the capability of blocking email from specified users, such as someone who just broke off a relationship and is still angry. People often use chat rooms to begin their dating experience because so many people can be screened so easily. People go into private rooms to talk, have cyber-sex, have a cyber-affair, exchange photos, arrange meetings, or exchange phone numbers.

Talkers
As with almost every other aspect of technology, popular communication vehicles are being combined to form hybrid and multi-dimensional tools. A very popular example of such a hybrid is known as the "talker," which combines elements of both chat rooms and bulletin boards. Talkers allow real-time communication while giving access to documents, pictures, graphics, or even websites to everyone involved.

MUDs and MOOs
These are sites on the Web and many derivations are text-based places where people take on the role of a character in a game or scene. All the

action is described in words on a screen, and people interact using keyboards to type words that appear upon everyone's screen synchronously. The early history of MUDs is interesting in that it demonstrates how quickly environments can evolve electronically, depending upon the needs and interests of users worldwide. Knowing about the origins of MUDs will help you understand their attraction.

The first MUD was developed in 1978 by Dr. Richard Bartle at the University of Essex, England. He called his program a "Multi-User Dungeon," loosely based on the popular adventure game known as "Dungeons and Dragons." In his MUD world, players competed for points with each other by slaying monsters and finding treasures. Although everyone starts on equal footing, after accumulating enough points, players advance to the next rank, which gives access to greater powers. This essentially evolved into a social hierarchy, ranging from "Newbies" (new players) to intermediate levels, and finally culminating in earning the title and powers of "Wizard."

Today, MUDs typically use similar ranking systems. These early fantasy-adventure MUDs have since evolved into over seven hundred different types of virtual environments throughout the Internet. Now the acronym MUD is used to refer to other derivations and subtypes, such as MOO (MUD, Object Oriented). A very popular example of the MUD concept is "LamdaMOO," maintained by Xerox Corporation. Its metaphor is that of a large, rambling house, where members interact through social activities that range from hanging out to flirting, and even to having virtual sex. This basic concept of creating virtual living space is optimized using newer technologies to create communities that form countless different purposes, including romantic or sexual activities.

What do people in these places do to form such deep connections? When entering such an area, people choose their gender, pseudo-name, abilities, and appearance of the character they wish to portray. People can then use a set of "actions" that are set up by the MOO or MUD to interact with others.

Popularity of Text-Based Environments

The amount of information transmitted in text-based environments is greatly limited, so why are these text-based environments so popular?

- People can participate anytime they want—no long waiting periods are necessary.
- They can assume an alias, an alternative name, and operate in the guise of someone else.
- If a person does not answer, it is possible to ask someone else a question.
- Even for a slow reader, the lines are often limited in length, and participants are identified by alias as the first part of their message, so it's easy to pick out whose conversation you'd like to follow.

○ The shortened message format requires an active imagination to grasp a participant's full meaning. The downside to this, of course, is a higher level of misunderstanding, due to errors in interpretation. Someone might choose a vague term or easily misread a phrase, and the recipient might get the wrong impression. Sarcasm seems to be more easily misunderstood, because of the limited nature of this environment.

○ People can screen dozens of others within an hour—looking for someone who strikes their fancy. Once such contact is made, it is possible to invite them to meet privately in a private chat room, in anonymous email, or other such secured arenas developed by dating website developers.

Non-Text-Based Environments

When people explore newer areas of the Internet, they can take advantage of many features that allow graphic and video capabilities.

Avatars

Avatars are cartoon representations. For example, they might represent a human quality that the user wants to experience in more depth, or may be customized to resemble the characteristics of the user. A woman interested in a cyber-affair may choose to interact with others through a particular sexual image, such as a prostitute, a buxom but inexperienced blonde, an innocent teenager, or an older and experienced matron. The avatar becomes a metaphor for the person, and that person can act out fantasies with others in real time.

Avatars can be made to change expression to happiness, sadness, surprise, or a number of other emotions at any time during a conversation. A user's voice can be transmitted through the computer as well to enhance the reality of the conversation. These avatars can also be placed in three-dimensional background settings. Therefore, a cyber-couple could watch a computer-simulated sunset on the beaches of Maui and gaze into the eyes of their partner's avatar while having romantic words whispered to them.

Video

Many types of video transmission programs, cameras, and microphones are currently available in computer stores. Some programs even allow you to hook up a camcorder to a computer and connect to places which can then serve as broadcast stations for the entire world to see. This allows for the possibility of teleconferencing. Other low-cost tools are beginning to flood the marketplace with options that do not even require a computer. ViaTV is a camera and cable system developed to connect a touch-tone telephone to a television set to offer video capabilities through telephone cables. Simply plug the TV and telephone into the ViaTV, and *voila!* You can see your loved one on your TV screen, talking into their telephone in real time as they speak to you.

There undoubtedly will be many more such products, and we'll have to learn new behaviors. Once that sort of synchronous connection is established, romantic possibilities abound, but personal privacy and anonymity diminish. It would not be surprising, however, to find that technology is developed to allow people to continue having aspects of anonymity while using video.

Video Bulletin Board System (VBBS)
This builds on video technology. A person using this technology would be able to watch a video camera, wherever it is pointed or focused, after connecting through a local telephone number. Pornographic sites now use this technology quite regularly.

Videomail
This is also becoming more commonplace. Recipients receive a video clip with attached sound, and can see and hear the sender's message being delivered on the recipient's screen.

Videoclips
Pictures can be captured from camcorders, desktop cameras, or videocassette recorders and transmitted to someone thousands of miles away. When looking at interactive video technologies, we can also see the best of all previous technologies come together. Existing equipment already includes many components of text-based environments, such as talkers, in that videoconferencing users can split their screens into quadrants, where in one quadrant they can see each other, and in another see themselves. They also can see a document they might both be referencing in a third quadrant. As if both were standing in front of a blackboard and drawing or writing something together, they can use the fourth quadrant of the screen to draw or write a list together, electronically. If preferred, any of these quadrants may be replaced by a home video, a cable TV show, or yet another live video-conferenced person or group. The possibilities are mind-boggling, but already available—and very real.

Caution
Some software programs are designed to help you monitor yourself. For example, Eudora, Qualcom's email program, has a Mood Watch feature, which warns users that the message they have written has the potential to be offensive to the receiver. The program uses chili pepper icons to warn the sender about the possible reception.

Conclusion

Undoubtedly, newer forms of technology will emerge as the Internet grows in size and capacity. These new technologies are astonishing and will challenge our values. Whether we like it or not, technology is transforming the ways we relate. Keep informed, but keep sane by staying connected to the real world and real people. Nature and loved ones will help keep you grounded when technology takes your emotions for a dizzying ride through cyberspace.

Appendix B: Emoticons and Acronyms

Emoticons

:)	Smile
: (	Frown
{{{{}}}}	Hugs
#:)	Bad hair day
: *	Kiss
–{–{–{–@	Long-stemmed rose
:- |	Disgusted
:- \\/	Shouting
: -(O)	Yelling
: -@	Cursing
: P	Sticking tongue out
: '-(	Crying
% -)	Confusion
: - 0	Uh–oh!
>: - >	Making a devilish remark
: -C	Feeling really bummed
: - /	Feeling skeptical
: I	Hmmm...
| -)	Hee hee
| - D	Ho ho
: - >	Hey hey
: -o	Oops, surprised, yawning
/'-)	Wink

Acronyms

<g>	Grin
<bg>	Big grin
<vbg>	Very big grin
AOL	America Online
ASAP	As soon as possible

AYT	Are you there?
BAK	Back at keyboard
BL	Belly laughing
BRB	Be right back
BTW	By the way
CWYL	Chat with you later
DBAA	Don't be an ass
DIKU	Do I know you?
F2F	Face to face
FAQ	Frequently asked question
FWIW	For what it's worth
FYI	For your information
GAB	Gimme a break
GGP	Gotta go to the bathroom
GIWIST	Gee, I wish I'd said that
HHOK	Ha ha, only kidding
HTH	Hope this helps
HTHBE	Hope this has been enlightening
ICLU	I cyber-love you
IM	Instant message
IMO	In my opinion
IMCO	In my considered opinion
IMHO	In my humble opinion
IMNSHO	In my not so humble opinion
IOW	In other words
IRL	In real life
ITRW	In the real world
ISO	In search of (used frequently in member rooms)
J/K	Just kidding
LOL	Laughing out loud
MOTOS	Member of the opposite sex
MOTSS	Member of the same sex
OH	Online husband
OHinL	Online husband-in-law
OIC	Oh, I see!
OTF(L)	On the floor (laughing)
OTOH	On the other hand
OTP	On the phone
OW	Online wife
OWinL	Online wife-in-law
PITA	Pain in the "acronym"
POV	Point of view
PTMM	Please tell me more

ROFL or ROTFL	Rolling on the floor laughing
S/AC	Sex, age check
TTFN	Ta ta for now
TTYL	Talk to you later
TU	Thank you
WRT	With regards to
WYSIWYG	What you see is what you get

References

ABC News. (2001, February 14). Online love. *ABCNEWS.com.* <http://more. abcnews.go.com/sections/gma/goodmorningamerica/gma010214online_d ating.html> [2001, July 26].

Barak, A., & Safir, M. P. (1997). Sex and the Internet: An Israeli perspective. *Journal of Sex Education and Therapy, 22,* 67-73.

Barrett, D. (1999). *Bandits on the information superhighway.* Collingdale, PA: DIANNE Publishing Co.

Bowen, M. (1978). *Family therapy in clinical practice.* New York: Jason Aaronson.

Brand, S. (1987). *The media lab.* New York: Viking.

Brody, H. (1995). Session with a cybershrink: An interview with Sherry Turkle. *Technology Review.* <http://www.techreview.com/articles/Fm96/ Turkle.html> [2001, Feb. 5].

Brown, E. (1991). *Patterns of infidelity and their treatment.* New York: Brunner/Mazel.

Bugental, J. (1981). *The search for authenticity.* New York: Irvingston.

Burns, D. (1985). *Intimate connections.* New York: William Morrow & Co.

Burns, D. (1989). *The feeling good handbook.* New York: William Morrow & Co.

Cairncross, F. (1997). *The death of distance.* Boston: Harvard Business School Press.

Carnes, P. (1989). *Contrary to love.* Center City, MN: Hazelton Information and Educational Services.

Carnes, P. (1991). Don't call it love: Sex addiction in America. New York: Bantam.

Cooper, A. (1997). The Internet and sexuality: Into the next millennium. *Journal of Sex Education and Therapy, 22,* 5-6.

Cooper, A. (1998). Sexuality on the Internet: Surfing into the new millennium. *CyberPsychology & Behavior, 1,* 181-187.

Cooper, A. (2000). *Cybersex and sexual compulsivity: The dark side of the force.* New York: Brunner/Mazel.

Cooper, A., Delmonico, D. L., & Burg, R. (2000). Cybersex users, abusers, and compulsives: New findings and implications. *Sexual Addiction &*

Compulsivity: The Journal of Treatment and Prevent, 7, 5-29.

Cooper, A., Maheu, M., Greenfield, D., & Boies, S. (in press). Sexuality and the Internet: The next sexual revolution. In F. Muscarella and L.Szuchman (Eds.), *The Psychological Science of Sexuality: A Research Based Approach.* New York: Wiley & Sons.

Cooper, A., McLoughlin, I. P., & Campbell, K. M. (2000). Sexuality in cyberspace: Update for the 21st century. *CyberPsychology & Behavior, 3,* 521-536.

Cooper, A., Morharan-Martin, J., Maheu, M. M., & Mathy, R.M. (2001). Random sampling of user demographics related to cybersex and other online sexual activity. Unpublished manuscript.

Cooper, A., Putnam, D. E., Planchon, L. A., & Boies, S. C. (1999). Online sexual compulsivity: Getting tangled in the net. *Sexual Addiction and Compulsivity, 6,* 79-104.

Cooper, A., Scherer, C. R., Boies, S. C., & Gordon, B. L. (1999). Sexuality on the Internet: From sexual exploration to pathological expression. *Professional Psychology: Research And Practice, 30,* 154-164.

Egan, T. (2000, October 23). Technology sent Wall Street into market for pornography. *New York Times,* 1, 20.

Freeman-Longo, R., & Blanchard, G. (1998). *Sexual abuse in America: Epidemic of the 21st century.* Brandon, VT: Safer Society Press.

Fromm, E. (1956). *The art of loving.* New York: Harper & Row.

Glass, S. (2000). Avoiding the slippery slope of infidelity. Workshop Presented at Smart Marriages Conference for Coalition for Marriage and Family Counselors and Educators (CMFCE): Denver, Colorado.

Glass, S., & Wright, T. (1991). Moving walls and windows to resolve extramarital triangles. Paper presented at the American Association for Marriage and Family Therapy Conference: Dallas, Texas.

Glass, S., & Wright, T. (1997). Restructuring marriage after the trauma of infidelity. In Kim Halford and Howard J. Markham (Eds.), *Clinical Handbook of Marriage and Couples Intervention.* New York: Wiley & Sons.

Greenfield, D. (1999). *Virtual addiction.* Oakland, CA: New Harbinger Publications, Inc.

Griffiths, M. (2000). Excessive Internet use: Implications for sexual behavior. *CyberPsychology & Behavior, 5,* 37-52.

Gwinnell, E. (1998). *Online seductions.* New York: Kodansha, Inc.

Hamman, R. (1996). Cyborgasms: Cybersex amongst multiple-selves and cyborgs in the narrow-bandwidth space of America Online chat rooms. *Cybersoc.* <www.socio.demon.co.uk/> [2001, Feb. 5].

Jacobson, E. (1959). *Progressive relaxation.* Chicago: University of Chicago Press.

Johnson, R. (1983). *We: Understanding the psychology of romantic love.* San Francisco: Harper & Row.

Jung, M., & Booth, R. (1996). *Romancing the Net: A tell-all guide to love online*. Rocklin, CA: Prima.

Laino, C. (2001, July 18). Click and tell. *MSNBC.com* <http://www.msnbc.com/new/596354.asp> [2001, Aug. 7].

Leiblum, S. R. (1997). Sex and the Net: Clinical implications. *Journal of Sex Education and Therapy, 22,* 21-28.

Lerner, H. (1989). *The dance of intimacy*. New York: Harper Perennial.

Lerner, H. (1993). *The dance of deception*. New York: Harper Perennial.

Levine, D. (2000). Virtual attraction: What rocks your boat. *Cyber Psychology & Behavior, 3,* 565-573.

Maltz, M. (1960). *Psycho-Cybernetics*. New York: Prentice-Hall.

Moore, T. (1994). *Soulmate: Honoring the mysteries of love and relationship* (p 221). New York: HarperCollins.

Offit, A. (1995). Are you ready for virtual love?: A psychiatrist looks at cybersex. <http://web2.airmail.net/walraven/cosmo.html> [2001, Feb. 5].

Pittman, F. (1989). *Private lies: Infidelity and the betrayal of intimacy*. New York: W.W. Norton.

Putnam, D. E. (2000). Initiation and maintenance of online sexual compulsivity: Implications for assessment and treatment. *Cyberpsychology & Behavior, 3,* 553-563.

Raphael, R. (2001, February 15). From E- to eternity: Email sparks new dating rituals. *ABCNEWS.com.* <http://abcnews.go.com/sections/primetime/2020/PRIMETIME_010215_emaildating_feature.html#3> [2001, July 26].

Rubenstein, C., & Shaver, P. (1974). *In Search of intimacy*. New York: Delacorte.

Sager, C. (1976). *Marriage contracts and couples therapy*. New York: Brunner/Mazel.

Schnarch, D. (1997). *Passionate marriage*. New York: Henry Holt & Co.

Schnarch, D. (1997). Sex, intimacy, and the Internet. *Journal of Sex Education and Therapy, 22,* 15-20.

Schneider, J. P. (2000). Effects of cyber-sex addiction on the family: Results of a survey. *Sexual Addiction and Compulsivity, 7,* 31-58.

Shaw, J. (1997). Treatment rationale for Internet infidelity. *Journal of Sex Education and Therapy, 22,* 29-34.

Spender, D. (1995). *Nattering on the net: women, power and cyberspace*. North Melbourne: Spinifex Press.

Spring, J. A. (1996). *After the affair*. New York: HarperCollins Publishers, Inc.

Sternberg, R. J. (1988). *The triangle of love: Intimacy, passion and commitment*. New York: Basic Books.

Subotnik, R., & Harris, G. (1994). *Surviving infidelity: Making decisions, recovering from the pain*. Massachusetts: Adams Media Co.

Tarbox, K. (2000). *Katie.com*. New York: Plume.

Vaughn, J., & Vaughn, P. (1996). Online affairs. <http://www.vaughn-vaughn.com/com010.html> [2001, Feb. 5].

Wallerstein, J. (2000). *Unexpected legacy of divorce.* New York: Hyperion.

Weil, B.E. (1993). *Adultery: The forgivable sin.* New York: Carol Publishing Group.

Weiss, R. (1975). *Marital separation.* New York: Basic Books.

Young, K. S. (1998). Internet addiction: The emergence of a new clinical disorder. *CyberPsyhology and Behavior, 1* (3), 237-244.

About the Authors

Marlene M. Maheu, Ph.D., is a licensed psychologist and a pioneer in the delivery of psychological services through the Internet. She is a member of the American Psychological Association, the California Psychological Association, the American Telemedicine Association, and the American Association of Marriage and Family Therapists. She is in private practice in San Diego, California.

Dr. Maheu is the Director of Telehealth for Alliant University, where she oversees a postgraduate training program in behavioral telehealth and e-health. She has served on numerous professional association committees related to telehealth and e-health, speaks regularly at professional conventions, conducts workshops and training seminars related to psychology and technology, and consults for companies and organizations developing technology-based behavioral healthcare services. She has appeared on dozens of radio and TV programs to discuss various aspects of Internet behavior.

Dr. Maheu is the editor in chief and founder of *SelfhelpMagazine*, the first privately held mental health website on the Internet. Established on November 1, 1994, *SelfhelpMagazine* is an informational and community website offering free services to a dedicated monthly readership from more than 106 countries worldwide. *SelfhelpMagazine* was featured in the Best 100 Websites of *Web Magazine*, as well as in the *Utne Reader*, *USA Today*, *US News and World Report*, the *Miami Herald*, the *L.A. Times*, and many other publications. *SelfhelpMagazine* was selected to represent new development in mental health technologies at President Clinton's Inaugural Expo, held at his 1997 inauguration. It was also chosen to accompany the National Institute of Mental Health to showcase their website in the Technology Tent on the Mall in Washington, D.C. As founder of this project, Dr. Maheu oversees a volunteer staff of more than seventy-five writers, programmers, artists, and support individuals.

Rona B. Subotnik, M.A., MFT, is a licensed marriage and family counselor, and is a clinical member of both the California and the American Association of Marriage and Family Therapists. She is in private practice in San Diego, California.

She received her M.A. in counseling from Trinity College in Washington, D.C. For eight years, she worked at A Woman's Place, an innovative counseling center that is a program of the Commission for Women of the Montgomery County, Maryland, government. There she conducted individual therapy and designed and led numerous workshops and counseling groups for women, one of which was called "Surviving Infidelity."

Mrs. Subotnik also taught in the Graduate Studies Department of Trinity College and the Women's Studies Extension Program at Mt. Vernon College in Washington, D.C.

Mrs. Subotnik has served as a member of the Commission on the Status of Women on San Diego's Committee on Sexual Harassment for three years, and its Committee on Domestic Violence for one year.

She is coauthor of one of the bestselling books on infidelity, *Surviving Infidelity: Making Decisions, Recovering from the Pain*, published in 1994 and updated in its second edition in 1999. She has appeared on the *Leeza Show* on national television, on national radio, and on Canadian radio discussing infidelity.

She has written a monthly column for the Internet psychology website called Here2Listen.com.

She is married, has three grown children, and lives with her husband in Palm Desert, California.

Index